Kindred Nature

Kindred Nature

VICTORIAN AND EDWARDIAN WOMEN
EMBRACE THE LIVING WORLD

Barbara T. Gates

THE
UNIVERSITY OF CHICAGO PRESS
*
Chicago & London

BARBARA T. GATES is Alumni Distinguished Professor of English and Women's Studies at the University of Delaware. She is the author of *Victorian Suicide: Mad Crimes and Sad Histories* (1988). Her edited volumes include *Critical Essays on Charlotte Brontë* (1989), *Journal of Emily Shore* (1991), and, with Ann B. Shteir, *Natural Eloquence: Women Reinscribe Science* (1997).

The University of Chicago Press, Chicago 60637
The University of Chicago Press, Ltd., London
© 1998 by The University of Chicago Press
All rights reserved. Published 1998
Printed in the United States of America
07 06 05 04 03 02 01 00 99 98   1 2 3 4 5
ISBN: 0-226-28442-5 (cloth)
ISBN: 0-226-28443-3 (paper)

Library of Congress Cataloging-in-Publication Data

Gates, Barbara T., 1936 –
    Kindred nature : Victorian and Edwardian women embrace the living world / Barbara T. Gates.
        p.   cm.
    Includes bibliographical references and index.
    ISBN 0-226-28442-5 (cloth : alk. paper). — ISBN 0-226-28443-3 (pbk. : alk. paper)
    1. Women—Great Britain—Biography.   2. Women naturalists—Great Britain—Biography.   3. Women authors—Great Britain—Biography.   4. Women social reformers—Great Britain—Biography.
HQ1595.A3G37   1998
305.4′092′2—dc21   98–34934
                                                                         CIP

♾ The paper used in this publication meets the minimum requirements of the American National Standard for Information Sciences—Permanence of Paper for Printed Library Materials, ANSI Z39.48-1992.

To Bev,

WHO WATCHED

Kindred Nature

GROW

CONTENTS

ILLUSTRATIONS

ACKNOWLEDGMENTS

A book ten years in the making incurs a catalog of debts, and I owe much to many. To the plants and animals with which I live and have lived and which I have watched since childhood, I may owe the most. They have both taught and sustained me as their counterparts did the Victorian and Edwardian women who thread the pages of this book. Then, to my father, Robert Timm, I owe my first hearing of the story of Tom, the Water Baby, which he patiently read to me from his own small library and which enthralled a small girl, fascinated by the water world.

Without patient and curious librarians on both sides of the Atlantic and by the shores of the Tasman Sea as well, I would have missed efficient direction to the right source at the right time. In London, Robert Sharp of the Science Museum Library launched me into the sea of women popularizers of science. Susan Goodman, Christine Ellwood, and Julie Oldfield of the Natural History Museum Libraries pointed me to work by women botanists, ornithologists, and entomologists. Christopher Mills, also of the Natural History Museum Libraries, helped me with finishing touches and permissions. Brent Elliott at the Royal Horticultural Society ushered me toward out-of-the-way books and manuscripts, as did the staff of the Library at Kew Gardens. And David Doughan at the Fawcett Library showed me the importance of Frances Swiney and feminist publications like *Shafts* to my project. To Ann Stevenson Hobbs of the Victoria and Albert Museum Library, I owe multiple thanks. Ann not only offered me access to the Lindner Collection and to her own extraordinary knowledge of the work of Beatrix Potter, she also took the time to introduce me to other Potterites—to Judy Taylor in London and Bob Peck of the Academy of Natural Sciences in Philadelphia, who in turn led me to Linda Rossi and other helpful librarians at the academy. In Sandy, at the library of the Royal Society for the Protection of Birds, Ian Dawson provided me both with archival materials about the RSPB's founders and with consistent support as I perused those archives. In Melbourne, I probed deeper into the Australian life of Louisa Meredith through the gracious agency of Trish Nash at Monash University Library, and in Berkeley, I received expert assistance in reading Gertrude Jekyll's garden plans, which are housed in the Beatrice Farrand Collection in the College of Environmental Design at the University of California, Berkeley. Here at home, at the University of Delaware Library, I have always been able to count on reference librarians Linda Lawrence Stein, Rebecca Knight, and Carol Rudisell to patiently guide me in my hunts for much-needed but maddeningly obscure materials. Thank you, librarians, one and all.

To colleagues in the profession I owe still further debts. Jonathan Smith helped me better to know Elizabeth Gould; Julie Early to see other sides of Mary Kingsley; Susan Morgan to rethink Marianne North's work; Bernard Lightman to look to Alfred Russel Wallace's correspondence for more information on Arabella Buckley's relationship to other scientists; and Lynda Birke and Sandra Harding to understand the importance of their kind of theory to my kind of enterprise. My good friend and coeditor of *Natural Eloquence,* Rusty Shteir, provided constant encouragement—and even accommodation in London—as I worked on this book. Rosemary Beresford willingly checked materials and ran errands to the London records offices for me when I was based in the United States. And Ann Ardis and Rosemary Jann read and offered very helpful comments on drafts of this book, each from her own perspective. To both of them, who borrowed time from their own administrative tasks and important research, I owe deep debts of gratitude, as I do to Susan Casteras, who helped me find the cover image for this book.

With the aid of research assistants from the University of Delaware's honors program, I saved many, many hours of my time on this project as they searched and filed and fetched and proofed and pondered. As they helped me with whatever needed doing, Carol Althouse, Jen Bodamer, Cynthia Cunningham, Mike Elder, Melissa Joarder, Deborah Lindinger, Michelle Lisi, Christine Redmond, and Chris Smith became like colleagues and will always have my sincerest gratitude. So will Rebecca Jaroff, who toiled to help me get the bibliography and birth and death dates for individuals for this book "just right," and Sara Trillet, who helped with the proofs. The University of Delaware also provided me with two summer research grants and a year's leave as a member of the university's Center for Advanced Study. These awards afforded me time in Britain to search, scurry, and research on my own and then an opportunity to write this book, free from other responsibilities. So did a summer residency at Blue Mountain Center in New York, where, among mountains and lakes, I wrote my first chapter.

Portions of chapters 2 and 3 of *Kindred Nature,* in preliminary versions, have appeared as "Retelling the Story of Science: Women Popularizers of the Nineteenth Century," in *Victorian Literature and Culture* 21 (1993); as "Revisioning Darwin with Sympathy," in *History of European Ideas* 19.4 (1994), used here with permission from Elsevier Science; and in the introduction to *Natural Eloquence: Women Reinscribe Science,* ed. Barbara T. Gates and Ann B. Shteir (Madison, University of Wisconsin Press, 1997). "Writing for the Birds," a section in chapter 4, was published earlier, in a longer version, in *Chattel, Servant, and*

Citizen: Women's Status in Church, State, and Society, ed. Mary O'Dowd and Sabine Wichert (Belfast: Institute of Irish Studies, 1995). I offer thanks to the various publishers of these essays, for their permission to reprint.

Finally, I would like to thank my editor at the University of Chicago Press, Susan Abrams, for her help and encouragement. I am also grateful to Rodney Powell, Mary Caraway, David Aftandilian, Joseph Claude, and Martin Hertzel, on the staff at the Press, for the enthusiasm with which they greeted my book and the care with which they saw it through the process of being published.

Kindred Nature

INTRODUCTORY

Throughout *Kindred Nature*, I kept thinking of William Holman Hunt's famous Pre-Raphaelite painting, *The Awakening Conscience* (1853–54), where an alert yet bedazzled Victorian woman begins to get up from a man's lap and stare out of an open window into the world of nature (see figure 1). If she has been her lover's source of "nature," she now pushes past him toward light and trees and fresh air. She revolves away from the hothouse parlor abruptly, away from the wallpaper patterned with flowers and toward the flowers themselves. Her image haunted me throughout this study. I wanted to know what she might find out there and, even more, what other women, not just men, might have been telling her about nature—her own, and the nature of light and flowers and trees. If, inside, Hunt's man was crooning a song of his particular sexual needs to this woman, what other siren song might she have been hearing? Outside, was a chorus of female voices swelling, many and varied women singing cheek to cheek?

In this book, I have set about discovering, recovering, and interpreting such voices. *Kindred Nature* centers on what a number of British Victorian and, later, Edwardian women said and did in the name of nature—what part they played in the cultural reconstruction of nature that transpired in the years just preceding the publication of Darwin's major work and in the wake of the Darwinian revolution. Naming, of course, implies power, the human power of the word over the thing named, the power of the word to bring into being through naming, the power to change situations by changing what they are called, the power of rhetoric to spin believable cultural myths. Always a significant agent in determining Western culture, the idea of nature came to exert even more formidable influence after Darwin. Since the theory of evolution seemed to have set limits to what humanity could do, learn, say, or be, the illusion of Promethean science seemed to fade in this new time frame, leaving "Nature" again in control of human destiny. Redefining and redetermining the meaning of nature, thoughtful people set out to devise conceptual constructions of evolution and a complex system of nomenclature—with illustrations to match—that helped give a semblance of control over biodiversity, human and nonhuman. Because of women's distinct position in British culture of that period—their separate, special education and their typical relegation to domestic spheres—women brought what Sandra Harding calls "different resources for understanding nature" to this

Figure 1.   William Holman Hunt, *The Awakening Conscience* (1853–54). Courtesy of the Tate Gallery, London.

enterprise ("Women's Standpoints on Nature" 189). They invested themselves more in general education—more in furthering their own education and in educating those outside the professions (children, the poor, and other women)—and more in feminine as well as feminist causes than did most men.

In recovering a link missing from the stories of nature and womanhood in the nineteenth and early twentieth centuries, *Kindred Nature* also encompasses a portion of the larger, more familiar story of men and women in this time frame. Darwin's revolution demanded not just a reordering of nature but a resituating of human beings in the history of nature. In Victorian Britain, as now, the dominant gender system socially constructed both women and nature. What women said about nature was, therefore, determined in part by what men said about nature and by what men said about women; what women said about nature was predicated in part upon the ways in which they themselves were constructed *as* nature. Women in this time frame struggled with an inveterate cultural attitude that forced this identification of women with nature, something George Sand must have had in mind when she quipped to Gustave Flaubert that he too was "nature" and had better get accustomed to the idea (8 July 1874, 351). Masculine presentations of "natural" woman—woman defined as inherently less intellectual and more close to nature than was man—and of womanly, maternal nature were two central Victorian/Edwardian fabrications that made it difficult for nineteenth- and early twentieth-century women to speak with authority and to be heard with respect on any subject, let alone on the subject of nature. In the process of defining masculinity, the cultural categories of "women" and "nature" had become oppositions to "men" and "mind." Without the pervasive feminization of nature and the naturalization of women, nineteenth-century Englishmen, like the young man in Holman Hunt's painting, could not have continued comfortably to relegate women to the realms of the erotic and the domestic and to exclude women from those of the public and the political, nor could they have allowed themselves the powerful illusion of (male) mind over (female) matter.

One effect of all of this was a general constriction of female voices in scientific discussions about nature, a constriction nevertheless loosened by moments of free flow. For example, at the turn of the eighteenth century and throughout the early decades of the nineteenth century, women spoke out mainly to popularize the work of *male* scientists, but they did so in considerable numbers and with considerable authority. The famous physicist Michael Faraday learned his first chemistry through scientific popularizations by Jane Marcet. Women like Marcet produced books which described scientific discoveries for an audience of women, children, and members of the working class, who had little or no access to specialist libraries or to universities. Such work offered a valuable service to a population isolated from formal education but eager for news of science.

In the 1830s and 1840s, women joined men in the widespread enthusiasm for natural history. Journals, experiments, and collections were all part of an enterprise that belonged to women as well as men. In the 1830s, generalist magazines like the *Penny Magazine* were, for example, quite willing to accept women's contributions for columns on natural history. By the 1850s, however, women were finding it harder to have their scientific insights or observations published in journals, in part because science was becoming more professionalized. In the

1850s and 1860s, more and more specialist natural history journals were established.[1] These journals targeted specific subjects and coteries of readers, and although their intent was to popularize, they were mainly directed by men to men. For example, *Scientific Opinion,* begun in 1869, declared that its mission was to advocate the "cause of Science and the interests of scientific men in England" and to seek "proper recompense and distinction" for men of science (qtd. in Barton 3, 4). Also in the 1850s and 1860s, the insidious equation of women with nature—already present in eighteenth-century pronouncements about women's lower intelligence being a matter of natural law—took on a new twist with the introduction of evolutionary ideas about natural selection. In this new view, women were seen primarily as reproductive vessels, selected by mates as bearers of the next generation of evolving human beings. Reacting against this sort of essentializing of female human nature, midcentury feminists like Elizabeth Garrett Anderson and Lydia Becker spoke up in a different voice about women's nature.

In the later decades of the nineteenth century, as women came more and more to redefine themselves politically and economically by seeking the vote and the right to work, they also became active in describing other species and in protecting animals both in their own and in foreign countries from threats like vivisection, hunting, and deforestation. More than half of the women who are most central to this book spent their most active years around the turn of the nineteenth century. Many—Beatrix Potter and Gertrude Jekyll, for example—found their voices in the 1890s and continued to write well into the new century. It was only a need for closure to their story that caused me to follow them only as far as 1918, when British women got the right to speak through the vote and when, as Virginia Woolf and others suggested, the world changed radically because of the Great War.

During the course of their lives, long-lived women like Potter and Jekyll turned their hands toward more than one enterprise involving nature. Potter worked with scientific illustration, published her famous "little" books for children, and evinced great personal dedication to the National Trust; Jekyll began as a painter and became a famous gardener. Other less well-known women found other spheres of influence.

Combing archives in search of traces of these overlooked women soon reveals the minimalization of both their numbers and their roles. Because both men and women in the Victorian/Edwardian period behaved like ethnographers—men in examining women and nature, and women in examining nature—and because both certainly held many of the biases of their culture, their

1. For this information, I am indebted to Ruth Barton, whose paper, "The Purposes of Science and the Purposes of Popularization: Some Popular Science Journals in the 1860s," I heard at the Australasian Victorian Studies Association meeting in Adelaide, Australia, in February of 1996, and to Susan Sheets-Pyenson's "Popular Science Periodicals in Paris and London: The Emergence of a Low Scientific Culture, 1820–1875," which I read in *Annals of Science.*

contrasting language and at times their contrasting choice of media have become a part of my subject. I have nevertheless tried not to privilege men's texts by setting them up as all-important controlling forces, male dictates that determined female responses to self or nature. Nor have I simply compared the work of men and women, except when doing so pointed directly toward women's accomplishments. Women's often passionate words cried out for center stage in this book.

Kindred Nature is thus neither a challenge-response historical study nor a comparative gender study but, rather, a feminist cultural study intended to recuperate and spotlight women's contributions in an effort to revise history. It is not meant to be fully comprehensive, nor to offer a new theoretical framework for understanding either literature or culture, nor to provide the last word on its subject. On the contrary, the book is intended to offer its readers starting points for further inquiry; most of the chapters in this book could themselves have become books.

Thinking about the shortcomings of the challenge-response theory in describing this cultural situation, I realize, as a feminist who is including women in a portion of history for years written solely by and about men, that I operate in a world still governed by such challenges. Despite a frequent desire to escape the chains of a male-centered system of discourse by featuring my women writers, I cannot claim to have solved this vexed problem. Walking hand in hand through hemlock woods on a sunny day, smelling the oozing sap and feeling soft needles underfoot, or nursing a tiny child who nuzzles and grasps at the female breast with small, red fists might lead women to essentialize themselves, to believe they belong to a universe of their own, to confirm that Victorian men were right—women are closer to nature. But sitting down to read or write a chapter about nature and European history soon involves us in a discourse in which nature functions as a mental and linguistic construct. The title of this book, *Kindred Nature,* is therefore not meant to suggest kinship in terms of "natural" womanhood but kinship in terms of a familiarity that was mentally and artistically apprehended and consciously and deliberately embraced. Eliza Brightwen, one of the women you will meet in these pages, expressed this idea of kinship well. Brightwen declined to be listed in *Who's Who* and sent a friend the only kind of entry she felt appropriate for herself. The entry might well serve many of the women who appear in *Kindred Nature:*

> *Name and title:* "A lover of Nature, protector of everything in fur and feathers." *Educated at:* "The shrine of Nature by no end of clever teachers." *Academical distinctions:* "Dame Nature does not bestow outward and visible honours, but she gives keen eyes, sharpened wit and ever-increasing pleasure." *Recreations:* "Searching for beetles and everything that flies and hops." *Address:* "At home everywhere in the world of Nature." (*Eliza Brightwen* xxx–xxxi)

In terms of cultural constructions of Victorian and Edwardian womanhood, there have been many studies written in the decade since I began this one. Bram Dijkstra's *Idols of Perversity*, Mary Poovey's *Uneven Developments*, Joseph Kestner's *Mythology and Misogyny*, Ludmilla Jordanova's *Sexual Visions*, Cynthia Russett's *Sexual Science*, Elaine Showalter's *Sexual Anarchy*, and Ornella Moscucci's *The Science of Woman* have all dealt with the ways in which the female gender was imaged or artificed and then naturalized by European men in the nineteenth century. Among other things, these books examine sexist beliefs of male artists or scientists and look further into biased constructions of gender as voiced in particular branches of science and medicine.[2]

I and the women in this book have attempted another course. They, a widely divergent group, used various strategies—sometimes reactive and sometimes not—to tell the story of nature in their time, and I have used theirs—sometimes by way of summary, more often by way of analysis or critique—to tell mine. Had we been listening for their voices all along, these women would have been asking us not only to revise their place in history but to reexamine our own definitions of the nature of nature and womanhood. Contemporary feminist theorists of science—Carolyn Merchant, Evelyn Fox Keller, Lynda Birke, and Sandra Harding, among them—have helped us to question the grounds of a masculinist science perpetuated through a language meant to be unbiased but in actual fact often quite the opposite.[3] Their work has set the stage for voices of another generation of women theorists. But the work of other, still earlier women—women of the eighteenth, nineteenth, and early twentieth centuries—set the stage for all of them. Until now, hearing the story of nature retold by contemporary women has generally been more important for us than recovering the fainter voices of these women of the past.

I have attempted this listening backward by probing the cultural time frame I know best—the Victorian period in Britain, along with the years just preceding and just following it. The voices of the women of this era seem fainter

2. Not only books but dozens of articles have been written in this area in recent decades. Among those most useful to me in this study—particularly in the first chapter—have been Flavia Alaya's "Victorian Science and the 'Genius' of Woman," in the *Journal of the History of Ideas;* Joan Burstyn's "Education and Sex: The Medical Case against Higher Education for Women in England, 1870–1900," in *Proceedings of the American Philosophical Society;* Lorna Duffin's "Prisoners of Progress: Women and Evolution" in *The Nineteenth-Century Woman: Her Cultural and Physical World;* Susan Sleeth Mosedale's "Science Corrupted: Victorian Biologists Consider 'the Woman Question,'" in the *Journal of the History of Biology;* Evelleen Richards's "Darwin and the Descent of Woman" in *The Wider Domain of Evolutionary Thought;* and Richard Allen Soloway's "Feminism, Fertility, and Eugenics in Victorian and Edwardian England," in *Political Symbolism in Modern Europe: Essays in Honor of George L. Mosse.*

3. In addition to the many books on this subject, two well-known essays on the nature of nature and the nature of women of special note here are Sherry B. Ortner's "Is Female to Male as Nature Is to Culture?" and Ludmilla J. Jordanova's "Natural Facts: A Historical Perspective on Science and Sexuality."

only because they are more distant now and harder to discern. Many rang out loudly and clearly in their own day. And although this book begins with what Victorian men said about Victorian women in the name of nature—a review, in chapter 1, of the context that made it so difficult for women to speak—female voices offer a counterpointing dissent right from the start. Subsequent chapters of *Kindred Nature* then reveal how actively, and with what diverse voices, Victorian and Edwardian women interrupted, revised, ignored, and sometimes disrupted masculine discourse as they participated in conceptualizing, describing, representing, and preserving the natural world of their time.

Women were not only more active but more persistent in their redefining of nature than we have previously allowed. Most of the women who appear in this book are distinctive in their fields but also typical of prevailing trends in women's writing, illustrating, or collecting. Sometimes their work offers but slight variations on men's, but at other times close examination of these women's work affords us a chance to detect distinctively female traditions in science and nature writing, for example. Many made it their agenda to be accessible to nonspecialist audiences. My own agenda, both in teaching and writing, is similar: although it is informed by the scholarship and theory of a number of academic disciplines—literature, art, history, history of science, and geography, for example—I hope that *Kindred Nature* will likewise be accessible to a general readership.

As a contemporary feminist, aware of class and race as important categories of current writing, I may be faulted for not featuring women of the working class in this study—except in rare cases like Mary Anning's—or for not discussing at any length the women of color who were a part of the British Empire at this time. Their important lives certainly belong to this time frame—to accounts of political challenge or of "natural" medicine—but their story is not mine here. Most of the women featured in this book—whether they be feminist or womanist or neither—were indeed "privileged" in the sense that they were highly literate, often well-to-do, and in touch with the intellectual currents of their day. Had they not been, in Victorian and Edwardian Britain they would not have been able to speak about nature even in the limited contexts available to women then; in turn, I would not have been able to speak about their texts at all.

And this is a text-based study, one in which a variety of texts are brought to light and discussed primarily for the sake of the cultural story they make available. *Kindred Nature* is divided into three parts: the first looks at women and natural science, the second at women crusading on behalf of nature, and the third digs more deeply into aesthetics and literary forms, relating them to nature writing. Each part highlights trends, conventions, or movements centered in women's differing addresses to nature. Throughout I have brought into prominence not just the words of one, or two, or even a dozen eloquent women who might join hands, bow their heads, and receive a blessing for their contributions to Western cultural history. Certainly, famous women like Frances Power Cobbe and Mary Kingsley stride through the pages of this book. But as a woman who grew up as a scholar in the age of feminist recovery and enjoyed discovering and learning about women previously unknown to me, I have deliberately tried to include the lesser known along with the better known. Moreover, when a point could be made equally well by addressing the work of a forgotten writer or artist, I have often done so. Journal-keepers Emily Shore and Muriel Foster have therefore gained greater prominence in this narrative than has Edith Holden, the Edwardian lady "country diarist" of some note, and agriculturalist Annie Martin has had more space devoted to her African farm than has novelist Olive Schreiner to hers.

Woven from strands of many women's discourses, my own text provides another fragment of the intricate fabric of Victorian and Edwardian cultural history. In telling this story of women and nature, I have been mindful of Donna Haraway's powerful insight that "scientific practice is a story-telling practice in which rival reconstructions of the history of nature contend to justify desired present worlds" (*Primate Visions* 4–5). Haraway's thoughts on science culture effectively apply to the making of a book like *Kindred Nature*. Nineteenth-century men told one story, nineteenth-century women another, and, in telling their stories in *Kindred Nature*, I am telling yet another story—one replete with respect for women's presence in the intellectual construction of nature, both then and now.

PART I

Women on the Edge of Science

CHAPTER

I

Who Can Speak in Nature's Name?

Setting the Scene

This chapter rehearses a capsule history of a nineteenth- and early-twentieth-century battle—a gendered struggle about naming, a turf war over the control of nature's voice. By "nature" I mean not the earth and sky "out there," not the too, too solid stones that sting human toes when we kick them too hard, but a mental construct that relies upon social consensus for its validity. In Darwin's century the term usually designated something more concrete: a physical non-human nature, tamed, as by cultivation or by science, or wild and unmediated and, as such, considered wholly separate from human nature. In order to project and evolve an ecosocial system that satisfied their intellectual and emotional needs, cultural spokespeople in the nineteenth century often felt compelled to gain control of this idea of nature—to define or circumscribe it. By so doing, they hoped to make human life in the larger world—which by then encompassed all of geological time and more and more of global space—more predictable and more comfortable for themselves and their kind.

Writers of course controlled nature through language, and many favored metaphoric language, which permitted them a powerful kind of ventriloquism. They created a personified Nature, a beautiful or fearsome dummy through which to pass their own pronouncements, an ultimate—if artificial—authority on the nature of nature. When, after Charles Darwin's *Origin of Species* (1859), the idea of nature became both more intriguing and more formidable, more Victorians began to practice this kind of ventriloquism. Interpreting the meaning of nature became second in importance only to interpreting the meaning of God. If the religious carried on culture wars in Victorian Britain—dividing into sects, skirmishing over biblical interpretations—so did the exponents of nature. Localized disputes among naturalists gave way to a full-scale battle to capture Nature's voice. Increasingly, it seemed more crucial to get Nature's story right—to locate not just creatures and nonhuman nature but "primitive" peoples and women as well on the evolutionary tree—to discern, interpret, and then enunciate what Nature had in mind for them. Since to most Victorian minds creatures and colonial people were *part* of nature, educated men spoke on their behalf. But where did that leave the women? Could a personified Nature speak for them, or only for men? If women, too, were thought of as "natural," were they, in consequence, too "natural" and too uneducated to help define the nature of this Nature? Could women, objects of appraisal *as* nature, be valued for their testimony *about* nature?

Without question, essentialist definitions of women's being made this difficult. Roland Barthes has shown how deeply the disease of thinking in essences underpins bourgeois mythologies of humankind ("Myth Today" 109–59). It ascribes not just fixed biological essences to women—like menstruation, pregnancy, and lactation; it also can ascribe emotional essences—like intuitiveness or compassion. Certainly, thinking in essences was at the bottom of mythologies about women and earthiness when Victorian scientists and social scientists joined ranks with men of letters to characterize women in terms of their own "nature," which to most of these men meant female sexuality and reproductive functions. This landed women squarely in (or as) the lap of nature. Listen, for example, to an anonymous writer for the *Journal of Psychological Medicine and Mental Pathology* in 1851, who sums up a paragraph about female anatomy with this comment: "In short, the posterior surface of the torso in woman is unquestionably the *chef d'oeuvre* of nature" (20). Listen again, this time to Havelock Ellis (1859–1939) some forty years later, discussing the importance of women to men's mental well-being: "Women are for men the embodiments of the restful responsiveness of Nature. To every man, as Michelet has put it, the woman whom he loves is as the Earth is to her legendary son; he has but to fall down and kiss her breast and he is strong again" (*Man and Woman* 426).

Such texts may bring a smile to the lips of enlightened, late-twentieth-century readers who can see that women are not nature—not even nature's masterpieces—nor any more "natural" than men are. Like men, women are reproductively, intellectually, and socially active beings. But if we take this position, we immediately isolate ourselves from an understanding of the many influential men and women who, in time past, thought quite the opposite. Equations of woman's sexualized, naked bodies with the essence of womanliness were all too common in Victoria's century. Evolutionists, eugenicists, psychologists, anthropologists, educators, poets, and painters alike tended to confer on women attributes of the "natural," and the biological differences between men and women that prompted such cultural leaders to place women closer to nature often became the basis for their social definitions of womanhood. This kind of biological determinism was so widespread that it can serve as an index to an entire set of discourses that typify Victorian and, later, Edwardian culture in terms of gender definition.

In "Oppressive Dichotomies: The Nature/Culture Debate," Penelope Brown and L. J. Jordanova have succinctly described how such deterministic distortions come about: by "(i) conferring attributes on each sex, (ii) speaking about the models and symbolism peculiar to each sex, (iii) reifying these attributes, making certain attributes universally associated with each sex, and (iv) attributing *naturalness* to these alleged differences" (229). This model typifies the thought process of those Victorians and Edwardians for whom anatomical sexual differences were confused with gender relations. In part because an organized women's movement was late in developing in the nineteenth century, in part because sexual determinism suited empowered men, such determinism gained a firm and initially unopposed stronghold. Its roots, however, are more elusive than is the fact of its existence. We could try to trace their beginnings to Darwin's first edition of *The Origin of Species* (1859), which made nature a female heroine, a *natura naturans*. But in this convention Charles Darwin (1809–1882) had predecessors dating back at least to Ovid and including Darwin's immediate precursor, geologist Charles Lyell (1797–1875). Moreover, just a year after the first edition of the *Origin* appeared, Darwin apologized for his personification and explained that he meant by the term only "the aggregate and product of many natural laws" (55). As Darwin seemed to realize, by midcentury it was late in the day to expect progressive intellectuals to resurrect Mother Nature. Skeptics like George Eliot (1819–1880) were already expressing doubt about the project as early as 1848, when Eliot playfully wrote her friends the Hennells that "Mother Nature—who by the bye is an old lady with some bad habits of her own—like other great names does her work by deputy and so gets both credit and discredit that don't properly belong to her" (*Letters* 272–73). Nevertheless, the influence of Darwin's first edition of the *Origin* prompted many not-so-progressive Victorians to engender the newly popular natural history as female.

Socializing Science, Sexualizing Woman: The Skirmish over Women's Intellect

Later, in his *Descent of Man* (1871), Darwin adventured beyond charting the evolution of other animals to take on humankind and explore the nature of secondary sexual characteristics. Over long periods of time, according to Darwin, human males had begun to differ from females in these characteristics, one of which was mental power—including reason, invention, and imagination. Because of his greater mental prowess, man can reach "a higher eminence, in whatever he takes up, than woman can attain—whether requiring deep thought, reason, or imagination" (2: 327). In addition, Darwin hypothesized that male mental power is strengthened through use during the lifetime of a given individual and can be transmitted to that individual's offspring through the inheritance of acquired characteristics. Fortunately for women, some of the mental power passes on to female offspring as well as to males; otherwise, said Darwin in an often-quoted and colorfully insidious analogy, "it is probable that man would have become as superior in mental endowment to woman, as the peacock is in ornamental plumage to the peahen" (2: 328–29).

Darwin's work with sexual selection and secondary sexual characteristics helped to reignite an eighteenth-century discussion about the supposed naturalness of women's supposed mental inferiority to men. Dictated primarily by religious and philosophical debate, the notion of this inferiority was transformed in the eighteenth century into what amounted to a natural law, the sort of social construction that Mary Wollstonecraft (1759–1797) had attempted to counter in her *Vindication of the Rights of Woman* (1792). In one of the first attempts to explain just what the "naturalizing" of women meant, Wollstonecraft discerned that because of social and educational constrictions which intellectually hampered them at every turn, women, "the first fair defect in nature," had "resigned the natural rights, which the exercise of reason might have procured them" (55). According to Wollstonecraft, women were first declared to be intellectually inferior and then made to be intellectually inferior, through the workings of a constraining social system. Wollstonecraft's call was for women to understand how this determinism worked, because, she reasoned, if they understood it, they would be better able to resist its working.

Wollstonecraft also contended that women had "natural rights" to intellectual development. Later, in the nineteenth century, the authority of biological science supplanted religion and philosophy in the business of manufacturing natural laws that extended to society. Always a part of a system of social practices, science began, after Darwin, to dominate those practices, which were altered in the process. Thus the open dynamism of Darwinian ideas about evolution was transformed into rigid social pronouncements about women's mental abilities and the relationship of those ostensibly limited abilities to women's ostensibly limited physical strength. And once again, these dicta were built into social structures.

In articulating pronouncements about women's inferior mental nature, it was sociologist Herbert Spencer (1820–1903) rather than Charles Darwin who led the way, and Spencer, far more than Darwin, who claimed to speak in Nature's voice. In his *Education: Intellectual, Moral, and Physical* (1861) and again in his *Study of Sociology* (1873), Spencer suggested that in terms of their evolution, women had been arrested intellectually in order to conserve their limited supply of energy for procreation. The agent behind this evolutionary development was, predictably, "Nature," and in turn her agency was the law of conservation of energy—a "law" which had been popularized by physicists in the 1840s. For Spencer, "Nature is a strict accountant; if you demand of her in one direction more than she is prepared to lay out, she balances the account by making a deduction elsewhere" (*Education* 179). In the case of women, babies would take the place of study or other intellectual pursuits, an assumption that Spencer's followers were quick to endorse. Humanity—and even Nature herself—

could be damaged by human willingness to ignore Nature's dictates, since, at least according to Spencer, "whenever requirements which have their roots in the order of Nature come to be enforced by an extrinsic authority, obedience to that extrinsic authority takes the place of obedience to the natural requirements" (*Principles of Ethics* 1: 542). Constrained intellectual development for women was the logical price to be paid for the continued biological evolution of humankind, a dictate made to come from Nature's mouth.

Spencer's arguments on women's intellectual development were immediately taken up by medical doctors, who were then called upon to determine exactly what level of intellectual endeavor was appropriate to women. For example, the question addressed to one of the day's leading psychiatrists, Henry Maudsley (1835–1918), was whether male models of education were fit for women. Based in Spencerian reasoning, Maudsley's answer in "Sex in Mind and Education" (1874) was that *no* male models were appropriate, since women were mentally inferior to men and in need of physically conserving their energy for their primary responsibility—motherhood. Maudsley clearly did not have Spencer's gift with the pen. In a sentence adorned with masculine verbs applied to his female personification, he claimed that "when Nature spends in one direction, she must economize in another direction" (467). The eminent doctor then offered his expert psychiatric opinion that there is "sex in mind as distinctly as there is sex in body" (468). The female brain had developed in correspondence with female reproductive organs, a "fact" which allowed Maudsley to conclude that women should simply not be faced with the rigors of an education paralleling men's.

By the time of Maudsley's pronouncements about their education, women had waged a decades-long battle to enter medical schools and had themselves become doctors.[1] Elizabeth Garrett Anderson (1836–1917) (see figure 2), who fought with everything she had to acquire her own medical education,[2] responded tartly to Maudsley in the May issue of the *Fortnightly*. To look at Maudsley's argument and then at hers is to reverse the stereotypes established by male doctors in the name of scientific "truth." Maudsley made four emotional appeals to personified Nature in the course of making his points and in the end withdrew to feature an American authority from Harvard, Dr. Edward H. Clarke, to round out his case. Distressed at Maudsley's appeals to sources other than his own knowledge, Anderson faulted her opponent for his "vagueness" (583) and then used traditionally "masculine" logic to engage him. Maudsley had claimed that "as women are marked out by nature for very different offices in life from those of men, the healthy performance of her [*sic*] special

1. What was in Victorian times, and still is, one of the most informative studies of British women's entrance into medicine is Sophia Jex-Blake's *Medical Women: A Thesis and a History*.

2. For an informative study of Anderson's life and an excellent summary of women's entrance into the medical field, see Jo Manton, *Elizabeth Garrett Anderson*.

Figure 2. Elizabeth Garrett Anderson. Courtesy of the
Wellcome Institute Library, Wellcome Centre for Medical
Science, London.

functions renders it improbable she will succeed, and unwise for her to perse-
vere in running over the same course at the same pace with him" (468). Anderson retorted that "this argument contains a *non sequitur.* The question depends
upon the nature of the course and the quickness of the pace, and upon the fit-
ness of both for women; not at all on the amount of likeness or unlikeness between men and women" (584). Moreover, if the expenditure of energy harms
women's reproductive capacities, Anderson queried why domestic servants did
not seem to have trouble with reproduction. She also faulted Maudsley's en-
listment of an American as an authority on the efficacy of English education
for English women. Not once did she enlist on her own behalf the Nature she
supposedly embodied.

By the late 1860s, intelligent women like Anderson had begun to enter the
Victorian debate about women's nature and its relationship to men's. Since
women were increasingly depicted as complements, their "nature" defined in
terms of its contrast with men's, women's mental capacities were further denigrated as the idea of complements became more popular. Gillian Beer reminds

Figure 3. Susan Isabel Dacre, *Portrait of Lydia Becker.* Courtesy of Manchester City Art Galleries, Manchester, England.

us that in the 1860s Victorian anthropology arranged "developmental patterns," with "the white, middle-class, European male as the crowned personage towards whom the past of the world [had] been striving" (*Open Fields* 77). Highly uncomfortable with ideas of inequality that were being promulgated at this time, educated women began to speak out in public forums, attempting to set the record straight on the question of female intelligence. In 1868, Lydia Becker (1827–1890)(see figure 3), a botanist and early feminist, presented her views to the Manchester Ladies' Literary Society, a group of which she was founder and president. In a paper entitled "Is There Any Specific Distinction between Male and Female Intellect?" she made a persuasive case against innate or natural distinction. Becker insisted that "the attribute of sex does not extend to mind" and that current distinctions were culturally determined by the "circumstances under which [the sexes] pass their lives" (484). A year later, in the pages of the *Contemporary Review,* she extended these arguments to the business of education. Building on the ideas expressed in her Manchester paper, Becker's "On the Study of Science by Women" advocated scientific study for contemporary women, arguing that science could save them from lives of "intellectual vacuity" (388) since "nothing that is real is considered insignificant by the naturalist" (389). All women are capable of observing and therefore contributing to scientific knowledge, a skill that would sharpen both their own sense of accuracy and their ability to verify others' work. In addition, she asserted, scientific societies and universities should be opened to women so that their mental abilities could be more fully challenged. Women need to be asked what they want, not told. Then, according to Becker in a kind of scientizing of Wollstonecraft's earlier arguments on behalf of women, life's stream might be peopled with "fish worth catching" rather than with "minnows and sticklebacks" (403)—a metaphor spawned to apply to small-minded women inattentive to their own minds.

Becker was far from alone in her concern about the undermining of women's intelligence in the name of Nature. In 1874, Emma Wallington delivered a paper to the London Anthropological Society, one of the newer professional societies which had bitterly argued against adding women to its ranks. Before this august group, Wallington presented a paper entitled "The Physical and Intellectual Capacities of Woman Equal to Those of Man." "Nature," said Wallington in a female appropriation of Nature's voice, "tells us that this [male physical and mental] superiority is shared by women" (553). She reminds us that women the world over perform some of the hardest of physical work, including soldiering, in which Ashantee women excel men, and she will also "declare" that women can excel mentally, when given the opportunity. To prove her Nature's latter point, Wallington cited examples of women like Mary Somerville (1780–1872), the well-known physicist and author of *On the Connexion of the Physical Sciences,* and Sophia Jex-Blake (1840–1912), the physician who had helped to institute medical education for women at the University of Edinburgh. According to Wallington, such women prove that "the intellectual capacity of woman does not differ from man's more than that of men differs among themselves; in other words, the differences are not so much of *sex* as of *individuals."* Men in "barbarous states do not show high mental powers at all; nor do men of science all show equivalent abilities" (559). Wallington had had enough of "dogmatizing on woman's supposed natural inferiority" (560).

Wallington's assumptions drew heavy fire. In a skirmish we can still reproduce, since *Anthropologia* printed not only the papers of the Anthropological Society but the discussions that followed the presentation of those papers, Wallington was first faulted for arguing in an "essentially feminine" way (560)—through exceptions like Somerville, rather than through the generally accepted rule. Next, all of her female exemplars were denigrated as purveyors of derivative knowledge, interpreters of male intellectual discovery. Finally, a decade-old argument about cranial capacity reared its authoritative head during the discussion following Wallington's paper.[3] To close the session, the society's president reflected the theory derived from European anthropological studies which had featured the measurement of craniums and presupposed that skull and brain size determined intelligence. The president put it this way: "Women have never attained the summit of any art or science" because their skull "resembles . . . that of an infant" and, furthermore, "the male European excels more the female than does the negro the negress; and hence, with the progress of civilization, the men are in advance of the women, so that the inequality of the sexes increases with civilization" (563).

The president's prejudicial statements were examples of exactly the kind of theorizing that Wallington despised. "An ounce of fact is of more worth than any quantity of theory" (555), she had boldly stated. In this dislike of "theory" about women, Wallington had good company. In 1878, Frances Power Cobbe (1822–1904), a fiery contemporary suffragist who detested the scientific establishment and found the medical community similar to "the priesthood of former times" in assuming the same "airs of authority" ("The Little Health of Ladies" 292), carried Wallington's concerns still further. She could not imagine why women needed to be studied by science at all. "Of all the theories current concerning women," pronounced Cobbe with Cobbe-like acerbity, "none is more curious than the theory that it is needful to make a theory about them" ("The Duties of Women" 66).

Influential men of the nineteenth century nevertheless continued to theorize about women's nature, continued to base conclusions on inconclusive evidence, and continued to argue by using the favored appeal to Nature with a capital *N*. Arguments from cranial size, for example, persisted as a popular way to explain women's presumed mental inferiority. Because women had smaller brains than men and, ostensibly in consequence, less intellectual capacity, they were believed capable of that much less intellectual endeavor. This theory wholly convinced George Romanes (1848–1894), an influential evolutionist who wrote three books on animal intelligence and consulted with Darwin in that area. In "Mental Differences between Men and Women" (1887), an essay already passé in its time, Romanes announced that it would "take many centuries for heredity to produce the missing five ounces of the female brain" (666). He found this unfortunate but incontrovertible and decided, like Maudsley, that the "missing ounces" made equality in education impossible. Claiming that he did so with sadness, he found he had to admit that "of all the pricks against which it is hard to kick[,] the hardest are those which are presented by Nature in the form of

---

3. For an interesting discussion of the storytelling that has come to surround the subject of the female brain, see Anne Fausto-Sterling, *Myths of Gender: Biological Theories about Women and Men*, 37–44.

facts" (667). Once again, because Nature's "facts" had decreed it, no amount of human education could in the foreseeable future bring women into mental equality with men.

Nevertheless, by the 1880s physicians put less credence in theories about brain size. According to John Thornburn, a Manchester obstetrician, "All the old-fashioned notions of women's brains being in some way inferior to men's are, I am convinced, utterly wrong. My experience shows me that they are equal if not often superior, but that this power is at present being frittered away by foolish attempts to ignore the physiological differences which exist between the two sexes" (*Female Education from a Physiological Point of View* 10). Despite his open-minded view of their brains, Thornburn went on to posit a highly limiting version of education for women, one based upon their uterus and their supposed bodily incapacity during menstruation. According to him, for one week out of every month women were totally unfit for rigorous intellectual work. Add this up, and one finds that for a quarter of each academic session women "can work as they do at other times only at the peril of mental or physical disablement, perhaps for life" (7). Following this line of reasoning, Thornburn concluded that women could not handle the curricula prescribed for men at either the secondary or tertiary levels and that "there is no scholastic or academic pitch-fork which can expel nature or render the disregard of its laws innocuous" (10). Thornburn sounds like a Maudsley who is simply a little flashier in choosing his metaphors. He was in fact a forward-looking man poised at the verge of the eugenics movement. For Thornburn also believed that higher education for women might send the bright girls to Girton and leave only "inferior women to perpetuate the species" (11). In one form or another, this elitist and classist view would underpin the eugenics movement and betray its conservative roots in the middle class.

There were, of course, dissenting voices among men as there were among women—men who could not make the leap from evolution to social policy with such ease and who saw classism for what it was. In *Darwinism and Politics* (1890), idealist philosopher David Ritchie (1853–1903) berated his privileged countrymen for their narrow-minded blindness, revealing them as always among the "first to prevent a race or class or sex from acquiring a capacity, and then to justify the refusal of rights on the grounds of this absence—to shut up a bird in a narrow cage and then pretend to argue with it that it is incapable of flying" (68–69). Concerned about the restriction of women in domestic settings, he called the bluff of their captors who "fly in the face of nature [and] fancy that they are influenced by scientific considerations, but they are really influenced by what they happen to have grown accustomed to" (62–63).

But Ritchie was in a minority. The new pseudosciences were busy proving that status quo social situations were indeed the work of nature and the way of the future. New fields like eugenics would enable their practitioners to comb present statistics in order to fashion methods of determining hereditary characteristics for the future. In 1869, Francis Galton (1822–1911), a cousin of Darwin's and considered the founder of eugenics, produced his first book on the subject. It was *Hereditary Genius,* a look into the origins of "natural ability" to seek and then reproduce the sources of originality of mind—in short, to breed a better race of intellects. For Galton, eugenics would both speed up and improve human natural selection. "What Nature does blindly, slowly, and ruthlessly, man may do providently, quickly, and kindly," Galton said later in *Essays in Eugenics* (42): from its very inception, the eugenics movement had taken "Nature" as its ally. Eugenicists like Galton assumed gender roles to be determined not by social requirements but by a configuration of genitals. They further believed it would be folly to change existing gender arrangements in terms of parenthood. Motherhood was women's supreme role, a role prescribed by Nature as utterly fulfilling for all women. Women—or at least, middle-class women— were of course expected to comply quietly with Nature's dictates. Nevertheless, eugenicists could not avoid the "woman question," as could earlier theorists. As we have seen, in their day the women's movement was well under way and female voices were demanding to be heard.

In response, eugenicists launched a propagandistic effort to convert women as well as men by promoting the idea of "race motherhood." The fittest classes were to be encouraged to breed with greater gusto so as to strengthen the race as a whole. Nature, it was believed, was more potent than nurture, and the lower classes were behaving more naturally than the upper and producing more children. Such fears surfaced in the last two decades of the nineteenth century and continued past the advent of the new century. To many, there seemed to be a general decline in the abilities of the British population. If entropy pointed to a general dispersion of energy in the universe, human decadence seemed to point to a waning of the species. What was needed was that the educated woman come to understand the importance of self-sacrifice for the good of the breed. If this sacrifice could be made, human nature as well as the human physique might improve.

Because such ideas developed alongside a budding women's movement, few disputable eugenic ideas went unchallenged. As once again the specter of Spencerian science was resurrected and women's alleged incapacity for much energy beyond that needed for conceiving, bearing, and raising children again was brought to the forefront, the New Women of the 1880s and 1890s took up the cause espoused earlier by Wollstonecraft, Garrett Anderson, Becker, and Wallington. If girls were not allowed to explore the intellectual parts of their nature, how were they, as women, to know for what endeavor they were really best suited? And what if nature, in view of the sweep of human evolution, had actually intended for enfranchisement and a greater role in political life for evolving women? These questions became the focus of a number of essays, pamphlets, and books as the century itself wound down and the eugenics and the women's movements simultaneously wound themselves up. At issue was a standoff concerning women's primary responsibilities: feminists were arguing for women's (actually, middle-class women's) right to self-determination; eugenicists were arguing for women's duty to motherhood. At the center of all of this controversy were the female body and the jurisdiction of nature, two contested areas in heated and sometimes humorous debates of the 1890s.

Enter the Dangerous "Wild Woman"

Take, for example, the debates over the "wild woman" that raged in the pages of *Nineteenth Century* in the early 1890s. In January of 1890, Lady Jersey, née Margaret Elizabeth Leigh (1849–1945), initiated the discussion simply by arguing that women's free choice of physical or mental activity in no way unfit them for motherhood. Diversity in womanhood should be countenanced just as should diversity in manhood. "It might," she suggested, with an eye to eugenics, "be better to take women as we find them, and to see what direction they can follow in order to attain to better things in future" (60). The next year, Eliza Lynn Linton (1822–1898), a prolific writer and social critic, escalated discussion to debate in her essay "Wild Women as Social Insurgents," which castigated all women who aspired to political or any other equality with men. "The desire to assimilate their lives to those of men runs through the whole day's work of the Wild Women," announced Linton, who associated such women both with savagery and with "the viragos of all ages" (598). For her, use of mental, decision-making power was somehow linked both with men and with primitivism. This apparent contradiction she neatly failed to explore, just as she failed to examine the contradiction in her linking wild women's temporal degeneration into savagery with their timeless state as "viragos of all ages."

Linton's lapses in logic were not lost on the outspoken feminist novelist Mona Caird (1858–1932). In dashing metaphors and graphic depictions, Caird countered Linton the following May, again in the pages of *Nineteenth Century:*

> To the time-honoured argument that nature intended man to be anything and everything that his strength of muscle and of mind permitted, while she meant woman to be a mother, and nothing else, the rebels reply, that if a woman has been made by nature to be a mother, so has a cow or a sheep; and if this maternal capacity be really an infallible indication of function, there is nothing to prevent this reasoning from running down-hill to its conclusion, namely, that the nearer a woman can become to a cow or a sheep the better. (818)

For Caird, nature's voice was not worth the capturing. She went on:

If popular feeling objects to this conclusion, and yet still desires all women to make maternity their chief duty, it must find another reason for its faith, leaving nature's sign-posts out of the question. On these sign-posts man himself is privileged to write and rewrite the legends, though of this power he seems at present to be unconscious, persistently denying it even while his restless fingers are busy at their work.

This dear and cherished appeal to nature, however, will never be abandoned by the advocates of the old order while breath remains to them. (811)

Caird suggested that if women should give all for motherhood, men should give all for fatherhood. Nature had designed them for this role. But then, nature had become merely a "fetish" when projected upon in this way (819). Nature really had no volition; "*Man* intends, *Man* desires, and 'Nature,' in the course of centuries, learns to obey" (820). Like George Eliot, Caird discerned the power of Nature-making but refused to play the game.

At about the time that Linton and Caird were sparring, a writer for the *Provincial Medical Journal* was attempting to lay to final rest arguments about the smallness of women's frontal lobes and the consequent smallness of women's intellectual capacity. Taking on the high seriousness of eugenics in its concern for the race, E. M. Bonavia, M.D., spoofed: "What are we to make of all this atrophy or degeneration of the female brain, which, if it be true, forebodes no good for the future of the British nation?" (358). The spoof continued: Is this "pauperization" due to disuse—as in lack of education—or is it due to evolutionary development, "the female size *never having* come up to the male level" (360)? Was this a case of nurture or nature? Bonavia went on to champion the gray matter of some females—Eleanor Ormerod (1828–1901), the entomologist, for example—who could hold their own in any enclave but were seldom given credit for their discoveries. In the end, nurture wins out in this essay, for, Bonavia avers, we have learned from Darwin's own frontal lobes that "there is no such thing as *fixed* or *unalterable* tissue or organism anywhere" (360), and we have seen what talented women with education can do. Social conditioning, not genitalia, determines the destiny of women.

Spoofing and reinterpreting Darwin's theories often had a serious social purpose. Consider, for example, two women who enlisted the idea of the missing link both on behalf of women and on behalf of the working class. In 1859, the year of *The Origin of Species* and the discovery of Neanderthal man, "L. N. R." (Ellen Ranyard, 1816–1879) wrote her *Missing Link; or, Bible-Women in the Homes of the London Poor*. Ranyard's missing link is the women of the working poor, who can "help the people to help themselves" (Beer, *Open Fields* 140). Ranyard believed that this doubly overlooked person—ignored not only because of her gender but also because of her social position—needed to be enlisted in the war against poverty. Forty years later, Margaret Harkness, another woman writing under the cover of a pseudonym—"John Law"—produced a naturalist novel in which the disenfranchised poor gained voice as the missing link. In her *Captain Lobe* (1889), Harkness forged an alliance between women and the working classes that permitted both to speak out against their grievances.

Despite spoofs, propaganda, and defenses on women's behalf, women's mental and physical constitutions continued to be minimized—and not only by men. In diminishing the strength of their sisters, women of authority sometimes spoke in concert with men. At the end of the century, when physical culture for women had become widely popular, physician Arabella Kenealy expressed deep concern for the bodies of women who too eagerly embraced sports. In her "Woman as Athlete," an essay on another controversial subject that surfaced in the pages of *Nineteenth Century,* she argued that muscle building was "bartered" for at the expense of femininity (639). Women would lose their moral as well as their physical identities if they persisted in athletics. Using the case of a hypothetical "Clara" to illustrate her points, Kenealy chose to speak through nature, as had her male counterparts.

> For Nature knows what are the faculties whence this new muscle-energy is born. She knows it is the birthright of the babies Clara and her sister athletes are squandering. She knows it is the laboriously evolved potentiality of the race they are expending on their muscles.
> Nature can but be disgusted with our modern rendering of baby. So sorry a poor creature the baby of this nineteenth century is, indeed, that he cannot assimilate milk. (643)

By walking for two miles a day, hypothetical Clara had not only lost her supple feminine sinews but had given the race indigestion in the bargain.

Nineteenth Century being a locus of timely debates, Kenealy was quickly answered, in the issue of May 1899. Her respondent was Laura Ormiston Chant (1848–1923), a suffragist and liberal crusader. Like Caird, Chant had heard enough cant about Nature. "In the words of the immortal Betsy Prig," she said, "'I don't believe there's no sich a 'person' as 'Nature' who 'knows' anything of the kind!'" (746). Referring to the information about Clara's muscles and Nature's disgust with the babies of the nineteenth century, Chant countered that if this is Nature, she has grown "cantankerous indeed" (746). Chant herself would trust to natural selection, which she did not think of as "cantankerous," to decide on appropriateness of musculature or anything else. "Let us modern women take heart of grace, and go on doing the best we can to develop muscular vigour, along with a sneaking fondness for frills and pleatings, and an openly avowed adhesion to the Eternal Baby, and its father" (754).

Behind Chant's comments, as behind many of the debated positions highlighted in this chapter, was Alfred Russel Wallace's stand on human selection. Wallace (1823–1913) had objected to any attempts to legislate selection.

"Improvement," he predicted in his essay "Human Selection" in the *Fortnightly Review*, "will certainly be effected through the agency of female choice in marriage" (335). Well into the next century, such statements were used both in support of the eugenics movement and in opposition to it. Feminists like Alice Drysdale Vickery, wife of the Malthusian League's first president, improved on Wallace's "improvement" by suggesting that women would need independence, both physiological and economic, before they could "exercise that natural selective power in the choice of a mate, which was probably a main factor in the . . . evolution of the race" (21). Others, like C. W. Saleeby (1878–1940), who was active at the height of the eugenics campaign in the early twentieth century, fought feminism in the name of eugenics. Saleeby demanded that "the very first thing that the feminist movement must prove is that it is eugenic. . . . [I]f it be contrariwise[,] . . . no arguments in its favour are of any avail" (6).

Saleeby had not just Vickery to contend with but opponents aplenty—often conflicted opponents, both inside and outside the eugenics movement. Female eugenicists who were also physicians, such as Mary Scharlieb (1845–1932) and Elizabeth Sloan Chesser (1878–1940), were in basic agreement with the aims of the eugenics movement in terms of the importance of motherhood, but they rejected stands like Saleeby's in their advocacy of increased physical and mental culture for women. The women physicians of their generation and the one preceding it of course occupied a difficult position with respect to the female body. Elizabeth Garrett Anderson and Sophia Jex-Blake, both of whom had waged such a long battle for medical education, also both wrote about the "naturalness" of women's joining the medical profession. Each in turn was then called upon to reargue the nature/culture debate, to avoid the trap of biological determinism. For if it was natural for women to be treated by women doctors—because a woman doctor herself inhabits a female body—it need not follow that women were necessarily further from culture or inadequate to carry out its aims. If, however, in arguing their suitability for medicine, these women claimed they were better equipped by nature to serve women patients, particularly as diagnosticians and gynecologists, they were arguing a position that essentialized women.

A generation later, Scharlieb and Sloan Chesser lived with this same contradiction and attempted to compromise with it in their position on race motherhood. If both of these women doctors strongly advocated athletics and education for young women, their reasoning on the subject came from eugenics, as did their classism. As Sloan Chesser suggested, "If we trace the evolution of motherhood, we find progress; survival of the higher species are dependent upon maternal care and maternal efficiency. Study the problems of motherhood and we find degeneration proceeds wherever maternal neglect and maternal exhaustion exists" (6–7). Like the male model of eugenic reform, Sloan Chesser's model focused upon improving the race by improving women as breeders and caretakers more than it did on educating them as purveyors of knowledge, important though that might be.

Scharlieb and Sloan Chesser lived and worked in the age of Havelock Ellis and Edward Carpenter (1844–1929), two advocates of sexual freedom for women who, despite their protests to the contrary, consistently had men at heart. If Carpenter wanted choice for women and in many ways argued on behalf of their rights, in *Love's Coming of Age* (1896) his main interest lay in women's power to lead men back to their "primitive" natures. He too wanted women "wild," but in the sense of "fearless and untamed." They must be passionate for nature and for men in order to lead civilization through open doors "to a new and a wider life" (72). Unfortunately, this kind of reasoning could lead to inferences of atavism: women were wild not because they had overstepped their social roles, as with Linton's wild women, but because they were simply less evolved. Atavistic thinking became popular enough to form the base for theories of criminality, as in the work of Cesare Lombroso (1835–1929), an Italian criminologist whose work was translated into English and who became celebrated for his insights into womanhood. Lombroso's research suggested that criminals were closer to primates than were most people, having craniums very apelike in appearance, an indication he profusely illustrated in his books. Carrying this theorizing into the realm of gender study, his *Female Offender* (1895) pronounced female criminals most "monstrous" of all. According to Lombroso, men were obviously more evolved than women, so when women lost the qualities of piety and maternalism that kept their atavism in check, they became "more terrible than any man" (150–52)—offenders in every sense of the word.

Rider Haggard's novel *She* (1887) shows the fate of a fictional woman "more terrible than any man." In the hands of Haggard (1856–1925), its heroine, Ayesha, or She Who Must Be Obeyed, transgresses both as a female ruler, a being wild in Linton's sense of the word, and as a sexual being, like Lombroso's women. Though seemingly the epitome of power and beauty, the zenith of an evolved master race, She dies a revealing and entropic death. She regresses first to an apelike thing by losing her erectness and then to something even more frighteningly reptilian. In the words of Haggard's narrator, Horace Holly, She "raised herself upon her bony hands, and blindly gazed around her, swaying her head slowly from side to side as does a tortoise. She could not see, for her whitish eyes were covered with a horny film" (221). Finally, in death She becomes only a "hideous little monkey frame, covered with crinkled yellow parchment, that once had been the glorious *She*." "Alas!" exclaims Horace, "it was no hideous dream—it was an awful and unparalleled fact!" (222)—that because they are so primitive underneath, women of power in the end will regress to the animal world. Holly's was certainly not the kind of "fact" about women that Wallington and Cobbe sought. If Haggard's story had a moral, it seems to have been a moral for men: to follow such a one as She is either to die with her, to pine for her, or to be compelled to retell her story as a cautionary tale.

Earlier in the nineteenth century, male cultural analysts had warned about the dangerous, primitive nature of women by depicting nature as difficult, cruel, and mythologically female. In fashioning or reviving myths about women, they put pseudoreligious forms and language to work for their own purposes. They thus clothed their ideas in the garb of ancient wisdom, empowering and authenticating their points of view through the venerability of myth (Auerbach, Dijkstra). As anthropologist E. B. Tylor (1832–1917) would realize, the "force and obstinacy of the mythic faculty" was revealed in "the processes of animating and personifying nature" (415). Earlier, in 1843, writer Thomas Carlyle (1795–1881) had sensed this power and typed "Nature, like the Sphinx," to be "of womanly celestial loveliness and tenderness; the face and bosom of a goddess, but ending in claws and the body of a lioness" (7). And later, in 1879, art critic John Ruskin (1819–1900) threw up his hands in exasperation at his own construction when he characterized nature as a puzzling and deceitfully Sphinx-like female in *Proserpina:* "Why the powers of nature should try to deceive us, is not our business to ask; nor if the question be put to her will the Sphinx reply; but it is a fact that she does, and that our life, when healthy, is a balanced state between a childish submission to her deceits, and a faithful and reverent investigation of her laws" (2: 531). Here then are yet more sources of dubious "facts" about nature and human nature: nature is woman both as coquette and as law-giving mother to men. And here too are even more tenuous myths about woman, who of course becomes nature in these same aspects.

Thinking of womankind in this cultural bind, Oscar Wilde (1854–1900) in his play *The Importance of Being Earnest* has Jack characterize Lady Bracknell as being "a monster without being a myth, which is rather unfair" (6: 50). It was "unfair" because mythologizing helped deal with the fearsomeness of this popular, male-authored phenomenon—the bestialized woman. But mythologizing also led men into a dangerous loop. When men turned to myth to understand the natural—natural cycles, workings of the sexuality of women, the nature of myth itself—and then pressed those same mythic structures into service to embody and embolden the female principle, as in Ruskin's and Carlyle's lioness-women and sphinxes, they paradoxically reempowered women through the very agency that disempowered them: the male mind. It is rather like Zeus giving birth to warlike and wise Athena. But the Greeks and Romans did not make Athena "natural" in the way that the Victorians did—they already had a pantheon of goddesses fulfilling a panoply of functions. In the Victorian construction, womanhood could absorb all of nature's power. Trapped in their own devices, men who wished to be natural had then to renaturalize themselves by giving over patriarchal law and rule. If they did so, however, they might feel in danger of losing on all fronts, abdicating mental and moral power and winding up as woman's (or nature's) thralls.

This was the case with Merlin the magician in Alfred Lord Tennyson's "Merlin and Vivien," one of the poems from the highly acclaimed *Idylls of the King*

(1859–85). Tennyson (1809–1892) was especially intuitive about the workings of this cycle of male renaturalization (Gilbert, James Eli Adams). His King Arthur emerges from the natural to establish a cultural code for his knights, but he returns to nature and the female both through Queen Guinevere and, again, through the three queens, with whom he drifts off to another world after the Lady of the Lake reclaims his sword.

Even Thomas Henry Huxley (1825–1895) found himself caught in this bind when, in 1860, he spoke on behalf of excluding women from the Geological Society. As Gillian Beer has pointed out, he made himself sound like a harpy when he argued:

> five-sixths of women will stop in the dollstage of evolution to be the stronghold of parsondom, the drag on civilization, the degradation of every important pursuit with which they mix themselves—'intrigues,' in politics, and 'friponnes' in science. If my claws and beak are good for anything they shall be kept from hindering the progress of any science I have to do with. (Qtd. in *Open Fields* 205)

On the other hand, in some ways it was beneficial for women to keep the myth of primitive wild women going. It perpetuated a myth of power, and it kept men guessing. George Egerton (pseudonym of fiction writer Mary Chavelita Dunne [1859–1945]), capitalized on this idea in her volume *Keynotes* (1893), when in "A Cross Line," she had her nameless heroine pronounce:

> The wisest of them [men] can only say we are enigmas; each one of them sets about solving the riddle of the *ewig weibliche*,— and well it is that the workings of our hearts are closed to them, that we are cunning enough or *great* enough to seem to be what they would have us, rather than be what we are. But few of them have had the insight to find out the key to our seeming contradictions—why a refined, physically fragile woman will mate with a brute, as mere animal with primitive passions and love him. . . . They have all overlooked the eternal wildness, the untamed primitive savage temperament that lurks in the mildest, best woman. Deep in through ages of convention this primeval trait burns,—an untameable quantity that may be concealed but is never eradicated by culture, the keynote of woman's witchcraft and woman's strength. (29–30)

Women's evolutionary nature could, of course, be read forward millennially as well as backward atavistically and mythologically. Two early-twentieth-century cultural analysts, H. M. Bernard and M. Bernard, attempted a millennial forecast in their pamphlet *Woman and Evolution* (1909). There they read increased freedom and educational opportunities for women as signs of a general human evolution which boded well for the evolutionary future of humankind. The Bernards believed that "the present demand for the enfranchisement of women [was] not an isolated phenomenon, but an inevitable movement forward, in accordance with the great evolutionary scheme which has led life onward and upward, from the minutest microbe that we can discern under the most powerful microscope, to Man" (7). For them, human beings were both biological and social organisms, and these two functions were interrelated. Women, with their knowledge of motherhood, might help the human race envision a kind of universal motherhood in which every person's child, regardless of its nature, might be nurtured.

And so the battle to interpret nature's voice vis-à-vis women raged on after the turn of the century, with strong proponents on both sides and the outcome of the fray still undecided. If essentializing women in the name of nature took on different guises in different times—depending on whether natural law, Nature, Mother Nature, Sphinxes, or natural selection did the dictating—the effects of this essentializing on women's roles in culture were similar. In every case of this sort, women were considered insignificant in terms of intellectual or public life and tended to become so as a result. Thus despite the sanguine claims of men like Patrick Geddes (1854–1932) and J. Arthur Thompson, who believed that "the social order will clear itself, as it comes in touch with biology" (270–71), women were culturally and socially circumscribed even more closely in the domestic sphere than they had been before the post-Darwinian, scientific reinscription of nature as reproductive rather than mechanical. Overly prized for their role as reproductive vessels, they were bound ever more tightly to their own physicality. Speaking out about nature or science from such a position could be highly uncomfortable. But bold and emboldened women did so as Victorians and would continue to do so as Edwardians.

Epilogue: Battle Won or Battle Lost and by Whom?
Two Case Studies

The first Contagious Diseases Act (1864) was passed *sub silentio* in Parliament, presumably because of the unsavoriness of the subject—the rounding up of women suspected of carrying venereal disease and the inspection of their bodies. According to a Victorian chamberlain for the City of London, "It happened that the public were in a state of alarm at the ravages of disease among cattle, and Parliament had passed various Acts under the title of 'Contagious Diseases (Animals) Act.' Few people outside Parliament did not suppose this was not another Animals Act" (qtd.in Hay-Cooper 34).

The earlier versions of the acts (1864–69), about which the chamberlain seems to have been speaking here, permitted the arrest of women even on the mere suspicion of their carrying venereal disease; required, by order of justices, a compulsory medical/gynecological examination once women signed a "voluntary submission" form declaring themselves liable to such examinations and

Figure 4.   Josephine Butler.

allowing themselves to be classified as "common prostitutes"; and further required, if women were found infected with venereal disease, their detention in
lock hospitals. Most women who signed the forms did not realize what they
were agreeing to, and women who refused to sign were often intimidated by
members of the special police force commissioned to enforce the acts. The primary purpose of the acts, first introduced by the secretary to the Admiralty, was
to protect servicemen, particularly those in ports and garrison towns; the primary protests were lodged on behalf of the legal rights of women and the un-
fairness of penalizing women's bodies for a disease also carried by men's. But the
implications of the acts went further. Via these acts, women were naturalized to
the extent that their human rights were withdrawn; they were bestialized by being classified only according to their sexual function.

Of the crusaders working to abolish the Contagious Diseases Acts, Josephine Butler (1828–1906) was far and away the most tenacious as well as the
most prominent (see figure 4). For nearly two decades, Butler mounted a per-

sistent campaign against the acts, working nationally and internationally to abolish the inspection and detention of women's bodies. Later she turned her energies to destroying the white slave trade. "I have seen," she observed, "girls bought and sold just as young girls were, at the time of the slave trade" (qtd. in Boyd 43). Although Butler led the ranks of those Victorians resisting the treatment of women's bodies like those of animals, she believed that her cause should not be "any more a woman's question than . . . a man's" (*Personal Reminiscences* 37). Butler wanted to save women from the degradations inflicted upon them by an abstract category—the stereotype of the female prostitute—that literally lessened their humanity by curtailing liberty in the name of sanitation. "We continue," she decried, "to mass all these victims under one great ban of social excommunication; to treat them as a *class,* to make exceptional rules and laws for them; and in our various police codes we continue to call them all by the ugly name of *prostitute,* and to pile on fresh penal clauses in order to deal with them more and more severely" (229–30).

Butler had been following the progress of the Contagious Diseases Acts for five years before she was mobilized into action. In her *Reminiscences,* she relates that before undertaking her crusade, she went into her garden and watched non-human nature, envying the birds who went about their business without perpetrating such crimes against their own kind. She embarked in 1869 upon her "abolitionist" crusade against these infringements of women's rights, organizing a Ladies National Association for the repeal of the acts. "Are these gentlemen to have protection for their vices, or will you retain your liberties?" she exhorted. "*We cannot have both*" (qtd. in Hay-Cooper 45). One result of her efforts was the famous "Women's Manifesto," printed in the *Daily News* on 31 December 1869, in which a "solemn protest" was lodged in support of the women affected by the acts. The manifesto protested the manner of passage of the acts, the dangers inherent to any constitutional government when a portion of its population can be so detained, the impetus not to practice "moral restraint" when prostitution is regulated by the government, the "brutalizing" of women by these acts, and the unjustness in punishing "the sex who are the victims of a vice" rather than its perpetrators. It further suggested that no such regulation had had the desired effects in countries in which it was practiced, something Butler would set out to investigate further in her travels to Europe and in her work with International Federations in the 1870s.

As the story of her Great Crusade has often been told, never more eloquently than in her own *Reminiscences,* here I only emphasize several of its elements that apply directly to the crusade against the construction of natural woman. From the outset, the acts were under suspicion because of the silent vote that initiated them. A group of men in Parliament had felt fully capable of conceptualizing and of passing this set of stipulations without full public support. As the crusade went on, their motives were thrown into bold relief. Since most of the women detained under the acts were impoverished, not only were the parliamentarians' own morals questioned but so were their views on womanhood and their positions on class. Thus as the lawmakers' motives for the passage of the acts were probed and questioned, the artificial labeling of women and the working poor as lesser and closer to nature was uncovered or discerned. In his consideration of the state of science at this time, Butler's biographer, L. Hay-Cooper suggests how science worked in tandem with politics to enable acceptance of the acts for nearly two decades. According to him, the post-Darwinian world was in such moral and intellectual disorder that men looked to doctors and scientists to validate moral positions. When they were told that there was a "biological necessity for vice," they became "hypnotised by the words 'Hygiene' and 'Sanitation'" (43–44); hence, the passage and enforcement of legislation like the Contagious Diseases Acts.

Not until after nearly two decades of struggle would Josephine Butler see the suspension of the acts and their ultimate repeal in 1883 and 1886. Throughout that time frame, Butler often endured male concern about the loss of her own femininity, which, they regretted, was being sacrificed to her political involvement in her crusade. Prime Minister Gladstone, who "was struck with the force of her mind" when he met her, was surprised to find her perfectly and rather remarkably feminine, "notwithstanding the said material which under a strong impulse of conscience she has had to handle" (qtd. in Bell, *Butler* 97). To his mind, as to many Victorian minds, good women did not roll up their sleeves and grapple with the equation of woman with nature. Doing so meant jeopardizing that other deeply ingrained Victorian construction: woman as helpless and ladylike, a creation that most women crusaders were quite willing to forgo. Once they determined to crusade to denaturalize womanhood, theirs became a risk calculated and taken with open eyes. They might (happily) lose the very things they were protesting against: the mythologies that served to silence them.

The Obverse

In 1893, six years after the repeal of the last Contagious Diseases Act, William Sharp (1855–1905), poet and essayist on literary subjects, became Fiona Macleod, prophetic, Celtic female writer about nature and myth.[4] The world knew little of this transformation, for until the end of his life Sharp concealed Macleod's "true" identity. His wife, sister, and a female secretary were the main parties in on the ruse, primarily because they assisted him in framing his delicate letters and helping to conceal the hoax from the public. After springing full-blown from the brain of Sharp, the newborn Macleod got herself a set of American publishers in Chicago, sent her emissary William Sharp to negotiate with

---

4. For an excellent study of William Sharp, see Flavia Alaya, *William Sharp—"Fiona Macleod,"* *1855–1905.*

them, and began producing dozens of books of romance, legend, and nature essays, with titles like *Pharais and the Mountain Lovers* (1895), *From the Hills of Dream* (1896), and *Where the Forest Murmurs* (1906). Only on his deathbed did Sharp reveal his female impersonation as Macleod.

In our post-Lacanian world, we might be tempted to read Sharp's hoax psychoanalytically. Affected by the gender confusion at the end of the nineteenth century—what Elaine Showalter by way of George Gissing has called "sexual anarchy" (*Sexual Anarchy* 3)—Sharp may have been effecting his return to the bliss of the mother. But looking through the lens of culture, not psychoanalysis, we can see that it is our old acquaintance and George Eliot's bugbear, Mother Nature, whose bliss is celebrated through the work of Macleod. Straw woman Fiona Macleod was meant to carry English culture's expectations of otherness—to embody a Celtic woman as more natural than man and more in touch with things romantic. Framing the introduction to Fiona Macleod's collected works, Elizabeth Sharp—William Sharp's wife and Macleod's editor—devised a Wordsworthian/Brontesque childhood for the fictional Macleod. The most significant influences on the young Fiona were "the wind, the woods and the sea" (*The Gold Key* 135), along with Gaelic songs and legends learned from Barbara, a family nurse. As writer, this child of nature then became a Sharp free to seek his Celtic roots in the wind, woods, and sea, to write romance—the womanly genre—and to quest for what he called "the Green Life," a transcendental ecstasy found in a oneness with nature, possibly in the "wild zone" that Elaine Showalter posits, lying beyond the borders of masculine symbolic order ("Feminist Criticism in the Wilderness" 262–63).

One thing is certain, Sharp's Fiona did not represent a latter-day version of Wordsworthian romanticism, a male union with female nature as earth or moon or nutting trees. Instead, Victorian Sharp created a female surrogate to enter the wild zone and seek his buried life in nature and Celticism while he carried on the more mundane aspects of his career as an English literary and cultural critic. Victim as well as maker of his culture, Sharp seems in time to have found that Fiona Macleod became as necessary to his self-creation as he had been to her initial conception. She was his way to redemption, his female savior. To reveal her as part of himself would have been to kill them both. In a strategy far more complex than any we have yet seen, Sharp, like many another man adduced in this chapter, projected nature's voice onto a woman of his own making. Depending upon how we choose to read this, he either ceded the arts of nature writing and romance to woman and did his authorial duty by the more stringent exercise of his critical faculties, or he completely co-opted the female voice in a near perfect hoax, rendering woman entirely silent. In either case, Sharp's move from ventriloquism to impersonation reveals the extent to which a male, turn-of-the-century writer was willing to go in associating women with nature and self with culture and suggests the extents to which women would have to go in pursuit of a voice of their own.

2

Retelling the Story of Science:
The Wonders of Nature

If Victorian women often found it difficult to speak in the name of Nature, they found it even more difficult to speak in the name of Science—"high" science, that is, the science of the laboratory or museum or scientific journal. As scientific discoveries continued to unfold in the nineteenth century, science was increasingly masculinized and professionalized (Heyck, Basalla, P. Phillips)—to such an extent that by the end of the century men of science may seem to have appropriated the sole right to gaze on nature. In their books explaining the gendered aspects of science, both Carolyn Merchant and Ludmilla Jordanova have showcased a telling representation, executed in 1899 and entitled *Nature Revealing Herself to Science* (see figure 5), a sculpture by Louis-Ernest Barrias that shows a young female unveiling her nude body (*The Death of Nature* 190–91; *Sexual Visions* ch. 5). Elaine Showalter has, in turn, suggested that if this image could only have been reversed in a companion piece entitled *Science Looking at Nature,* "it would have depicted a fully clothed man, whose gaze was bold, direct, and keen, the penetrating gaze of intellectual and sexual mastery" (*Sexual Anarchy* 145). I agree with Showalter's observations about Barrias's representation and its implications. But I also believe that frequent refocusing on an image like Barrias's reinforces our cultural stereotypes of nineteenth-century European intellectual life and may cause us to overlook those many women who themselves did the gazing and then went on to create a distinctive language not just about nature but about science.

Because British educational and political opportunities were so strongly biased in favor of men in the nineteenth century, major breakthroughs in scientific discovery and theory remained a male prerogative. Yet many women took an intense interest in those discoveries and throughout the century sought knowledge of the workings of the universe, often at the urging of other women. Lydia Becker's essay "On the Study of Science by Women," for example, exhorted women to realize that

> many particulars respecting the commonest of our wild plants, animals, and insects are as yet imperfectly understood; and any woman who might select one of these creatures, and begin a series of patient observations on

Figure 5. Louis-Ernest Barrias, *Nature Revealing Herself to Science* (1899). Bronze, ivory, gilding. Musée des Arts Décoratifs, Paris. Giraudon/Art Resource, NY.

its habits, manner of feeding, of taking care of its young, of communication with its kind, of guarding against danger, on its disposition and temper, and the difference in character between two individuals of the same species, would find such occupations not only exceedingly entertaining, but, if the observations were carefully noted, the result would be something of real, if not of that great, scientific value. (389)

Investigation of the natural world became over the course of the century an activity passionately engaged in by amateurs, with a number of scientific fads sweeping the nation—botany, the fern craze; geology, the rock-collecting craze; entomology, the bug-hunting craze. All of these crazes were increasingly female more than male pursuits (J. F. A. Adams, Merrill). Novelist Charlotte Brontë (1816–1855) made a pressed fern collection while away on her honeymoon. And *Glaucus* (1855), a book written by Charles Kingsley (1819–1875) to inform a hypothetical London merchant about the wonders of the seashore, asks the merchant to look at what pleasures his daughters have gained from their "pteridomania" over ferns and to imagine what equivalent joys he himself might find in a study of the seashore (4–5).

In the nineteenth century, women were in fact enthralled with gazing at the wonders of nature, participating in a virtual "romance" with natural history (Merrill) that matched their love of literary romance. Denied formal higher education, they also constituted large portions of the audience at public lectures on science and read whatever was available to them on the subject. From the late eighteenth century onward they could quite easily find the works of other women who had written the story of science by emphasizing its wonders: the puzzling or seemingly indecipherable, the new, the remarkable, the odd or amazing story of a creature or a plant that was previously little discussed or little known. Within the system of scientific practices defined by their culture, such women writers functioned not as the groundbreakers but as educators and popularizers, carefully explaining new views of the physical and natural world—translating scientific discourse into the vernacular.[1] Typically, the scientific theories they conveyed were those which had become accepted; they eschewed the controversial, partly in order to enhance their own authority. Their function was to transmit specialized scientific knowledge, the received wisdom of professionals in the field, to a general public often composed largely of women. The originality of these women popularizers therefore lay less in the theories that they were trying to recapitulate than in the kinds of discourse they evolved as they told the story of science.

1. For two particularly cogent and useful essays on the general subject of scientific popularization and its implications, see Roger Cooter and Stephen Pumfrey's "Separate Spheres and Public Places: Reflections of the History of Science Popularization and Science in Popular Culture," and Richard Whitley's "Knowledge Producers and Knowledge Acquirers: Popularisation as a Relation between Scientific Fields and Their Publics." See also Gates and Shteir (1997).

At the dawn of the Victorian era, William Whewell (1794–1866) observed that women were particularly good at scientific popularization. "We believe," he said, "that there are few individuals of that gender that plumes itself upon the exclusive possession of exact science [in short, men], who may not learn [from *On the Connexion of the Physical Sciences*, by Mary Somerville (1780–1872)] much that is both novel and curious in the recent progress of physics" (56). Whewell was certain that women made the best popularizers because they had clear, comprehensive minds. And, like Whewell, women popularizers themselves believed they were unhampered by their gender: their writing gave them voices and in many cases livelihoods as well. These women had found their audience, and they liked the job of informing it. In her autobiographical *Recollections*, Somerville herself took pride in realizing that "age had not abated my zeal for the emancipation of my sex from the unreasonable prejudice too prevalent in Great Britain against a literary and scientific education for women" (345).

Up until the end of the century, when women began to be "edged out" of science popularization as they seem to have been edged out of the "high-culture novel" by several of the mainstream publishers (Tuchman 5),[2] their volumes sold as well as men's. When George Eliot and George Henry Lewes arrived in Ilfracombe in 1856, awkward and ill-equipped novices in seashore life but ready to learn enough for Lewes to be able to write *Sea-side Studies* in 1858, they would have been as likely to have been carrying Anne Pratt's *Chapters on the Common Things of the Sea-Side* (1850) as they would Philip Gosse's *Aquarium* (1854) or Kingsley's *Glaucus*. As W. H. Brock has shown, seaside books were "heavily derivative and symbiotic" (27), and by midcentury male writers drew from women's texts as well as from men's. But if both men and women popularized science, women nevertheless established a set of narrative paradigms which in the end they made their own. These paradigms reveal a great deal about women's writing and women's authority in nineteenth-century culture and are important enough to make us pause for a moment to trace their roots in the late eighteenth century.

Dialoging

Women's popularizations of science in the late eighteenth century heavily favored dialogue as the means of telling the story (Myers, "Fictions and Facts" and "Science for Women and Children"; P. Phillips; Gates and Shteir; Shteir). These dialogues certainly do not offer what Showalter calls "the penetrating gaze of intellectual and sexual mastery" (*Sexual Anarchy* 145). Nor do they offer the hard edge of the third-person "objective" scientific paper—of the expert

2. Margaret Stetz's work with publishing houses such as Lane and Heinemann suggests that not all publishers followed the example of Macmillan; see her *England in the 1890s: Literary Publishing at the Bodley Head.*

writing for the expert. Most of the early women popularizers preferred to imagine their audience as receptive but uninformed women and children who would function as virtual tabulae rasae, querying and then waiting to receive the scientific word. Dialogue was found to be the perfect vehicle for conveying to women those "many things which were thought to be above their comprehension, or unsuited to their sex," to quote Maria Edgeworth (1768–1849) in her *Letters for Literary Ladies* (1795). Dialogues could include catechism and letters and had the virtue of acknowledged and endorsed literary value. They recalled Socratic inquiry and had been Galileo's chosen means of disseminating knowledge. What was more, they could foster drama, conference, and debate.

They also encouraged consensus. Dialogic narrative proceeds by a series of interrupted statements and explanations that continue until some consensus is reached. In addition, it challenges the authority of specialized language: the inquirers on both sides need again and again to make sure that they and their interlocutors are speaking the same tongue, one accessible to all participants. As in a class in foreign-language skills, this process of interruption and realignment of language continues until the knowledge involved becomes the property of all members of the dialogue. Since the intended audience of women popularizers did not consist of specialists, fictional authorities in the dialogues—most often women characters with scientific know-how—could afford to be sufficiently patient to get to the heart of the matter they were explicating while providing their pupils with enough time in which to learn. They were not required to foretell, but carefully to retell. The experiments they purportedly ran and the observations they made were all directed to the goal of furthering others' learning. These fictional authorities, like their authors, did not project the image of a lone scientist on the eve of a new discovery but of an alert woman sharing an interest in the world around her. While altering the shape of science writing, they added a social dimension to the story of science. Thus, while creating a scientifically literate population, women popularizers contributed to the "art of teaching" as well.

Many nineteenth-century writers of dialogues were motivated by a commitment to natural theology. In describing the wonders of nature, they believed they were also describing the wonders of creation and, ultimately, of a creator who was made more accessible through their writing. For Priscilla Wakefield (1751–1832), in *Domestic Recreation; or, Dialogues Illustrative of Natural and Scientific Subjects* (1805), "the curious phenomena that nature presents, is [*sic*] one of the most rational entertainments we can enjoy: it is easy to be procured; always at hand; and, to a certain degree, lies within the reach of every creature who has the perfect use of his senses, and is capable of attention" (77–78). For women like Wakefield, moral education and scientific observation went hand in glove: observing and teaching about the natural world amounted to a calling.

Since women saw themselves as the moral educators of each other and of the young, it only made sense that they should be the ones to offer a proof-laden version of natural theology to women and children. They became important purveyors of what I shall call the "narrative of natural theology." This category of scientific storytelling complements Greg Myers's two categories: (1) the "narrative of natural history," which refers to a popular account of nature that is diverting, full of anecdotes, and nontheoretical—the sort of thing one finds in contemporary natural history magazines, and (2) the "narrative of science," which describes a work that meets the standards of a discipline and is heavily committed to model-building (*Writing Biology* 142–43, 194–96). The primary purpose of the narrative of science is to establish the credibility of a scientist within the scientific community. Students of the nineteenth century will notice that Myers's distinctions, which are applied to the twentieth century, can easily apply to the Victorian era as well. For example, Thomas Henry Huxley and many mid- to late-nineteenth-century women popularizers utilized the narrative of natural history; Charles Darwin, the narrative of science. But this is to anticipate my own story.

At the turn to the nineteenth century, William Paley (1743–1805), not Darwin, was the figure to be reckoned with. His *Natural Theology* (1802) claimed that each discovery of natural science was new proof of the wisdom and power of a divine creator. If Paley's deity had personality and was separate from nature, Paley's nature was nevertheless valuable primarily as a means of deducing deity. For half a century, Paley's work served as the basis for popularizations of natural history, supplying the theological underpinnings for narratives of natural theology. Margaret Bryan (1769–1858), one of the best-known turn-of-the-century women who taught science both in her home and by way of her pen, prefaced her *Lectures of Natural Philosophy* (1806) with the statement, "I have followed the very excellent divine Dr. Paley, in his Natural Theology:—a work comprehensive in its nature, important in its application, and extensive in its elucidations of the divine wisdom and omnipotence of our great Creator" (n.pag.).

If for the substance of their narratives of natural theology women popularizers often took Paley's work as a model, as a paradigm for their narrative discourse they took the work of an animal lover and mother of twelve, Sarah Trimmer (1741–1810). Trimmer's *Easy Introduction to the Knowledge of Nature* (1780) was written in the form of a sequence of conversations between a mother and her two children. Together, the three take outdoor walks and talk over issues of morality and the wonders of nature, often moving through a catechism of questions and answers. In 1796, Trimmer followed the *Easy Introduction* with her immensely popular *Fabulous Histories, Designed for the Instruction of Children, Respecting Their Treatment of Animals. Fabulous Histories* features the Benson family, who become recipients of their mother's knowledge of and sensitivity toward animals as she moves her children toward understanding "the *divine principle* of UNIVERSAL BENEVOLENCE" (227). Trimmer, like many of the women popularizers who would follow her, invented stories to convey facts and created female figures as repositories of the wisdom essential for sensitizing growing children to nonhuman nature.

In *Fabulous Histories,* the children are learning about the British birds—including just about everything there is to know about robin behavior—and, like real children, they ask difficult questions. Young Harriet, for example, wants to know why it is so important for British birds to be left free to pursue wild lives while canaries are caged. The canaries, Mrs. Benson replies, are "little foreigners who claim my hospitality. This kind of bird came originally from a warm climate, and they are in their nature very susceptible of cold, and would perish in the open air in our winters; neither does the food which they feed on grow plentifully in this country; and as they are always here bred in cages, they do not know how to procure the materials for their nests abroad" (32). She goes on: "I remember once to have seen a poor Canary, which had been turned loose because it could not sing; and surely no creature could be more miserable. It was starving for want of victuals, famishing with thirst, shivering with cold, and looked terrified to the greatest degree; whilst a parcel of Sparrows and Chaffinches pursued it from place to place, twittering and chirping with every mark of insolence and derision" (32–33). Harriet of course wants to know the end of this sad story—what ever happened to "the little foreigner"? The answer: Mrs. Benson caught, caged, and—she believes—saved the bird. Here, in the early discourse on sensitivity toward other creatures, caging is not called into question as it would be later in the animal rights movements nor is the xenophobia inherent in discussions of the "little foreigner." Instead, what is most important is the cultivation of the children's sympathy. They are to be responsive to a morality propounded by women. Harriet's query speaks to the kind of sensitizing that Mary Wollstonecraft's *Vindication* advocated for young women—an awareness of the implications of metaphors like those of caged birds and their application to the situation of young women in patriarchal society.

Trimmer's work was influential for decades and became a model for writers like the poet Charlotte Smith (1749–1806), who also produced *Rural Walks in Dialogues Intended for the Use of Young Persons* (1795)—in her case to support her own children. The task proved trying, as Smith laments in her preface: "I wished to unite the interest of the novel with the instruction of the schoolbook, by throwing the latter into the form of dialogue, mingled with narrative, and by giving some degree of character to the group. I have found it less easy than I imagined" (iv). Smith's preface also reveals her worry that her work might be judged harshly and appear "insipid" to those for whom it was not intended. Readers must realize that she is not to be blamed by "persons who seem not sufficiently to consider that such books were not meant for their entertainment, but for the instruction of the rising generation" (v). Disclaimers like Smith's became an important part of the tradition of women's popularizations of science. They not only emphasized the self-consciousness of women who felt themselves excluded by the scientific community; more importantly, they also created a bond between the women writers and their less well educated audiences that paralleled those between the teachers in the dialogues and their pupils.

In this way, yet another aspect of the dialogue reinforced a model of education that enabled the conversion of the authoritative into something internally persuasive. Even Jane Marcet (1769–1858), unquestionably the most popular of the women writing scientific dialogue in the nineteenth century, used disclaimers in her prefaces. Marcet attended lectures by Humphry Davy (1778–1829), and her own work was in turn read by Michael Faraday (1791–1867), a young bookbinder's apprentice who went on to achieve scientific fame and who credited his own entry into science to her. Nevertheless, in her *Conversations on Chemistry, Intended More Especially for the Female Sex* (1805), a book that sold 160,000 copies in its day and went through sixteen editions in less than forty years, Marcet felt it "necessary to apologize for the present undertaking, as her knowledge of the subject is but recent, and as she can have no real claims to the title of chemist" (v).

Marcet evolved an important variation on the dialogue, the "conversation," devised as a result of her own needs in learning science. When she first attended lectures in experimental chemistry, Marcet found herself overwhelmed by the rapidity of the demonstrations. But as she began to have conversations with friends about what she had heard and seen, she realized that the subject of chemistry came clearer. She therefore decided that "familiar conversation was, in studies of this kind, a most successful source of information; and more especially to the female sex, whose education is seldom calculated to prepare their minds for abstract ideas, or scientific language" (v). Marcet invented a set of characters who became familiar to generations of readers: Mrs. Bryan, a teacher, and Emily and Caroline, her pupils. As in many dialogues by women popularizers, in Marcet's conversations one of the two students has already acquired some knowledge of the subject to be discussed. This allowed Marcet to speak both to readers with a degree of sophistication and to those with little or none. As the fictional Mrs. Bryan reflected the real-life Margaret Bryan, her appearance signals the beginnings of a female tradition in women's popularizations and a special tribute to the power of women's word in the teaching of science. In Marcet's book on chemistry, the three women converse their way through the discoveries of Cavendish, Lavoisier, Davy, and others. In both this book and *Conversations on Natural Philosophy* (1819), the fictional Mrs. Bryan carefully controls the conversations in order to make her points. "I do not," she remarks, "wish to confine you to the systematic order of a scientific treatise: but if we were merely to examine every vague question that may chance to occur, our progress

Figure 6. Frontispiece, *Conversations on Mineralogy* (1822), by Delvalle Lowry.

would be but very slow" (2). Marcet's characters never wasted time with dialogue but nonetheless took time to get things right by conversing productively.

After Marcet's successes, the dialogue was even more widely adopted by women and sometimes by men as well. In 1827, Charles Lyell (1797–1875) began writing "Conversations in Geology," intended to be a companion volume to Marcet's work on chemistry. But the eminent geologist reconsidered and set to work on one of the century's most famous narratives of science instead—his *Elements of Geology* (1838). The conversation form already had distinct overtones of women's talk and thus might have undermined the authority of Lyell's topic. Certainly throughout the 1820s and 1830s conversations were employed by women to introduce nearly every branch of science. In 1822, Delvalle Lowry offered a two-volume *Conversations in Mineralogy* (see figure 6), noting that "the mode of conversation has not yet been adopted in this branch of natural history" (v). In her preface, Lowry praised Marcet's format yet, despite her admiration, found problems as she herself began to experiment with the form. As a teacher, Lowry was dedicated to direct observation and hands-on experimentation, but as a writer she felt that she was offering something far less. As she carefully warned in her preface, "very little knowledge of Mineralogy can be obtained from books, without an acquaintance with Minerals themselves" (ix). In part, Lowry got around this dilemma through the ample use of illustrations in her text. Strongly believing that the systematic study of nature required direct observation of minerals, Lowry also referred her readers to museums of mineralogy, to encourage them to see collections firsthand. But she remained frustrated with other shortcomings of the conversation format. For example, the way taxonomy had been handled in earlier conversations troubled her and led to her streamlining her references: "As it did not appear consistent with the nature of conversations to particularize all the different synonymes of Minerals, I have inserted the principal in the Index; placing them after the English names. I have avoided as much as possible the use of technical terms in my descriptions; as a great many . . . have been generally adopted by English Mineralogists, I have endeavoured to define them in the first part of the work; and near the end is an Alphabetical List of one hundred and eighty-seven names of Minerals, with their derivations from the Greek, Latin, and German" (vii).

Although Lowry wanted to move closer toward representing the observations and experiments of what was already moving toward "high" science, other women continued to deliver Paleyan narratives of natural theology. In *Harry Beaufoy; or, The Pupil of Nature* (1821), a popular fiction about a ten-year-old boy, author Maria Hack (1777–1844) tells her readers: "Though I have purposely avoided placing the formidable words '*Natural Theology*,' in the title-page, yet parents will perceive, at a glance, that the admirable work of Dr. Paley has been used as the basis of this little volume" (ix). Hack goes on to spin the story of Harry and his mother, who instructs him in everything from the ligaments in chicken legs—by snatching a bird from her maid's platter—to gardens and microscopes. Through dialogue placed in the context of a more discursive fictional narrative, young Harry is made to see the wisdom and ingenuity of a divine artificer at every turn. Women like Hack were driven to keep alive the story of natural theology. They wished to continue to add moral values to the study of science, a practice many non-Paleyites would also continue in science popularizations throughout the nineteenth century. Such additions helped, in turn, to continue the romance of nature—an idea that came to annex a morality implicit in early romantic literature of poets like William Wordsworth.

Eventually the narrative of natural theology and widespread use of dialogue both dwindled in importance. The religious component of natural theology would persist in other forms, like animal anecdotes, late into the century. Nevertheless, by midcentury, evolution was in the air, and Paley, the natural philosopher and theologian, was being displaced by new scientists. In general, people were better informed scientifically by then, partly because of the dialogues themselves. But the dialogue form had begun to outlive its own credibility. Learning by question and answer was satirized in the 1850s and 1860s—by Charles Dickens (1812–1870), for example. In *Our Mutual Friend* (1864–65), his Miss Peecher and Mary Anne fall into a mock dialogue of "learning": wherever she goes, whatever she is asked, young Mary Anne reels off the expected rote answer, so inured is she to interrogation. Accordingly, John Ruskin found out to his dismay that dialogue books on natural sciences were no longer so popular when, in 1865, his book of dialogues on mineralogy appeared—and sold poorly (Myers, "Science for Women and Children," 171).

Still, for half a century the scientific dialogue had suited both its women practitioners and their audiences. Certainly, it established women as experts in knowledge. Questions imply answers, and authorities of one sort or another are needed to supply them. The female instructors in the dialogues, whether they were mothers, teachers, aunts, or older cousins, knew what they were talking about—so much so that when, in 1869, Charles Kingsley decided to write a popular book of lessons in geology for children, he titled it *Madame How and Lady Why*. Kingsley's book, addressed to young boys, made these two female figures aspects of Nature herself, the ultimate authority on how and why. Of course, the real-life female instructors were experts, too. Like all good educators, they studied their subject well enough to translate it from professional jargon into the vernacular and to cull just the right examples from their store of knowledge to impress their pupils with self as well as science. Indeed, some of these women seemed to be reappropriating the idea of Mother Nature, turning this myth into both a new kind of intellectual reality and a new kind of authority.

Journeying

By the 1840s, other forms began to enhance and ultimately replace the dialogue in science popularizations. In her *Young Naturalist's Journey* (1840) and its reissue as *The Young Naturalist; or, The Travels of Agnes Merton and Her Mama* (1863), Jane Loudon (1807–1858) (see figure 7) offered a type of narrative that would certainly widen its scope. In Loudon's "journey," a fictional young girl and her mother travel throughout the British Isles and meet, query, and parley with people who own or have extensive knowledge of exotic animals. Anecdotal in the extreme, Loudon's book was informed by other vehicles for popularizing science. When she was turning over the pages of the *Magazine of Natural History* searching for information about animals, Loudon was prompted to write her own book. "Stripped of their technicalities," the magazine articles could, she believed, "be rendered both interesting and amusing to children" (ix). The Mertons, Loudon's fictional mother and daughter, were patterned after her own daughter and herself. Loudon wrote *The Young Naturalist* and dozens of other books in order to support the two of them after the death of her husband, John Claudius Loudon (1783–1843), an eminent landscape gardener, horticulturalist, and author.

In *The Young Naturalist,* the subject that most interests Loudon is animal

Figure 7. Jane Loudon.

adaptation—like that of a mole to its underground hideaways. If there is some Paleyan reference to the beauty of adaptation in Loudon's book, the chief emphasis is on the creatures themselves, not on a conjectured creator. Take, for example, the story of a captive marmoset that Agnes and Mrs. Merton come to know in a railway carriage on the first leg of their journey. The woman to whom it belongs tells them the story of its adaptation to civilization. Captured by traders in Brazil, it would at first not allow itself to be touched. In transit over the ocean, the marmoset did not lose its wildness so much as adapt to a new diet and surroundings, darting after and feasting on cockroaches. When it arrived in the colder British climate, the little monkey suffered so much that it needed artificial warmth and was so insecure that it dragged around its cage as a potential refuge. Finally, it allowed the Mertons' fellow passenger to hand-feed it—not cockroaches, which it apparently associated with the difficult voyage across the Atlantic—but fruits. This story of adaptation to exotic places and foods both fascinates and alarms Mrs. Merton, who wants her daughter to know both about wild things and about animals' feelings but fears the marmoset's bite. Cautiously she observes: "Animals in a domesticated state often appear to lose their natural antipathies. Do you think it safe to allow my little girl to touch your monkey?" (9). The Mertons' journey is to be a lesson in adaptation and otherness, but not a source of danger. Mrs. Merton is representative of those midcentury British who approved of the domestication of exotic species but then liked to imagine that their wildness might reemerge. This not only proffered excitement but made domestication by cage and leash more morally acceptable.

Loudon's is unquestionably a railroad journey, not a turn-of-the-century, romantic-style walk in nearby rural surroundings like the rambles of her predecessors. Not only the thrills of natural history but the thrills of railway travel are described. Agnes has never previously traveled by rail and is "very much struck with, almost frightened at, the number of carriages" (1), just as she is struck with and almost frightened by the marmoset. She watches the "crowd of people who bustled about, all eager to secure their places, and all seeming in the greatest hurry and confusion; while the porters passed to and fro, each with a kind of wheelbarrow, loaded with almost innumerable trunks and carpetbags" (1–2). With railway travel a possibility for more and more people in Loudon's time and with women eager to think of themselves journeying away from their homes if only on imaginary trips via children's literature, Loudon found a medium that perfectly suited her audience. Fictional railway journeys enabled Victorian readers to view wider worlds through the windowpanes of both natural history and geography, worlds that women writers were particularly eager both to explore and depict. Mrs. Merton and Agnes call in at Birmingham, stop off in Shropshire, and go down to Dartmouth; and in all of those places they visit menageries and meet people who take them mentally not just to Brazil but to the East Indies, to other parts of Europe, and to Egypt and the Barbary Coast. When at last they return to their home in Bayswater, they are in possession of a monkey from Sumatra. With fear conquered and knowledge gained, the wonders of the empire are delivered to their doorstep.

Loudon's book, no doubt coupled with her many authoritative studies of botany for women, led to imitations like Margaret Plues's *Rambles in Search of Ferns* (1861), a first-person, fictional handbook describing a long holiday with friends in various parts of England. Plues's narrator makes visits in order to see the ferns indigenous to each part of the country, then authoritatively explains them to her native but less well-informed hosts and, of course, to her readers as well. Loudon's botanicals—for instance, her *Ladies' Flower Garden of Ornamental Annuals* (1840) and *British Wild Flowers* (1846)—were part of a movement celebrating botany that had attracted British women as illustrators and enthusiasts throughout the second quarter of the nineteenth century. These books were designed to familiarize women with native British plants that they could see with their own eyes and grow with their own hands.

But a still wider, international world of botany, much like the wider world of animals described by Loudon in *The Young Naturalist*, was opening to reading and traveling women in the 1840s and 1850s. In 1868, Elizabeth Twining's beautifully wrought *Illustrations of the Natural Orders of Plants with Groups and Descriptions* (1849–55) was specially prefaced to promote this new catholicity of vision. Twining (1805–1889)—whose family owned tea plantations in several corners of the British empire and who was known also as a philanthropist and promoter of women's education—wanted to show British plants in relation to those of other nations. "By thus placing our native plants in groups with foreigners, we acquire a more correct idea of the nature of our Flora, and the character it has when compared with that of other countries" (ii), she explained. Proud of her pioneering efforts at popularizing comparative botany, she helped her readers to see their favorites in a new light. Loudon and earlier popularizers had sympathized with women's difficulties with the Linnaean system of classification, which classified plants according to their reproductive parts. Yet Twining chose an even more difficult system to follow—Candolle's—a system which supplanted Linnaeus's for the experts. Augustin-Pyrame de Candolle (1778–1841) offered a "natural" system of plant classification according to a number of characteristics, not just reproduction. In time, the adoption of his system by professional botanists began to separate those amateur practitioners schooled in Linnaean classification, as women and children still were, from scientists who read the specialists' journals. Twining used the new scheme because she wanted her readers not to be left behind in this transition from one system to another. Candolle's ordering would allow her readers "a ready perception of the geographical distribution of any particular tribe. Also what proportion our British Flora bears, both in quantity and quality, to the whole range of the Natural Orders" (ii) (see figure 8).

By the mid-1800s, women popularizers may have favored taking readers in search of wider worlds because they themselves felt the constrictions of British society and its scientific community. Going beyond British borders offered women horizons against which to shine as authorities, granting them a stature more equivalent to that of men. Rosina M. Zornlin (1794?–1859), author of over half-a-dozen books popularizing science—among them, *Recreations in Geology* (1839), *The World of Waters* (1843), and *Outlines of Geology* (1852)—praised the work of travel writers and believed it was allied to her own work: "Descriptions of small and detached portions of the earth's surface kindle in us a desire to become acquainted with all that is remarkable on the face of the globe: in short, with all that descriptive geography . . . can impart to us" (*Recreations in Physical Geography* 4). This desire could then lead to a need to understand physical geography and, hence, to her book—which, like all of her books, was amply illustrated with wonder-producing plates of faraway places.

By midcentury, audiences for scientific writing had certainly become more demanding and more sophisticated. Speaking on behalf of the reader or student of science, Patricia Phillips explains in *The Scientific Lady* that "women were no

Figure 8.   Elizabeth Twining, *The Teazle Tribe.*

longer content to be supplied with their science in a haphazard manner" (191). Writers responded to this discontent by expanding the world of popularizations and bringing new sciences before new audiences. Nevertheless, female devotion to moralizing science remained a force to be reckoned with. Zornlin, so aware of the far-ranging, so devoted to getting an accurate picture of geology and geography to the working classes—"to the cotter no less than the large landed proprietor, to the artisan as well as the master manufacturer, to the miner as well as the owner of mines" (*Physical Geography* vii)—and so convinced of the "truth" of science, nevertheless clearly stated that truth was "God's" truth (*Recreations in Geology* 365). And Margaret Gatty (1809–1873) (see figure 9)—writer of the

Figure 9.   Margaret Gatty.

authoritative *British Seaweeds,* completed in 1862 after fourteen years of pains-taking research—continued for decades (1855–71) to reissue editions of her *Parables from Nature,* one of the most popular books of the last half of the nine-teenth century. Gatty's two-volume *Seaweeds* was intended to supplement Wil-liam Harvey's *Manual of British Algae* (1841); the *Parables,* although also based in scientific knowledge, was meant to illustrate morals. In "A Lesson of Faith," for example, the stages of metamorphosis become demonstrations of patience. In the course of this narrative, an impatient caterpillar eventually learns that it will become a butterfly—but in nature's time, not its own. One cannot will beauty or sudden, utter transformation. If one is a caterpillar, nature bestows the gift; if a child, God does. Another parable, "Knowledge Not the Limit of Be-lief," displayed Gatty's scientific knowledge more specifically. In this parable, a zoophyte, a seaweed, a bookworm, and a naturalist parley about a controversy that had earlier interested Gatty: whether a zoophyte was or was not a plant, and whether a seaweed was an animal. The naturalist solves the problem by show-ing that despite popular opinion and the bookworm's protests, the zoophyte is animal, the seaweed a plant. Even the two creatures themselves are humbled by this discovery and become "disciples" of a higher power—the naturalist—as children must in turn become disciples of God.

Reenvisioning Darwin

As they challenged themselves to popularize science in more sophisticated and less amateurish ways, women like Gatty and Zornlin continued to carry the re-sponsibilities of moral teachers because injunctions for this role had been deeply entrenched in their society. Laid down by a female tradition in children's books by writers like Mary Wollstonecraft and Sarah Trimmer, at the same time these injunctions had been further reinforced by such influential figures as Erasmus Darwin (1731–1802). In his *Plan for the Conduct of Female Education in Boarding Schools* (1797), Darwin had recommended that women inculcate in other younger women "sympathy, when any thing cruel presents itself; as in the destruction of an insect" (47). Darwin went on to illustrate his point: "I once observed a lady with apparent expressions of sympathy say to her little daugh-ter, who was pulling off the legs of a fly, 'how should you like to have your arms and legs pull'd off? would it not give you great pain? pray let it fly away out of the window': which doubt not would make an indelible impression on the child, and lay the foundation of an amiable character" (47).

This kind of moral responsibility had been still further reinforced in "how-to" books on teaching—like one by Elleanor Frere Fenn (1743–1813), *The Ra-tional Dame; or, Hints towards Supplying Prattle for Children* (c. 1800), in which dames were instructed that "nothing could more effectually tend to infuse benevolence than the teaching of little ones early to consider every part of nature as endued with feeling" (vi). Such caveats persisted into mid-Victorian times in conduct books such as Maria Grey and Emily Shirreff's *Thoughts on Self-Culture, Addressed to Women* (1851), where women were still charged with the duty of inculcating in the young sympathy and benevolence for all "inferior beings."[3] And even later in the nineteenth century, Erasmus Darwin's grandson, Charles, would influence Patrick Geddes and J. Arthur Thomson in their widely read study *The Evolution of Sex* (1889), which characterized women as having evolved "a larger and habitual share of the altruistic emotions" and as excelling "in constancy of affection and sympathy" (270–71). The role of the altruistic teacher who respected the lives of other species was thus allocated to women for the whole of the nineteenth century. Conduct books influenced not just the novel, as Nancy Armstrong has suggested,[4] but, I would suggest, women's science writing as well.

Small wonder, then, that a need and even a desire to sympathize remained with women even when a new generation of post-Darwinian popularizers of biology appeared toward the end of the nineteenth century. Remarkable among these was Arabella Buckley (1840–1929), Sir Charles Lyell's secretary. Personally familiar with the leading scientists and scientific theories of her day,[5] Buckley was a knowledgeable and authoritative popularizer of science who also accepted the woman's social responsibility to teach morality to the uneducated and the young. After Lyell's death in 1875, Buckley was considered expert enough to write the scientific portions of the entry about him in the *Encyclopaedia Britannica* (9th edition, 102–3). Although she had the mental know-how to enter formal scientific discourse, she followed a more acceptable route for women of her day and practiced gendered science, becoming an important popularizer of science rather than a scientist herself. In her first book, *A Short History of Natural Science* (1876), she recalled with a firm voice how she "often felt very forcibly how many important facts and generalizations of science, which are of great value in the formation of character and in giving a true estimate of life and its conditions, are totally unknown to the majority of otherwise well-educated persons" (vii–viii). This is to say nothing of children, who are fed only a few elementary and scattered facts about science, and therefore are unprepared "to follow intelligently the great movement of thought" (viii). Buckley's own book was

---

3. See, especially, their chapter 7, "Benevolence."

4. See Nancy Armstrong, *Desire and Domestic Fiction*, 63.

5. Alfred Russel Wallace wrote both familiarly and admiringly of Buckley in his letters, praising her to Darwin for the essay she wrote in 1871, published in *Macmillan's*, on Darwin's work (see *Alfred Russel Wallace: Letters and Reminiscences* 216–17). In a letter to Wallace ten years later, Darwin wrote that Buckley had helped him to draw up a memorial to Gladstone "with respect to your services to science" (*Wallace: Letters and Reminiscences* 257).

intended to "supply that modest amount of scientific information which everyone ought to possess, while, at the same time . . . form a useful groundwork for those who wish afterwards to study any special branch of science" (viii) and, as such, was praised by Charles Darwin.

When Buckley raises questions in her books, she makes it clear that it is she herself who has both the discernment to pose scientific questions and the knowledge to answer them. This is also true in her second book, *The Fairy-land of Science* (1879), where she expatiates on the dangers of questions and answers as she instructs children in the wonders of a science that should seem to them as magical as the wonders of fairyland, and far more accessible. Buckley advises her young readers not to be constantly asking questions of other people "for often a question quickly answered is quickly forgotten, but a difficulty really hunted down is a triumph forever" (13). Learning becomes something more than parroting. Buckley is teaching her readers how to *think* science. In *Fairyland* and its sequel, *Through Magic Glasses* (1890), Buckley generated interest in her scientific subjects by borrowing the language of fairy stories and wizardry to reinforce her belief that the wonders of science not only parallel but surpass the wonders of fairyland. *The Fairy-land of Science* is introduced with an epigraph from folklore, suggesting that fairy tales imprint the memory in ways that Buckley hopes science will. After briefly telling the story of Sleeping Beauty, on her second page Buckley asks: "Can science bring any tale to match this?" Her answer is a resounding yes; her fairies, "forces" like magnetism and gravity, will be every bit as fascinating as Sleeping Beauty, Aladdin's genie, or Ariel and Puck. In the sequel, *Through Magic Glasses,* Buckley would focus more closely on what childlike eyes can see, here with the help of the telescope, stereoscope, photo camera, microscope, and a fictional guide, a magician whose chamber—and eyes—we enter in the first pages of the book.

In both of these books, Buckley was attempting to transcend—and also to call attention to—the limitations not only of the human eye but of supposedly objective language as adequate focalizers and descriptors of natural phenomena. In several ways children's books left Buckley freer to do this than the treatise and scientific papers had left Darwin. As Gillian Beer (*Darwin's Plots*) and James Krasner (*The Entangled Eye*) have both noted, Darwin's biology seems to have made his writing more difficult for him. When Darwin chose to tell the story of evolution, he realized that the tale of life and its origins and development need an omniscient narrator but, given the evolutionary short-sightedness of *Homo sapiens,* could not really have one. He had to settle for describing nature through the inadequate lens of the human eye and with the inadequate verbal constructs of a realistic literary tradition. Hence his careful presentations of metaphoric tangled banks, his brilliant attempts to compensate for omniscience through the proliferation of written detail about nature. After Darwin, the imperfect eye of the physical human organism, still suggesting as it did the inter-preter's own evolutionary deficiencies, became a bane of science writing. Work-ing in the areas of scientific popularization and children's literature, Arabella Buckley could, however, write science with a difference. Transgressing the bor-derlands of acceptable scientific discourse, Buckley defied the limitations of both realistic language and human sensory experience. In *Fairy-land,* she could comfortably use the language of illusion to describe an impalpable world of reality, and then in *Magic Glasses,* she could reinforce the importance of access to machines designed by humans that help expand limited human sensory perceptions.

Before delving more deeply into these two books, I would like to backtrack a moment to briefly examine the writing of Sir Charles Lyell. Like Darwin's, Lyell's work was highly visual, but its sights were set less on detail and more on the larger picture. Lyell liked to envision the scope of things, to play with images that worked as museum-like panoramas or cross sections, sending the reader's eye back through time or downward through the unseeable layers of the earth's crust. In doing so, he did not choose to limit himself to the range of the human eye but asked his readers to imagine looking through the eyes of other crea-tures—to try to see both land and oceans, for example, through the eyes of an imaginary amphibian with human powers of understanding. Then, according to Lyell, one "might ascertain, by direct observation, the action of a mountain torrent, as well as of a marine current; might compare the products of volcanos with those poured out beneath the waters; and might mark, on the one hand, the growth of the forest, and on the other that of the coral reef" (*Principles of Geology* 1: 99). Such vivid, persuasive, and compensatory narrative strategizing was well known to Buckley, who worked closely with Lyell from 1864 to 1875, taking dictation for the geologist, copying his texts, and no doubt discussing his writing as they worked alongside one another.

But in *Fairy-land,* Buckley went further than Lyell. Like him, she wanted to depict the invisible in terms of the forces that shaped earth's history; like Dar-win and John Tyndall (1820–1893), she wanted to show those forces visibly at work. But in writing for children, she could count on her audience's curiosity, properly addressed, to make leaps from make-believe to science. If Darwin's dis-course was marked, as Krasner believes it was, by a tension over "misprision, il-lusion, and limitation" (5) that led him and other scientists to an empirical self-consciousness, Buckley's exploded the worry and self-importance implicit in such self-consciousness. Writing on the periphery of established science, Buck-ley came to envision nature writing as a more accurate and correctable form of fiction and told her readers so at every turn. If such writing was grounded in em-pirical evidence, it was nevertheless a mental construction, based strongly in inference as well as in observation. Here her emphases differ from Tyndall's in

particular. Although both writers stressed observation, Buckley chose to emphasize the importance of imagination to her young readers. In his essay "Alpine
Sculpture" (1864), Tyndall, on the other hand, had pointed out that

> imagination is necessary to the man of science, and we could not reason on
> our present subject without the power of presenting mentally a picture of
> the earth's crust cracked and fissured by the forces which produced its up-
> heaval. Imagination, however, must be strictly checked by reason and by
> observation. (182)

Comparison of the frontispieces of the two writers's books also point up their
different emphases. Tyndall's *Fragments of Science* had a frontispiece depicting
his own "Fairy Land of Science"—a long glacier fading off into the distance,
pointed to by three men with staffs (see figure 10). Note the differences between this and Buckley's frontispiece, with its fanciful, ice-encrusted medieval
castle with knight and lady (see figure 11). Never-never-lands and Sleeping
Beauties were acceptable in Buckley's fairyland of science because, according to
her, "exactly all this which is true of the fairies of our childhood is true too of
the fairies of science" (*Fairy-land* 6).

Why, then, should children or anyone else bother to read science at all? One
reason lay in its greater utility, which Buckley was ever clear about. Take Buckley's own example: the story of a knight who attempts to cross a raging torrent
and just before being swept away is saved by a water nymph who guides him to
the opposite shore. A Victorian person could be like this knight of old and attempt to dash across a torrent, hoping for rescue by a supernatural water nymph.
Or that person could turn to and be informed by a scientific principle which
would enable him or her to read the currents and make for the shore in due
course and due time. Both water nymph and current reading are learned constructions, but the one is more likely to save one's life than the other. Buckley
shows her readers how to grow from one set of beliefs to another, from water
nymphs to trigonometry and liquid flow, telling them what equipment they will
need to make the journey with her.

First of all, they must open their eyes; they must learn to look at what is
around them in the universe. Then they must also learn to exercise their imaginations, for much is "hidden in the things around them" (*Fairy-land* 13).
Buckley's young niece once wanted to know why there was a mist on her bedroom window in the morning. Buckley then breathed on the windowpane,
showed her the mist, and reminded her that "Cissie and auntie have done this
all night in the room" (14). This, according to Buckley, is how scientific knowledge can best be assimilated; forces can be understood only if one first discerns
them at work and then questions the mystery that they represent. Finally,
Buckley's readers must learn something of the language of science. "Not hard

Figure 10.   *Fairy Land of Science,* frontispiece, *Fragments of Science* (1879), by John Tyndall.

scientific names, for the best books have the fewest of these" (15), says Buckley, but simpler words, like "liquid" and "solid," so that readers may enter the land of science like well-equipped travelers, knowing its tongue.

Here language and the eye are foregrounded once again, but they are strongly mediated by imagination, whose powers Buckley pushes to the forefront. Buckley is careful to warn that she does not mean for children studying science to exercise "mere fancy, which creates unreal images and impossible monsters,

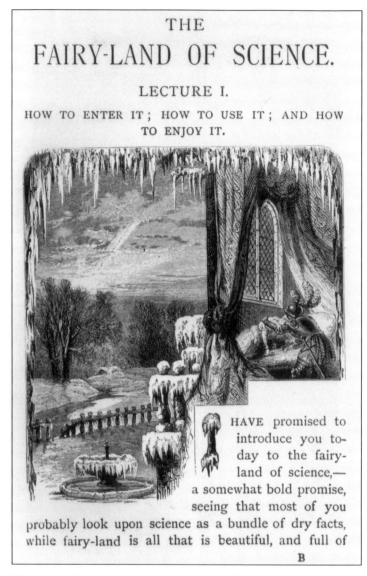

THE

FAIRY-LAND OF SCIENCE.

LECTURE I.

HOW TO ENTER IT; HOW TO USE IT; AND HOW
TO ENJOY IT.

HAVE promised to introduce you to-day to the fairy-land of science,— a somewhat bold promise, seeing that most of you probably look upon science as a bundle of dry facts, while fairy-land is all that is beautiful, and full of

B

Figure 11.   First page, *The Fairy-land of Science* (1879), by Arabella Buckley.

but imagination, the power of making pictures or *images* in our mind, of that which *is*, though it is invisible to us" (7). This distinction between fairy stories and science stories is an important one. Buckley will impart knowledge that will allow the young to see the invisible within the visible not, ultimately, by visualizing a gothic being, as in romantic literature, but by apprehending contemporary and revisable scientific theory, which is also based in human imagination.

If this too is a fiction, its probability and revisability bring it closer to describing what we see with our own two eyes. The human mind thus corrects for the human eye, and the two function together in shaping a view of the world.

Although Buckley's rhetoric and written genre afforded her a greater degree of freedom from empirical self-consciousness than most scientific papers and scientific treatises might have allowed, Buckley still faced the problem of presenting the limitations of the human eye as an instrument of discovery. Here again, her genre was a help. Women popularizers had been writing primers about microscopes and telescopes for over a century, hoping to bridge a gulf between what Barbara Stafford calls mere "'curious' *watching* and a rational, tasking, language-driven *observation*" (96). In Buckley's own time, Mrs. Ward had produced popular works on the telescope and on the microscope, hoping in the second of these to "attract those readers who, unversed in microscopic marvels, might possibly feel repelled by a complete and lengthened treatise" (*The Microscope* v–vi). Her aim was to promote "watching," and her chapters set out to describe what one could see with the aid of a microscope. Along the way, Ward also felt obliged to describe the workings of the human eye peering at the eyes of other animals through the enhancing lenses of the microscope. But rather than imagining life through other eyes, as had Lyell, Ward advocated objectifying the vision of other species in order to understand it.

If Ward's was a standard way of popularizing optics, Buckley characteristically again tried something else. Drawing in readers by setting the scene of a mysterious laboratory inhabited only by moonlight and a magician, she begins *Through Magic Glasses* with illusion. Before long, however, she demystifies her magician. He is, in fact, a knowledgeable principal of a school for boys of the artisan class—a man of science, and a teacher. Buckley seems only to have snared us with her talk of magic; our attention once captured, we are ushered into a lecture hall and are readied to learn optics. All human beings, we now learn, can sharpen their sight and become true magicians, which in this book means scientists. But they must first study their visual equipment—which means the human eye, along with telescopes, microscopes, and other devices—and realize its strengths and shortcomings. Like so many popularized versions of scientific discovery, *Through Magic Glasses* then asks its young readers to contribute to scientific inquiry. In her magician's words to his boys, "the value of the spells you can work with my magic glasses depends entirely upon whether you work patiently, accurately, and honestly." If they do so, the magician's students can then "look deep below the outward surface of life . . . and help to pave the way to such grand discoveries as those of Newton in astronomy, Bunsen and Kirchhoff in spectrum analysis, and Darwin in the world of life" (*Glasses* 54).

The magic of science is not arcane and black, Buckley seems to be saying, but discernible and white. It involves Stafford's "language-driven *observation*." Simple language and simple analogies can make science available to everyone and help correct for ignorance of the universe, just as improved optical devices can make it possible better to visualize that universe. "In these days, when moderate-priced instruments and good books and lectures are so easily accessible," says Buckley in her preface, "I hope some eager minds may be thus led to take up one of the branches of science opened out to us by magic glasses; while those who go no further will at least understand something of the hitherto unseen world which is now being studied by their help" (*Glasses* v). Word and eye can facilitate each other's work.

Still, scientific mysteries will remain, and these give Buckley room to develop her own metaphors. As we have seen, Buckley's is a science of both subjects and objects. *Through Magic Glasses* concludes not with what we might see through optical devices but with what we might not see—the visionary and the imaginative. In its final chapter, Buckley remystifies the old magician, who now sits alone in his study, concerned about how to present the story of evolution—of earth and its inhabitants, not of sky. Like Lyell and like Buckley in her earlier works, he must fall back upon "a waking dream" (210) based upon partial knowledge of the scattered fossil record. Puzzled, his students do not know why he seems possessed, with a "far-away look in his eyes" (226)—those same eyes that they had seen so effectively at work with optical devices enabling even better sight. The boys strain to understand that he has "passed through a vision of countless ages" (226) and returned to tell them a yet incomplete story. Here Buckley evokes the self-consciousness of contemporary science, aware of itself as nature trying to read nature with inadequate sensory and intellectual capabilities. But Buckley seems also to have realized that these very weaknesses in perception and lacunae in the material facts of science offered her her main openings as storyteller. If at the turn of the century Buckley and other women who were scientifically educated were not yet culturally deputized to carry the burden of scientific discovery, scientific popularization gave them entryways and elbowroom to explore—and even to enjoy—the fictiveness of science writing.

Human history obviously fascinated Buckley, as did analogies between scientific forces and imaginary fairies, but neither of these gave full scope to her distinctive penchant for narrative. Only the story of evolution did that. Thoroughly grounded in evolutionary theory and in all aspects of the new geology, Buckley set out this knowledge in a series of books whose narratives are brilliantly original. It is difficult to imagine a popularizer of Darwin who could out-narrate Darwin's own remarkable story, with its high drama of struggle and its presiding Nature who both is and is not the principle of natural selection. But, as Darwin himself knew, the story of evolution was many stories. His revisions and his own later comments on what he meant by natural selection show his own openness to reinterpretation. Buckley, then, like Huxley, was one of many later interpreters of Darwin who took advantage of the capaciousness of the story of evolution.

This she did in two highly imaginative volumes, *Life and Her Children* (1881) and *Winners in Life's Race* (1883). In these books, Buckley presented seven divisions of life: *Life and Her Children* covers the first six, from the amoebas to the insects, and *Winners in Life's Race,* the seventh, the "great backboned family" (as the book's subtitle styles it). Life, or the life force, is only a partial heroine in this story; it drives creatures to continue their species but does not exhibit the sympathy that Buckley most admires in a heroine. The quality of sympathy is reserved for the vertebrates of the animal kingdom. In this way, as in many ways, Buckley's story does not recapitulate Darwin's, with its confusion between a seemingly benevolent natural force, Nature, and a more indifferent one, natural selection.

In *Life and Her Children,* Buckley reviewed the struggle for existence and the various adaptations of the simpler animals, concluding with an interesting appraisal of ants—a scenario that prepared for her second volume. Her entire chapter on ants is highly authoritative: Buckley supports every observation and anecdote with scientific accounts by eminent authorities and leads us to consider ant colonies throughout the globe. But ants left her with a final troubling question: whether these creatures, with all their socialized behavior, were also marked by sympathy. Her conclusion was that the ant's place in Life's scheme need allow for no such thing—ants are devoted to community, not to each other. It remained for the backboned creatures to illustrate kindness.

Winners in Life's Race shows these backboned creatures in far greater detail than its predecessor had depicted the invertebrates and reveals the original ways in which Buckley handled narrative problems that had also faced Darwin. Having written a history in her first work, Buckley knew well how to depict events imagined through time. But the story of evolution called for a different kind of history, a different kind of time. The need to get beyond life spans, not just of individuals but of entire species, forced Buckley to reach past the strategies she had previously relied upon. The need to describe a history that was preverbal and antecedent to human consciousness sent her deep into images. In this second book on evolution, Buckley recalls how "with a history so strange" she wishes to "open the great book of Nature still further, and by ransacking the crust of the earth in all countries . . . try and find the explanation, which will no doubt come some day to patient explorers" (210)—the explanation of the "missing links." What stops Buckley in her long and colorful recounting of the evolution of species is a "strange blank"—the mysterious end of the age of reptiles. All this is told as spectacle, with a panoramic vividness that paints pictures rather like the museum dioramas beginning to be popular in the 1880s, the "blank" functioning like an empty case. This blank sends her back to a "history"

(342) of the mammals and humankind's appearance on the scene, which in turn affords her a place for her favorite improvement upon Darwin: her belief in the evolution of sympathy.

In *The Descent of Man* (1871), Darwin had bridged some of the perceived gap between human nature and nonhuman nature by dispelling the myth that the two are sharply divided and by laying to rest the special creation of human beings. But he did not go on to make particular pronouncements about morality as a special preserve unique to humans or about competitive advantages deriving from altruistic behaviors. He acknowledged the altruism displayed by parents toward their young but did not offer an explanation for its evolution. As James Rachels has pointed out, he was "mystified" by this issue (154). In Darwin's words:

> With respect to the origin of the parental and filial affections, which apparently lie at the basis of the social affections, it is hopeless to speculate; but we may infer that they have been to a large extent gained through natural selection. (Qtd. in Rachels 154)[6]

In *Winners*, Buckley rushes in where Darwin feared to tread and addresses altruism more directly. But before she launched into her explanation of altruism in this, her second book on evolution, Buckley looked a while at adaptation, then instinct. These observations ushered her into the realm of feeling, exactly where she wished to be. The loyalty of pet snakes, the sacrificial miming of injuries by parent birds trying to distract enemies away from their young, the instinct of herding for protection—all these led her to speculate that "one of the laws of life which is as strong, if not stronger, than the law of force and selfishness, *is that of mutual help and dependence*" (351). This law was not a special gift to human beings, as Christians might like to believe, but a gradual development through the animal world. In considerable contrast to the social Darwinists of her day, Buckley concludes her book with the very particular pronouncement, "The great moral lesson taught at every step in the history of the development of the animal world, that amidst toil and suffering, struggle and death, the supreme law of life is the law of SELF-DEVOTION AND LOVE" (353). For Buckley, the raison d'être for evolution was not just the preservation of life but the development of mutuality as well.

Buckley's last book, *Moral Teachings of Science* (1891), was devoted to this idea and written to unite science and philosophy—to study morality from "within outward" and "without inward" (4). For Buckley, "these are not really

---

6. "Darwinism and Religion," Buckley's essay for *Macmillan's* in 1871, spoke directly to Darwin's statement and attempted to show that Darwinism was not contrary to religious morality, especially in terms of altruism. Nor was it in conflict with utilitarianism at its best.

two, but only different methods of arriving at one result, namely, the knowledge of laws by which we and all the rest of nature are governed" (5). Life for
her had become universal; she set out to examine a natural and human world
where struggle predominates but mutuality works to benefit individuals of all
groups, including human beings. Although Buckley plants us firmly in the world
of sympathy, as a post-Darwinian she moves us away from the pre-Darwinian
moral order of William Paley. "We must remember," she reminds us, "that this
[evolution, development] has not taken place by special guidance along certain
beneficent lines, since degradation and partial deformities result as by-products
of the struggle for life; but that the overwhelming preponderance of healthy,
happy, and varied existence has been brought about by the steady working of
natural laws among which the struggle to survive and the constant action of
natural selection are the most important" (54).

In this championing of Darwin, as in her belief in mutuality, Buckley looked
more to the future than to the past. One could, of course, view Buckley's deep
concern with cooperation as distinctly Victorian sentimentality or look backward and see it as an aspect of the female tradition of inculcating sympathy that
I have described—and could, accordingly, minimize its significance on both
grounds. But one could as easily leap ahead and see in Buckley's vivid and lively
work something more visionary, and also more original—a rewriting of Darwin for the future. Buckley was an early Darwinian who realized the tentative-
ness in Darwin's thought on the development of moral qualities in the animal
kingdom, set out in his discussion of "social instincts" in the *Descent of Man*.
Far from being daunted by this aspect of evolution, Buckley, with her title *Life
and Her Children*, made parenting her central metaphor and continued Darwin's observations with far greater emphasis on mutuality.

In this, she was a pioneer. Her work is concurrent with Karl Kessler's "On the
Law of Mutual Aid" (1880), the lecture that stimulated Pyotr Kropotkin (1842–
1921) to reexamine Darwin. Kessler died in 1881 (the year that saw the publication of Buckley's *Life and Her Children;* it then took Kropotkin ten years to challenge Huxley, in the pages of *Nineteenth Century,* over the importance of mutual
aid and another twenty to formulate his classic *Mutual Aid: A Factor in Evolution* (1902). Huxley had claimed in 1894 that "cosmic nature is no school of virtue, but the headquarters of the enemy of ethical nature" (*Evolution and Ethics*
75). Had Buckley been writing for a different audience, her work might have
entered the debate, helped counter Huxley, and filled an intellectual lacuna
that, because of Kropotkin's hesitations, was left agape for over twenty years.

Though it may be attractive today, Buckley's moral ecology was not embraced by her contemporary Alice Bodington, whose *Studies in Evolution and
Biology* (1890) attempted to bring the story of evolution scientifically up-to-
date for turn-of-the-century readers. Bodington's whole tone is an even greater
departure from that of earlier women popularizers than is Buckley's. Buckley

found no need for disclaimers; Bodington found them wholly absurd. Her preface, entitled "To the Reader," makes this fully clear. She complains:

> A stigma is supposed to rest, for some mysterious reason, upon the person who ventures to write upon any branch of science without being an original discoverer. I am at a loss to imagine why it is considered almost wrong to write about physical science without having made original experiments. A historian is not required to have fought in the battles he describes, nor a geographer to have personally traversed the wilds of Africa. Why cannot a wide view be taken by some competent person of the results of the labours of hundreds of scientists, so that we may more clearly see what manner of fabric is being reared? (ix–x)

This is a direct plea on behalf of the expansiveness of the narrative of natural history—a preserve that women shared with men—versus the narrative of science—the more narrow, more exclusively male preserve. Bodington wanted to be able freely to enter the shared preserve without risking scientists' condemnation. She especially wanted an unobstructed right-of-way in her attempt to supplement Darwin's narrative where Darwin seemed passé.

She made this clearest in her essay "The Mammalia: Extinct Species and Surviving Forms," where she took exception, as had Buckley, to Darwin's idea of natural selection. The "great master," as she calls him, "had only grasped one form of the law governing evolution . . . whereas we now see that the infinite, delicate variations in the world of organic beings are owing to the intense irritability and susceptibility to molecular changes of protoplasm, and the consequent action of the environment upon it" (22). What she objected to in Darwin is what Buckley objected to in Paley: his determinism. To her, "natural selection evoked some unknown force vaguely of the nature of will. The action of the environment upon protoplasm requires nothing but ordinary and well-known phenomena of organic chemistry" (23). Bodington preferred this explanation because it gave natural selection a lesser role in "the great drama of development" (23).

Bodington went on to discuss post-Darwinian theories of extinction. To her mind, catastrophism was utterly dead, killed by frequent, new discoveries of missing links. She therefore proposed a natural law of her own, one "*governing the duration of species*" (27). Species and even orders of animals "may be *prematurely* destroyed by glacial epochs, or drying up of marshes, or inundations of the sea, but if they are exposed to no possibility of perishing by external accidents, *the species dies out of old age*" (27). Ever the popularizer, Bodington used her ready wit to name these "Liberal-Conservative animals," those who have the best chance of long-term survival because they "do not change too quickly or slowly" (27). When she concluded her essay on mammals, Bodington identified her intended audience—nonprofessionals who do not realize that, despite the many discoveries since Darwin's time, obscurities still veil the story of "the appearance, duration, and disappearance of species" (60). This permitted her to urge her readers, especially the travelers and anthropologists among them, to continue hunting for missing links.

In its choice of audience, Bodington's post-Darwinian work makes an interesting contrast with Buckley's. Bodington was clearly not writing for children but for intelligent adults, which gave her room to poke fun at the fanciful, Buckley's stock-in-trade. Whereas Buckley illustrated the romance of science and of geologic history, Bodington employed wit and humor to drive home the peculiarities of species' evolutionary adaptations. Spoofing science fiction, she complained of its tired exploration of beings from other planets, who "always turn out to be distressingly like ourselves." She would have preferred "a planet inhabited permanently by a set of old maids, where gentlemen were grudged even a few days of life, and one matron presided over the whole community, where there were no paupers and no starvation, and children were brought up as in the Republic of Plato" (20)—her unique demonstration of female sympathy and compassion. But more interesting still would be a world "where everyone had their mouths in the middle of their bodies . . . and their eyes at the ends of their fingers and toes" (20), like some of the animals she had just been describing. These adaptations would play havoc with the accustomed style of dinner party but would probably also be too much for the human imagination. "We might," suggests Bodington, "find our reason tottering, as that of the clergyman did, who wished that all his congregation had tails they could wag when they were specially pleased with his sermons" (20). With this kind of playful wit, Bodington's essays capture humor along with their subjects. Bodington's main thrust was to educate; she wanted to make "clear and plain" to persons of "ordinary intelligence" those many new observations of scientists who "buried" their work "in the pages of scientific journals, to be read only by specialists" (143). All the same, she could see no reason not to make the narrative of natural history as amusing and pleasurable as possible.

Nor at the end of the century could many others. Bodington worked the same vein as did men like the Reverend John George Wood (1827–1889). Although women like Arabella Buckley lectured on the subjects in which they had expertise, science lecturing was still predominantly the domain of men, themselves often hopeful amateurs whose lectures helped them to build scientific reputations or to sell books. Wood, for example, developed a unique technique that he called "sketch-lecturing." He would speak, then illustrate his subject before his audience's eyes, dramatically conjuring up huge images of hydrozoa, fish, or other animals in colored pastilles, which he applied directly to a large black canvas. When he died, the year before Bodington's *Studies in Evolution and Biology* appeared, Wood was heralded as the great popularizer of his day; when he wrote his *Boy's Own Book of Natural History* in 1883, the year of Buckley's *Winners in Life's Race*, he staked claim to the field, suggesting that there was no other "work of a really popular character in which accuracy of information and systematic arrangement are united with brevity and simplicity of treatment" (iii).

Yet Buckley's and Bodington's works supply these elements. Moreover, both of these women were supporters of the theory of evolution, which Wood, with his conservative religious bias, had trouble condoning. By the end of the century, women popularizers were often perceived as competitors in a literary struggle for survival and, because of this, were not infrequently discounted, as by Wood, or devalued. In a supposed tribute to the popular natural history writer Eliza Brightwen that introduces her posthumously published autobiography *Eliza Brightwen: Life and Thoughts of a Naturalist* (1909), Edmund Gosse, for example, all but kills his subject with condescension. "This little book," he says of Brightwen's autobiography as he compares it with her natural history, "in its simplicity, in its *naïveté*, will not be comprehended by any but those who are already in sympathy with its author and in measure conversant with her methods" (x). By implication, then, women's methods were depicted as simple and naive, rather like Charles Kingsley's description of the young women's "pteridomania" mentioned earlier in this chapter. Kingsley had minimized the young women's pursuit in order to make his intended audience, the London merchant, feel superior to his daughters. They had only taken up ferns in preference to "the abomination of 'Fancy work,' that standing cloak for dreamy idleness" (*Glaucus* 4); whereas the merchant should take up the study of seashores as an amateur naturalist.

As the century wore on, botany too was becoming the province of men, although it certainly had been the science most attractive to women. In 1887, an essay in *Science*, "Is Botany a Suitable Study for Young Men?" written by J. F. A. Adams (1844–1914), advocated plant science as an excellent area for study by "able-bodied and vigourous brained young men" (116) as well as women. Adams's attitude, like Kingsley's and Gosse's, reveals how, late in the century, scientific endeavor had become linked to masculine intellectual qualities. If women's success in purveying the narratives of natural theology and in producing botanical primers showed the importance of those books to the culture of the earlier nineteenth century, women's diminishing presence in science books for children at the end of the century does not show a lessening cultural interest in science but, instead, a shift in the popular narration of the scientific word from female to male voice. Science for the masses had become too important to entrust simply to the care of women. More male popularizers entered the field, and from the 1870s onward more intellectuals, including scientists, began to publish in nonspecialist journals and magazines (Beer, *Open Fields* 231–32). By the 1880s, Huxley, Spencer, and other well-known figures involved themselves in enterprises like the International Science Series, meant for popular consumption.

Women's loss of status in popular science writing also occurred because women's special audience of home-based children and women had decreased. Natural history education had reached the schools—first girls' schools, then boys', and had reduced the need for science books in the home. In the first half of the century, mothers and grandmothers had purchased books by women popularizers and had virtually educated themselves along with their children. Anne Brontë's Helen Huntingdon carefully educates her young son at home in *The Tenant of Wildfell Hall* (1848), and he is proud to show off his new book of "natural history with all kinds of birds and beasts in it, and the reading as nice as the pictures!" (487). And my own copy of Anne Pratt's *Chapters on the Common Things of the Sea-Side* was a gift from a grandmother to her grandson in 1852. But as time went on, mothers and grandmothers were progressively less responsible for children's knowledge of science.

Concomitantly, formal education in natural history for girls, an important ingredient in their curricula for decades, was lessened, while at the same time it was increased for boys. Young men became more knowledgeable in science, more apt to learn their science from men, and more likely to become the major disseminators of the narrative of natural history as well as the narrative of science. Ironically, this overall "demise" of science as a female interest was especially noticeable after the Taunton Commission's report of 1868–69 (P. Phillips, *The Scientific Lady* ch. 8). The commission was the result of a large-scale governmental effort to inspect schools in order to assess the nature of the education provided. Because of the intervention of Emily Davies (1830–1921)— founder of Girton College, Cambridge, and a feminist determined to improve the education of women—women's schools were included in the commission's assessment. Young women, in contrast to young men, were found to be receiving adequate scientific education but inadequate training in classics.

It was after this report that the focus of women's education shifted from the natural sciences to the classics, ostensibly to help make women's study equivalent to men's, and men's education was shifted more toward the sciences. By the mid-1890s, many of the bright young women in secondary schools who showed a special desire to study science were discouraged from taking classes in scientific subjects and encouraged instead to work to perfect a knowledge of classics. Thus in the name of equalizing formal education for women, fewer young women were given access to narratives of science in secondary schools, while at almost the same time, fewer were reading narratives of natural history in their homes. Ironically, the economics of the book trade and the masculinization of science—through appropriation by and education of men—joined educational reforms reputedly on behalf of women to prevent those very women from teaching freely in nature's name.

3

Cataloging the Natural World: Case Studies

of Women Naturalists

For most of the Victorian period, women were kept just out of reach of scientific cultural preserves, and the means of their exclusion were many. Up until the last decades of the century, women were not, for example, permitted to share tertiary science education with men. Then only a few women, like Marie Stopes—paleobotanist and, later, sex education and birth control advocate—began to receive scientific higher education at a few universities such as the University of London. Even when educated separately and given laboratory experience, as they were at the women's colleges at Cambridge from the 1870s onward, women needed to create their own scientific subculture, most often as laboratory instructors and lecturers in elementary subjects. This subculture helped perpetuate itself, but it did not lead to professional distinction for women (Richmond). From the time of the 1830s, men had worked hard to elevate the professional status of science (Basalla, Heyck), and throughout the nineteenth century they remained reluctant to admit women into the ranks of scientific professionals.

The exclusiveness of professional societies paralleled that in higher education. Women were not admitted to the Linnean Society until 1905—and then only after persistent challenges. Take, for example, Marian Farquharson's attempt to join that august body. Fellows of the Linnean needed to demonstrate an "active interest in a branch of natural history, supported if possible but not necessarily by publications and a signed recommendation by a Fellow or Fellows, and the capacity to pay the current annual subscription, followed by approval of the Council and balloting by Fellows at a General Meeting" (Gage and Stearn 195). Because Farquharson, a cryptogamist and member of the Royal Microscopical Society, felt herself qualified on all of the grounds required for admission, she petitioned for membership in 1900. Although the Linnean's charter did not expressly deny membership to women and although Farquharson was sponsored by a number of prominent members, for eight years she was consistently and sometimes rudely rebuffed. Eventually, in late 1904, fifteen women were permitted to join the society; Mrs. Farquharson, however, was blackballed for the trouble she had caused the society and not granted membership until 1908.

The Linnean Society was not alone in resisting or guarding against female membership. Thomas Huxley—who also set up the famous X Club in 1864 to polish the image of science and maintain a coterie of nine male friends near the center of things scientific—actively kept women out of the Geological Society, as we have seen in chapter 1. Even in professional societies to which women had been admitted earlier in the nineteenth century—as in the Botanical Society of London, which had granted women membership from 1836 on—women achieved their membership status at a later age than men did and then primarily on the basis of their social standing or their family's interest in science. Never did they constitute more than 10 percent of the membership, nor did they present papers. And if as early as 1838 women were permitted to attend meetings of the British Association for the Advancement of Science, even there, their activities were curtailed. They were, for example, barred at one point from the section on natural history "on account of some of the papers belonging to the Zoology section" (Alic 180)—papers having to do with issues concerning the reproduction of marsupials. In short, science for women was viewed mainly as a female "accomplishment," like the ability to play a musical instrument or demonstrate competence in archery; it was not considered a route to professionalism (D. E. Allen, "The Women Members of the Botanical Society of London").

Nevertheless, women contributed significantly to scientific knowledge—especially to the development of the natural sciences—and not just as popularizers of previously established theories. To reemploy a term coined by Steven Shapin in his discussion of skilled but uncredited seventeenth-century laboratory workers, women in the nineteenth century were often the scientific community's "invisible technicians" (Shapin ch. 8). The hidden, behind-the-scenes nature of women's work in the fields of science concealed many individual accomplishments. Yet without women's help, Victorian scientific endeavor would have been considerably diminished, although most often this help went sorely unacknowledged. In this chapter, I would like to turn the tables and discuss three areas in which women contributed particularly strongly to the enterprise of natural history: through collection, illustration, and close observation. This set of disciplined and interwoven pursuits has often been backgrounded in histories of science in favor of breakthrough discoveries and theoretical conjectures. Moving this triad of scientific practices to the foreground refocuses on nineteenth-century women's struggles to assume scientific authority, struggles that were far more difficult than, for example, the pursuit of literary recognition in the same time frame.

Collector's Collectors

Devaluation of all three pursuits—collection, illustration, and close observation—still exists today. As Kuklick and Kohler have said of scientific fieldwork, "defining scientific rigor by the standards of the laboratory, scholars have judged the field to be a site of compromised work: field sciences have dealt with problems that resist tidy solutions, and they have not excluded amateur participations" (1). This was true from the outset. In the first three quarters of the nineteenth century, women were rarely acknowledged or the value of their work as observers or collectors.

Take the case of Mary Anning (1799–1847) (see figure 12). Amateur in one sense of the word, Mary Anning was a professional in another—an unerring collector who had great impact on science yet whose area of expertise has certainly been "compromised." Anning provided extraordinarily fine fossils for well-known geologists like William Buckland (1784–1856), Sir Richard Owen (1804–1892), Henry De la Beche (1796–1855), and for countless amateurs as well. In 1811, when she was only eleven and exploring the Dorset Lias near Lyme Regis, she found the first *Ichthyosaurus* fossil and had it carefully removed, entirely intact. Now it resides in the British Museum of Natural History in London; then it was argued over by Buckland, De la Beche, and William Conybeare (1787–1857), and drawings of it were sent to Baron Georges Cuvier (1769–1832) before it was duly named and classified. Meanwhile, Anning found other fossils of previously unknown creatures, among them four kinds of *Ichthyosauri*, two *Plesiosauri*, and a *Pterodactyle* sufficiently important to make Cuvier review and retract his earlier theories. Notwithstanding these contributions, Mary Anning was rarely heralded by scientists for the deep knowledge she evinced and the extreme care she took in her work of collecting and preserving the specimens that enabled geologic theorists to decipher the fossil record. Thomas Hawkins (1810–1889) reported this conversation, recalled from his first visit to the fossil beds of Lyme: "'You will never get that animal,' said Miss Anning, as we made our devious way towards Lyme through the mist and flashing spray, 'Or if you do, *perchance,* it cannot be saved . . . because the marl, full of pyrites, falls to pieces as soon as dry. That I can prevent. Can you?'" (qtd. in Lang 159). Hawkins could not, but he did take Anning's advice and learned how to save the specimen. Nevertheless, Hawkins was something of an exception.

Others did not care so much about *how* Anning worked as they did about *that* she was working: her specimens were their commodities. Despite this tacit disparagement, Anning herself was duly proud of her skills and discernment in developing the fossil-hunting profession she had embraced from girlhood. When the king of Saxony visited her in Lyme and his companion, Dr. Carus, asked her name in order to record it in his account of their trip to the British Isles, she is reported as having replied, "My name is well known throughout Europe" ("Mary Anning, Fossil Finder" 62). But Anning's remains a name less well known in science than in supply. Even today, when she is remarked about at all, she is generally thought of as a woman with commercial interests. Yet, in

Figure 12. *Mary Anning, Pioneer Fossil Collector of Lyme Regis, Dorset* (before 1842), portrait by an unknown artist. With the permission of the Trustees of The Natural History Museum, London.

fact, Anning sold her fossils at reasonable prices—the first *Ichthyosaur* cost its purchaser only twenty-three pounds. Ultimately impoverished, she wound up living out her days on a small grant from Lord Melbourne, requested for her by Buckland.[1]

Anning did have a scientist's curiosity and methodicalness about what she was doing. Her letters to Buckland show that she was capable of preparing exact descriptions of her finds. Her work was observed by others who were amazed at its thoroughness and proficiency. One woman who watched Anning work, Lady Harriet Silvester (1753–1843), described in her diary how adeptly Anning "fixes her bones on a frame with cement and then makes drawings and has them engraved" (qtd. in Torrens 265). Anning also collected live specimens from the environs of the beds containing her fossils so that the geologists with whom she dealt might make comparisons between living and extinct species (letter of 21 December 1830, qtd. in Lang 155–56). Her observations on squid ultimately led Buckland to speculate accurately about ink sacs in marine fossils.

So why has this heavy contributor to the foundations of modern geology been little acclaimed as such in the history of science? Mainly because, as Ruth Ginzberg has shown, we fail to recognize something as science that has not been called science all along—primarily because that something has not already been "awarded the honorific label of 'Science'" (70). This certainly seems to have been true of the "science" performed by collectors who were women; their work was prejudged with an unfair, "unscientific" bias. They were seen as helpmeets and enablers, rarely as professionals in their own right. Like the women at home, they provided services. Anning, who collected and knew well what she was collecting, was viewed in this light.

But Anning faced still other biases in her culture. Not well-educated except in finding and identifying fossils, she was unlike other women discussed in this book. She did not write well enough either to establish herself as an expert in a new branch of scientific knowledge or to leave personal journals or memoirs by which others might have established her reputation later. In addition, her few remaining letters, once part of the Owen collection, have been scattered. Class attitudes also may have played a part in Anning's case. Listen, for example, to the tone of Gideon Mantell (1818–1852), famous for his work on the dinosaur *Iguanodon*, the star of the show at the great Crystal Palace Exhibition in 1851. In his journal, Mantell described a visit to Anning in a flippant, denigrating prose that indicates something of Anning's double bind as both a single woman and an impoverished tradeswoman. Mantell sports with Anning by calling her "the geological Lioness." Then, he goes on to describe her:

---

1. Hugh Torrens's fine, recent article, "Mary Anning of Lyme," which also features Anning as a collector of great value, suggests that it may have been either Owen or Buckland who "wheedled" (269) this grant.

We found her in a little dirty shop, with hundreds of specimens piled around her in the greatest disorder. She, the presiding Deity, [proved] a prim, pedantic vinegar looking, thin female; shrewd, and rather satirical in her conversation. (Qtd. in Torrens 268)

In the end, in addition to her stipend from Lord Melbourne, Anning was given an honorary membership in the Geological Society, bestowed a few months before her death, and, ultimately, a dedicatory window in a local church, installed posthumously. In 1865, over two decades after Anning's death, an anonymous writer for Charles Dickens's magazine *All the Year Round* wrote a latter-day tribute to Anning. He/she concluded: "Her history shows what humble people may do, if they have just purpose and courage enough, towards promoting the cause of science. The inscription under her memorial window commemorates 'her usefulness in furthering the science of geology' (it was not a *science* when she began to discover, and so [she] helped to make it one)" ("Mary Anning, Fossil Finder" 63). Mary Anning had indeed helped make geology what it was in the nineteenth century; unfortunately, this fact still needs reinforcing today.

Few women contemporaries fared even as well as Anning. The final reputation of Anna Atkins (1799–1871), a collector of British seaweeds, is more typical of women in the second quarter of the nineteenth century. Atkins spent ten years not only collecting but reproducing images of marine algae and in 1843 privately published the first book of natural history to be illustrated by photography, *British Algae*. Before Atkins, the only illustrated catalogs for botanicals were hand drawn, which made her book what Larry Schaaf calls "the first realistic attempt to apply photography to the complex task of making repeatable images for scientific study and learning" (8). Although Atkins called her photos "photographs," they were actually photograms whose plates were made by ordering the specimens directly on light-sensitive paper. With no negative or camera involved, the object is placed in the sun and its shadow cast directly onto the recording surface, leaving a perfect image. The surface, usually writing paper, is coated with ferric ammonium citrate and potassium ferricyanide and, after exposure, simply washed with water. The result is a blue-toned photogram, or cyanotype, a perfect background for images of marine algae.

Atkins was encouraged in her enterprise by her father, a fellow of the Royal Society, librarian and keeper at the British Museum of Natural History, and friend of Sir John Herschel (1792–1871), who invented the cyanotype. Before photogramming the seaweeds, Atkins had illustrated her father's translation of Lamarck's *Genera of Shells* in 1823 with more than 250 hand drawings and was also adept at lithography. When she turned her hand to marine algae in the 1830s, she was working in an area in which British women already had made a place for themselves. Ever since Robert Kaye Greville (1794–1866) introduced his *Algae Britannicae* (1830) with a tribute to women who worked with marine algae, women had been respected in this particular field—which, as we have seen, would later become the province of Margaret Gatty as well.

Unfortunately for her own reputation as a collector, Atkins chose a precarious medium for her presentation. In an age of quickly changing technology like Atkins's, a scientific work could fast become out-of-date because of its presentation, let alone its "science." I would like to interrupt the story of Atkins's work for a moment to indicate just why. Natural history and its "crazes" of the earlier nineteenth century had started with observation, with the enjoyment of particulars rather than theories or abstractions, and with an eye to beauty, all of which attracted women in large numbers. The human eye was trusted as an appropriate instrument of observation, and a focus on seeing became a hallmark of Victorian culture, a culture obsessed with sight (A. Briggs, Krasner, Crary). As the character Rhoda Gale says in Charles Reade's novel *A Woman-Hater* (1877), "the humblest spot in nature becomes extraordinary the moment extraordinary observation is applied to it" (89). Retraining the eyes for close inspection of natural processes kindled the excitement of a personal rediscovery of the everyday world, but it took some patience and some talent to become an adept in natural history. Women and men who wanted to contribute to the field needed to pass through what Edwin Lees (1800–1877) in 1838 termed the "ordeal of study . . . which no ingenuity or tact of observation can enable [the natural historian] to dispense with" (297). Many Victorian women were willing to run this gauntlet.

One of them, Emily Shore (1819–1839), whose personal journal extended to twelve volumes, often wrote of what she saw around her. A prodigy who died at age nineteen, Shore developed considerable skill in both botany and ornithology. She watched birds in every season and at every hour of the day, keeping precise records of their movements and behavior and then writing two essays on bird behavior for the *Penny Magazine* that were published in 1835 and 1837. When she turned her eyes from birds to plants, she set out with similar aspirations to accuracy. "I shall," she said, "study botany this year in a very different way from that which I have been accustomed to pursue, for I find that I have hitherto been a very superficial botanist, attending to little besides the uses of plants, as I do the habits of birds. I might just as well call myself an ornithologist, if I knew only in what tribe to place a bird, as call myself at present a botanist" (89). The rage to see and then classify in order to understand and order came to dominate science.

Yet as early as the 1820s and 1830s, numerous experiments conducted on the eye itself had revealed it to be an unreliable instrument—limited physiologically and bounded too by individual subjectivity. Science, as we have seen in the discussion of Arabella Buckley, was requiring something more dispassionate, something more objective than the human eye to help determine its truths (Krasner, Crary, Daston and Galison, Horton). And not only was the subjectivity of the observer called into question but so too were the things seen. As Jonathan Crary has noted, "the problem of the observer is the field on which vision in history can be said to materialize, to become itself visible" (5). To do creditable scientific work, one had to get the field in sharpest possible focus; consequently, new optical devices were brought in to aid in this refocusing. Enter not only the photographic camera but a host of other inventions, like the stereopticon. And reenter, too, Anna Atkins with her cyanotypes. Atkins seemed to have sensed what was in the air in the 1830s. As Lorraine Daston and Peter Galison have described it, science was more and more eager to let nature describe itself, removing the observer as much as was possible. And all sciences needed to deal with the "problem of selecting and constituting 'working objects' [representative specimens], as opposed to the too plentiful and too various natural objects [individuals of a species]" (85). Atkins's cyanotypes lent this aura of objectivity to her study; in her medium the objects themselves provided their reimaging.

There were, however, several problems with Atkins's medium. The individual algae Atkins chose were not necessarily typical of their kind. A composite illustration of an idealized object, drawn from several specimens, might have been more representative of a class than were the separate samples she photogrammed. Moreover, Atkins was unfortunate enough to choose a new medium that would soon be made technically obsolete by further developments in photography. Suggesting waterlike tints of the sea, the blue cyanotype backgrounds lent enormous beauty to her studies of sea plants, but the translucence of many of the plates could also mislead some of the people relying on Atkins's book for clues to identification in the field. In addition to the technical defects inherent in her medium, Atkins herself was not careful to note precisely where all her algae were found, rendering her collection of little use to most scientists—professional or amateur. She also did not produce an index to her work. In one sense, then, her achievement remains what Schaaf has determined it to be: "a seminal contribution to book illustration" (40).

Atkins's work does not, as Gatty's does, supplement Harvey's *Manual of British Algae* (1841); it does not expand it in the way in which her handwritten introduction suggested it might. Instead, it offers an ecological vision of sea and seaweed. Whereas Harvey's images are stiffer and set starkly against white pages, Atkins's plants are artfully arranged to suggest a living organism swirling in an appropriately liquid blue medium. But in another sense—if we take Atkins's failed experiment both as a contribution to the history of beautiful book design and as an attempt at a more accurate form of cataloging—she is also a pioneer. Her brand of photography did not prove useful in accurately representing species. But then, neither would photography itself—and for exactly the reasons that her work might be criticized: because photographs of individuals do not make good composites of species. Scientific illustration has proved itself the more accurate form of atlasing. Nevertheless, Atkins's cyanotypes do suggest the variety and large numbers of marine algae and the decided individuality of some members of given species. Atkins wanted to offer the "impression of the plants themselves" (handwritten introduction), to give a sense of living nature. Like the work of midcentury natural history illustrators, her many hundreds of plants are drawn from life.

The Art and Science of Illustration

Accurate scientific illustration has often been the purview of women. Yet few Victorian women, and that includes a cyanotype producer like Atkins, entered the ranks of scientific illustrators in order to gain recognition for their achievements. Most worked for love or money. Emily Bowes Gosse (1806–1857), who had studied with John Sell Cotman (1782–1842) and was a landscape painter, executed all of the underwater landscapes for *The Aquarium* (1854) (see figure 13), a stunningly and colorfully illustrated book by her husband, Philip Gosse (1810–1888). This book bears the subtitle *An Unveiling of the Wonders of the Deep Sea*, a designation that clearly points to the importance of its illustrations. If one recalls Louis-Ernest Barrias's sculpture *Nature Revealing Herself to Science*, Philip Gosse is here unveiling and revealing nature—in this case, the sea—through his written text. But Emily Gosse's illustrations are both more dramatic and more accessible to the uninitiated than are Philip Gosse's accompanying words. She is the real unveiler for the public. Nevertheless, although the sale of books like *The Aquarium* was in large part dependent upon the quality of their pictures (Dance 200, 206), Emily Gosse's contribution went unacknowledged by her husband. The pictures are unsigned, the title page does not mention the illustrator, and the plates are labeled simply "P. H. Gosse, delt [delineated]."

Elizabeth Gould (1804–1841), one of the world's finest bird illustrators, was similarly unacknowledged. Gould died at an early age, having virtually given her life for her husband's passion for compiling bird atlases. Overworked by producing both the illustrations for the seven-volume *Birds of Australia* (see figure 14) and a family of eight children, Elizabeth Gould was only partially revealed as the illustrator of those books. John Gould, her husband, signed all of the plates "J & E Gould del et lith [drew and put on lithographic stone]," which disabled reviewers from discerning exactly who did what, something Edward Lear (1812–1888) would complain of when he worked as an illustrator for Gould. Of course, it is important to keep in mind that the text in books like the Goulds' was the primary part of the volume; despite Lear's demurral, artists would have known this. As Ann Shelby Blum points out, typically writers "'owned' and bore responsibility for . . . intellectual contents, including the illustrations" (9). Thus the *Naturalist* could review *The Birds of Australia* by pointing out that the plates were "executed with the hand of a master; and we particularly admire the representations of the genus *Malurus*, where the heads are finished as usual, and

Figure 13.   Emily Bowes Gosse, *Star Fishes*, illustration from *The Aquarium* (1854), by Philip Gosse.

Figure 14. Elizabeth Gould, *Swift Lorikeets and "Eucalyptus gibbosus,"* illustration from *The Birds of Australia* (1840–48), by John Gould.

the rest of the bodies sketched in a light and excellent style. The colours, too, are as judiciously and accurately laid on as we could desire, and Mr.GOULD has not failed even where the tints are most brilliant and difficult to obtain the freshness and vividness of Nature" (47). Although John Gould was in charge of all of his volumes, the plates of *Malurus*—the wrens—were actually Elizabeth's,[2] as was the idea to learn about and draw native plants in conjunction with native birds—to represent a larger ecosystem of bird and bush. In a letter to her mother in England, Elizabeth Gould wrote from Australia: "Just now during John's absence I find amusement and employment in drawing some of the plants of the colony [Tasmania], which will help to render the work on Birds of Australia more interesting" (9 January 1839, qtd.in Chishom 49). Elizabeth Gould, like the many women in Charles Darwin's family and acquaintance who collected and experimented on behalf of Darwin's work, did not see herself as seeking fame. Avant-garde in her ecologically sophisticated illustrations, she simply saw herself as enhancing her husband's book by representing animals in their native environment. This was her role in science.

Illustration could thus be a thankless task within the culture of science. Illustrators—female and male—worked under the direction and at the whim of both scientists and book producers. It was with no small edge that in 1869 the botanical illustrator Walter Fitch (1817–1892) complained that it was dangerous to artists to be too exacting in depicting flowers: "It might tend to upset some favourite theory, or possibly destroy a pet genus—an act of wanton impertinence which no artist endowed with a proper respect for the dicta of men of science would ever be wilfully guilty of!" ("Botanical Drawing," qtd. in Blunt, *Botanical Illustration* 276). Unlike Fitch, women botanical illustrators were unlikely to complain and generally drifted into anonymity. One need visit the Botanical Library at the Museum of Natural History in London only briefly to find hundreds of drawings signed by women whose careers and lives are impossible to trace.

For some women, the work of scientific illustration might incur rather than alleviate debt, a painful fact that author-illustrator Sarah Bowdich Lee (1791–1856) eventually discovered. Lee's first book, published in 1825, was a completed version of her husband's *Excursions in Madeira and Porto Santo*. Lee took sole responsibility for the book when her husband, Thomas Bowdich (1791–1824), died of fever on that trip. Left with debts to pay and children to support, Lee began her own writing career by prefacing her husband's work and supplementing it with a number of appendixes, including all of the natural history drawings for the text. Three years later, with the publication of the beautiful

---

2. Elizabeth Gould illustrated all but one of the wrens in volume 3 of *The Birds of Australia.* The illustration *The Beautiful Wren* (Pulcherrimus) is the work of Henry Constantine Richter, as are all of the "supplemental wrens" in volume 7.

Fresh Water Fishes of Great Britain Drawn and Described by Mrs. T. Edward Bowdich, subsidized by herself in order to gain her reputation, Lee embarked on an independent career. What made her forty-four watercolors so remarkable was her experimental use of gold and silver foil to give them a sense of the metallic iridescence of fish scales. Like many of the women who entered natural history illustration wishing to draw only "from life," Lee wanted to be on-site when her fish were caught in order to capture such living color.

As an early Victorian gentlewoman, Lee felt it unseemly to catch her own specimens. "It has never," she disclaimed, "been my intention to touch upon the manner of catching the Fishes I have delineated, for that demands an experience and skill that a female cannot be expected to possess" (iv). What she did instead was to sit alongside the fishermen who caught fish for her, as she tells us when recounting her trip to a trout stream: "The colours of the trout change directly after they leave the stream; but I was lucky enough to avail myself of the skill of a friend, who supplied me with a succession of them as I sat on the bank, and by which I secured the tints in all their delicacy and brightness" (iv). Still, Lee knew she needed specimens from all over the British Isles, much further than she could travel personally. She was often frustrated, first, by her attempts to get living specimens through the post—packaged and sent in bladders—and, second, by variations in the same species of fish pulled from the waters of different parts of Britain. The Parr of the south, she found, was very different from the Parr of the Tweed—just the sort of observation that would aid taxonomers to determine accuracy in developing sciences like ichthyology.

Despite inconveniences and handicaps, Lee persisted with her volume, determined to produce authoritative work. For a time her primary concern became the defining of riverine versus estuarine fish. In the case of the Thames, she decided to establish a simple rule for herself: all fish constantly found above London Bridge she labeled as freshwater; all below, estuarine. With this determined, she took up a post on a small island in the Thames near Henley-on-Thames and spent day after day there. Local inhabitants of the island and town helped her by catching fish for no remuneration other than the right to look at the exquisite drawings. Figure 15 offers an example of what they saw: a representation of a perch, from the mill-pool at Henley-on-Thames, ablaze in Lee's choice of gold and silver foils (see figure 15).

Studies like Lee's were pioneering works and served an important function in pre-Darwinian science, when classification was of the utmost importance. But Lee herself went on to write books on Baron Cuvier and on taxidermy and also works of fiction—all of which took less time, effort, and expense on her part than had the book on fishes and all of which she hoped would net her greater profits than had the privately printed, beautifully produced, and ultimately debt-inducing *Fresh-Water Fishes.* Scientific illustration did not earn a living for Sarah Bowdich Lee, as it had for Elizabeth and John Gould. Nor was commercial illustration a fully respectable profession, at least for women who

Figure 15.   Sarah Bowdich Lee, *Perch,* illustration from *Fresh-Water Fishes of Great Britain, Drawn and Described by Mrs. T. Edward Bowdich* (1828), by Sarah Bowdich Lee.

had other means. Beatrix Potter met parental opposition when she stated her wish to be a professional scientific illustrator.

Nevertheless, women who could persisted in working in this field, none to more acclaim than Jane (Jemima) Blackburn (1823–1909)(see figure 16), a Scotswoman and amateur ornithologist who—like Lee with fish—took pride in painting birds "from nature" rather than from skins or dead models as had the Goulds and John James Audubon (1785–1851). Blackburn hung from ladders to capture the sight of owls in their tree, struggled with frozen paintbrushes as she depicted swans in the cold, and peered over cliffs to view sea eagles in their nest. If Bessie Rayner Parkes (1829–1925) poetically immortalized the famous feminist Barbara Leigh Smith Bodichon (1827–1891) as daring the wilds in her plein air landscape painting,[3] Jemima Blackburn celebrated herself by

3. According to Pam Hirsch, Bodichon was known to paint out-of-doors for twelve-hour stretches. Bessie Rayner Parkes depicted her as:
> Perched on a crazy paling,
> Deep in a hawthorn hedge.
> On briny air inhaling
> Which whirls by ocean edge:-
> Wherever Nature calls
> Will this brave artist speed.
>   (Qtd. in Hirsch 176)

Hirsch also notes that in 1849 Bodichon wrote a fictional work entitled "A Parable. Filia," in which she describes a daughter of nature who goes to Scotland—Blackburn's country—to learn that Nature is the primary book for a landscape painter to study (171–72).

Figure 16.   Jemima Blackburn.

sketching herself painting birds. A friend of John Everett Millais (1829–1896) and the Ruskins, she adhered to the Pre-Raphaelite qualities that Ruskin had espoused, paying utmost attention in her work to truth to nature and to the precise capturing of every detail. Blackburn was always given credit for this strength in her work, but it is important to recall that this was not a strength peculiar to her. As we have seen with Bowdich Lee, women had for many years prided themselves on sketching or painting from life. As early as 1816, in Brookshaw's

New Treatise on Flower Painting; or, Every Lady Her Own Drawing Master, women were encouraged to equal or surpass men as floral illustrators and to do so by copying from nature, not from other art "because Nature . . . has nothing gaudy in all her works" (33). William Holman Hunt, who in 1853–54 painted the image of a hothouse woman (see figure 1) that opened this book, forty years later, in 1893, painted another archetypal woman, this one fully out-of-doors in a garden, in *The School of Nature* (see book jacket illustration). By 1893, perceptions of womanhood had altered, and Holman Hunt's central female figure had correspondingly altered. Like Blackburn, she is immersed in her work, studying the world of the nature as she readies herself to draw.

Jemima Blackburn was an especially painstaking observer of nature who knew well the habits of the birds she drew. In one instance, her careful observations served as a corrective to John Gould. In his *Birds of Great Britain,* Gould had suggested that host birds accidentally destroyed their own young when making room in their nests for a cuckoo chick. But Blackburn had seen and drawn a young cuckoo ejecting the nestlings of its host parents. Testing her observations by replacing the young of some pipits in a nest only to find them again thrown out by an interloping cuckoo, she wrote up her first formal account of this behavior in two children's books, *The Pipits* and *Caw! Caw!* in 1871. As Blum has suggested, in the later nineteenth century "the ever-growing literature of popular natural history . . . continued to meet and cultivate a taste for prose and pictorial descriptions of whole animals in nature" (*Picturing Nature* 318–19), and Blackburn contributed strongly to this descriptive literature. When she was encouraged by friends to republish her findings in more scientific publications (in addition to her popular books), she did so in a letter in *Nature* (14 March 1872). In a rare case of popular science informing more official science, Gould would also publish her drawing in *The Birds of Great Britain,* with a corrigendum acknowledging his earlier mistake about the cuckoo.

Blackburn's own *Birds Drawn from Nature* (1862) received widespread recognition but did not satisfy its very particular author-illustrator, who immediately set about expanding and revising it. Blackburn reworked the plates, some of which had been damaged, and for her second edition there was unqualified praise. Hailed as the best bird illustrator since Thomas Bewick (1753–1828), Blackburn was appropriately complimented by art critics and scientists alike. The eminent naturalist Joseph Wolf (1803–1857) wrote her a long letter in which he favorably compared her with John Gould:

> In avoiding hard outlines of single feathers and over precision of their markings you have preserved an agreeable breadth and have produced pictures of birds as birds are generally seen. The reverse of this subordination of detail forms a great fault of Gould's drawings; his pastel plumage without light shade or perspective in the markings spoils the form flattening it instead of showing the round body of a bird it often looks more like a map

Figure 17.   Jemima Blackburn, *Cuckoo,* illustration from *Birds from Moidart and Else-where* (1895), by Jemima Blackburn.

> of its markings. Besides as Mr Gould has never drawn birds direct from the life his figures must be more or less conventional and consequently there are very few of them so characteristick [*sic*] as those of yours which are done direct from the life. (Qtd. in Fairly 58–59)

Lady Eastlake (1809–1893) compared Blackburn to Joseph Mallord Turner (1775–1851), suggesting that both artists had "studied *Nature*" (qtd. in Fairly 70).

Thus praise for Jemima Blackburn came freely, as praise had come for Mary Somerville's study of physical science. Each of these women moved in circles literate and scientific, and each had a temperament that was pleasing to others. Blackburn was, for example, self-effacing, a quality openly demonstrated in her work. In her preface to *Birds from Moidart and Elsewhere* (1895), she sounds much like those women popularizers who disclaimed scientific authority. "I do not," she says, "attempt to give a complete collection of British birds, or even those of Moidart, still less to describe them scientifically (all of which has already been admirably done by Yarrell), but only to represent such birds as I have known personally, and to add simply, and I trust truthfully, a few observations which I have had the opportunity of making on their life and habits" (1) (see figure 17). Such self-effacement not only characterized the work of women popularizers of science; it also, George Levine reminds us, characterized the world of Victorian science at large, where the "denial of specialness—of genius, of heroism—is a mark of much nineteenth-century narrative, and a further gesture in the intellectual imperialism of nineteenth-century science" ("Objectivity and Death" 281). I believe that in its eradicating of the subject-self and its foregrounding of the subject or object studied, women's self-effacement was akin to the objectivity sought after in mainstream scientific observation. In this way, the modest disclaimers of many women illustrators and writers of natural history reinforced the entire movement toward scientific objectivity that grew with the unfolding of the nineteenth century.

Putting Oneself into the Picture: Scientific Women of the 1890s

When women began to popularize science, literature and science were not categorically separated in the way in which they are now. The word "scientist" was not even coined until 1840, when William Whewell realized: "We need very much a name to describe a cultivator of science in general. I should incline to call him a Scientist" (*Blackwood's Magazine* 273). But as the century progressed and a more professional scientific class arose, its professional readership would read and validate scientific content, as well as reinforce its own identity, via scientific publications such as specialist journals and monographs. Gillian Beer characterizes this kind of writing as "a concentrated technical address to like-minded and similarly prepared readers, emphasizing specification of meaning and offering few means of entry to non-specialists" (*Open Fields* 160). In biology, such writing was eventually dominated by a coterie of men who worked for major museums or institutions of higher learning in places like London's South Kensington or Kew, which were largely state-supported and staffed by full-time researchers (Outram). By the end of the nineteenth century, when women began to be edged out of scientific popularization, they were rarely permitted to enter the ranks of these scientists. This did not, however, mean that women did not scrap to enter the scientific enterprise and be recognized for their scientific experiments and intuitions.

Take the case of Beatrix Potter (1866–1942) and her work in the field of mycology as a first example. From 1887 until 1901, Potter intensively gathered and studied fungi in Perthshire and the Lake District. After examining them through microscopes, photographing them, sketching them in separate sections with special attention to the attachment of the gills and stems, and heeding her friend Charles McIntosh's advice to study them from life and carefully learn the scientific nomenclature that verbally described them, Potter produced over three hundred detailed scientific drawings of fungi (see, for example, figure 18). As she got deeper and deeper into mycology, Potter began to experiment as well, keeping exact records of the germination of spores, checking her specimens every few hours, and drawing the germinating spores she had examined at high

Figure 18.   Beatrix Potter, *Illustration of Fungi—Yellow Grisette ("Amanita crocea") and Fly Agaric ("Amanita muscaria")*. © Frederick Warne & Co., 1966. Reproduced by kind permission of Frederick Warne & Co.

magnifications. She was a pioneer in discovering the molds that accompanied higher fungi and worked diligently to grow them, realizing that "there are enormously more moulds than have been specified" (*Journal* 420). At an earlier juncture in the history of natural history, this alone would have qualified her as an expert. In the field of spore experimentation, she succeeded in germinating *Basidiomycetes,* something that no one in Britain had ever done before her.

At this point, Potter decided to present her work to the experts at Kew Gardens. First, she offered a set of drawings illustrating her discovery, but the authenticity of these drawings was doubted by Kew's chief mycologist and assistant director, George Massee (1850–1917). They were nevertheless provocative enough to enable her to obtain an admission ticket to Kew. Second, she wrote up the result of her findings in a paper which she typed herself and took to Sir William Thiselton-Dyer (1843–1928), Kew's director. Despite her family's connections with Thiselton-Dyer, Potter in her correspondence—suggesting that Massee was wrong and that the Germans would outstrip the British in mycology if her own researches were ignored (3 December 1896, *Letters* 38)— totally irritated Thiselton-Dyer. He told her that he had not had the time to look at her drawings and curtly dismissed both her work and herself. Dauntless, the far-from-self-effacing Potter tells us in her journal that she just as curtly "informed him that it [her discovery] would all be in the books in ten years, whether or no" (*Journal* 426).

With the aid of her uncle, Sir Henry Roscoe (1833–1915), who was known in scientific circles, Potter next set about preparing a formal paper for the Linnean Society. Meanwhile, Massee began growing the same mold spores that Potter had been studying. In Potter's journal, she indicts him for being slow and narrow in his focus: "It is extraordinary how botanists have niggled at a few isolated species and not in the least seen the broad bearings of it. He [Massee] would never have found out the bearings of the lichen" (426). What Potter refers to here are her own experiments with the new theory of the German scientist Simon Schwendener (1829–1919), who contended that lichens were dual organisms, a fungus growing in tandem with an alga. Having thought through this duality for some time and having had some doubts about the details of Schwendener's work, she turned away from the gates of Kew and toward the British Museum of Natural History, where she confronted George Murray (1858–1911) with a series of questions based upon her own theorizing. These questions, she says, tested Murray's knowledge of lichens beyond the bounds of his current understanding. At this point, Potter grew wary of imparting too much experimental knowledge to too many scientific experts. She tended to make them prickly, and they might, in reaction, never acknowledge her work. As she said of *A. velutipes* in a letter to Charles McIntosh: "Unless I can get a good slide actually sprouting it seems useless to send it to the Linnaean [*sic*]. I should be obliged if you would *not* mention it to any one [*sic*] concerned with botany, until the paper is really sent, because without meaning to be uncivil they are more inclined to grow the things themselves than to admit that mine are right" (22 February 1897, *Letters* 41).

Eventually "On the Germination of the Spores of *Agaricineae*" was presented at the Linnean Society on 1 April 1897. In what can surely be seen as dramatic irony, it was read by a George Massee on behalf of a "Miss Helen B. Potter." As we have seen, at this time women could not be members of the Linnean Society; nor could they read before that august body. There is no evidence as to whether Potter's accompanying drawings were shown at the Linnean (Noble 123) nor whether the entire paper or only a portion of it was read. Thiselton-Dyer, not Massee, is listed as the main speaker of the day. Although Potter was subsequently told that her paper was "well-received," she was also informed that it needed more work. Whether or not it got that reworking, we also do not know.[4] Potter stopped keeping her journal, the source of most of this information about her attempt at scientific recognition, before the paper was delivered, and the paper itself does not survive. Potter was not one of the botanists' number

---

4. What we do know—and for this information I owe Anne Stevenson Hobbs yet another round of thanks—is that in 1997 the Linnean Society offered an official apology to Beatrix Potter in April, one hundred years after the original presentation of her paper.

Figure 19. Margaret Fountaine.

and no longer seems to have cared to be. By the turn of the century, she had be-gun writing her little books for children, where she could freely utilize her knowl-edge of mycology in other ways, illustrating and fancifully describing the fungi that had so fascinated her scientifically.

Potter's story in the halls of science has been well-documented because her life is well-documented (Taylor, Whalley, Hobbs, and Battrick; Noble). But her case is not unusual. By the late nineteenth century and on into the twenti-eth, there was not just a cleaner line of demarcation between the amateur scien-tist and the professional scientist; professionals were by then more determined to maintain science as a limited preserve. Even if Margaret Fountaine (1862–1940) (see figure 19) seems to have succeeded in entomology where Potter failed in mycology, having published more than twenty scientific papers on but-terflies in journals like the *Entomologist*, the *Entomologist's Record*, and the

Transactions of the Entomological Society of London between 1897 and 1935 — she, like Potter, received little acknowledgment from her contemporary associates. In a final tribute paid to her by Norman Riley of the British Museum of Natural History, whom she had often consulted in identifying rare specimens not discussed in existing books, he blamed her for his own denigration of her: "This short sketch falls far short of evaluating Miss Fountaine as an entomologist," says Riley, "but regrettably this is largely her own fault for recording so little of her work in print or in any systematic form. She was rather a loner, with few really close friends even amongst entomologists, and this and her uncontrolled wanderlust, may partly account for it" (Riley typescript).[5] A lifetime of far-ranging travels in search of rarities; a collection of over twenty-two thousand butterflies, preserved in mahogany cases and willed to the Norwich Museum; and a large collection of beautiful and scientifically accurate watercolors depicting the life cycles and food sources of the butterflies she raised in order to observe and document them, willed to Riley's museum — all are dismissed as desultory pastimes; Fountaine was not systematic enough, did not publish enough. Part of Fountaine's problem, according to Riley, could be laid at the doorsteps of collectors in general. In his words, those naturalists "who take pride in building up a valuable collections are notoriously bad at recording their observations for the benefit of others" (4). Another part of the problem may have resided with Riley's envy of a person with sufficient time and money to spend a lifetime "wandering" in search of lepidoptera. Scientific voyaging and collecting were expensive. Only people of independent means or those whose journeying was supported by institutions like the large natural history museums, the Colonial Office, or other forms of patronage could go.

But the underlying problem was just whose observations were to be considered of value to institutionally based scientists like Riley who were establishing the main sightlines of the discipline, the hegemonic, official methods of seeing. Official sight is not empirical but constructed, not objective but social. It only appears to be "natural"; in reality it has been focused through the lenses of some aspect of culture. Vision is thus continually reenvisioned through the technology and social codes and cultures that make up any given moment in time. By the turn of the nineteenth century, professional, scientific modes of seeing were hegemonic. The close scrutinizing that had marked the age of Victorian natural history observation, open to all people in the gathering of information about species, was no longer officially sanctioned sight, and nature study, the forte of women, was no longer considered science. What Martin Rudwick calls "the science of specimens" (266 – 69), referring to the art of collecting, sorting, and classifying those specimens, gave way to a more precise and technologically

5. For the use of this typescript, I am indebted to the kind generosity of Julie English Early, who has shared not only her photocopy of it but also many of her ideas about both Fountaine and Mary Kingsley with me.

sophisticated examination of specimens. In fields like entomology, men like Riley had appropriated what was proper to see and therefore to know; thus his diminishment of Fountaine's work was not pronounced with an edge of disdain or even disrespect but with the ring of authority. His was the official word, based on official seeing; it was what every self-respecting scientist would propound. Self-taught field naturalists were simply less and less valuable to the scientific enterprise—and, for the most part, women landed in the camp of the self-taught and unofficial.

This meant that women who had the means, or the knowledge (or both) to dedicate themselves to collecting had to find special ways of making their collections count or of getting their scientific work recognized. They could not afford simply to be "eccentric pack rats" (Altick 17), as could so many amateur men and women of an earlier generation. If Margaret Fountaine gave her many cases of butterflies to the Norwich Museum, there to remain a monument to her industry and a resource for further reevaluation, another entomologist, Eleanor Ormerod (1828–1901) (see figure 20) found a field in which she could excel and at the same time receive full recognition as a partner in science.

Ormerod helped to establish the new field of economic entomology, a science that was high on utility and so made her knowledge indispensable to the Victorian economy. She was also a woman with a perfect sense of timing. She began, as so many women had, as a well-to-do collector of objects from natural history. In 1869, she responded to an item in the *Gardeners' Chronological and Agricultural Gazette,* printed at the request of the Royal Horticultural Society, calling for collectors of "insect friends," "gardener's enemies," and "insects beneficial and injurious to man" (qtd. in Ormerod 55). Until this time more casual in her collecting, Ormerod now became highly disciplined. By 1877 she was expert enough to put together "Notes for Observations of Injurious Insects," a questionnaire and call for further collections and information, which led to her editorship of an ongoing series of annual reports. Ormerod collected the collectors. Her "Annual Reports on Injurious Insects," which ran until 1900, utilized the insights of numerous members of British entomological societies. Self-published, they became essential material to amateurs and experts alike and built Ormerod's reputation as a prime figure in economic entomology, an expert on the botfly and Hessian fly, the uses of pesticides, and the ecology of bird and insect.

Throughout the life of these reports, Ormerod was widely consulted for her knowledge. In 1878, she was also elected to the Entomological Society of London and in 1882 became what she calls "official Consulting Entomologist" (68) for the Royal Agricultural Society of England. As a result, she was in high demand by agriculturalists, prepared monthly and annual reports for the Royal Agricultural Society, and was frequently called in as an expert witness in court cases. That same year, along with men like Riley and Thiselton-Dyer, Ormerod was invited by the lords of the Committee of Council on Education to become

Figure 20.   Eleanor Ormerod.

a member of a "committee to advise on the improvement of the collections relating to Economic Entomology in the South Kensington and Bethnal Green
Museums" (87). In the early 1880s, she wrote *Guide to the Methods of Insect Life*
(1884) and delivered lectures on economic entomology for the Royal Agricultural College. By 1892, she had written the definitive *Text-Book of Agricultural
Entomology*.

I have chronicled rather than analyzed Eleanor Ormerod's career because
the story of her life, in contrast to most women's lives in her day, can be read
like an entry in the *Dictionary of National Biography*. Although Virginia Woolf
wrote Ormerod into her "Lives of the Obscure" in *The Common Reader* in 1925,
envisioning the scene of a young Victorian girl watching water grubs devour
one another, we must nonetheless plainly recognize that by the turn of the century there was little that was obscure about Ormerod. She had worked to authorize herself in an area just outside "high" science, an arena in which she could
readily interact professionally with both scientists and agriculturalists. No one

seemed to daunt her. A friend to experts such as Thomas Henry Huxley and Sir Joseph Hooker at Kew, she nevertheless had no compunctions about criticizing those who were inaccurate in their observations or conclusions. Referring to a professor of biology at the Royal Agricultural College, she stated with authority: "My reference work is to the leading men of the world—those who are known, literally, as the authorities above all others on the special points; thus I am in no way derogating from the respect I bear to Professor Harker's knowledge, but who that knew anything would have cared for his opinion on *Icerya purchasi* (scale insect of orange trees)?" (79) Eleanor Ormerod did know something of this species, as of so many others—enough to be awarded an honorary doctor of laws degree from the University of Edinburgh in 1900, the first awarded to a woman. And, certainly, she was the only woman to have been called "the protectress of agriculture and the fruits of the earth, a beneficent Demeter of the nineteenth century" (qtd. in Ormerod 96).

Ormerod was an exception, a rarity among women, and one who complicates arguments like Lynn Barber's in *The Heyday of Natural History* which suggests that Victorian women's science existed in a metaphorical "boudoir" and that "illustration was the only form of natural history in which women really excelled" (126). Nevertheless, Ormerod quite literally paid a price for her success. She was in actuality a "beneficent Demeter." Well-to-do, in the beginning of her career she took no remuneration for her work in order, as a woman, to establish herself. Later, believing that this practice had kept her work pure and free from external influence, she continued to decline offers of money, although her research unquestionably enhanced the coffers of agriculturalists. She also refused to accept the assistant she was offered in 1899 because, she said, she was quite well assured of her own abilities and accustomed to her own careful way of working. Independence of means allowed her these choices, but Ormerod made her decisions based on her conception of the challenges facing women in the field of entomology. She deliberately held herself back from competing with men and remained aloof from the sexual politics of contemporary science by donating her professional services. The honorific "beneficent Demeter" accurately described a role she herself had constructed as a means of self-survival.

Not all the women of Ormerod's generation had either her independent means or her canny instinct for new and commercially viable fields. Most had to find other routes to recognition. Mary Kingsley (1862–1900) (see figure 21) wrote and spoke her way into the history of ichthyology and geographic exploration through travel narratives and public lectures. It was under the purview of the internationally most authoritative and scholarly scientific expert on fish, her sponsor Albert Günther (1830–1914) of the British Museum of Natural History, that Kingsley first set out to gather fish specimens in West Africa in the 1890s. As a woman in men's provinces, Mary Kingsley should have been like a fish out of water. Yet Kingsley not only saw and collected but wrote her own

Figure 21. Mary Kingsley.

accounts of what she found and validated them with an unusual combination of seriousness, humor, self-irony, self-deprecation, and bravado. Small wonder, then, that recent appraisals of Kingsley have had trouble pinning down the nature of her self-authorized female voice, crying out about fishes and fetishes from the wildernesses of the Dark Continent (Stevenson, Mills).

One can detect a strategic elusiveness from the first page of Kingsley's *Travels in West Africa* (1897), where she describes herself with an earnestness undercut by irony. There she becomes a person who traveled under an important edict: "'Go and learn your tropics,' said Science" (1). What better auspices to set out from than those of Science? What more authorizing aegis than that of Science herself?—that is, if we believe such a persona exists. Kingsley, for one, knew otherwise: in reality, "Science" was a collection of male authorities who had deputized one another to hold forth on scientific subjects in journals, books, reports, and lectures, and Kingsley was well aware that her own investigations would have been perceived as very much at the periphery of their work. Kingsley, who gathered, processed, reported, cataloged, and wrote up data—much like an advanced Ph.D. candidate today—wanted to be a part of the scientific band. Earlier, she had written to Macmillan, her publisher: "I went out there as a Naturalist, not as a sort of circus," and suggested *The Log of a Naturalist* as a title for her work, hoping to have the book valued as scientific account, not a travel narrative (letter to George Macmillan, 18 December 1894).

Nevertheless, Kingsley was adept at providing her narratives with circuslike sideshows—for instance, one in which a giant catfish lands in her boat and she uses the occasion to both honor and spoof men of science while foregrounding herself. This particular anecdote reveals how Kingsley sported with the very authorities she purported most to admire, in this case her beloved "ju ju," or magical mentor, Albert Günther. Kingsley had in all likelihood originally read Günther's important and influential *Introduction to the Study of Fishes* (1880) in her father's library, but she used the book virtually as a Bible during her voyages. Upon her return from the 1893 trip, she went to see Günther at the British Museum of Natural History, carrying with her the fish she had so carefully collected and preserved in large bottles of spirit. Impressed by the fish, though not by their condition, Günther commissioned Kingsley to find both more specimens and better ways to preserve them. Partly to that end, she set off for a second time, equipped with professional kits, formaldehyde, and an intention to travel the Ogowé River (now called the Ogooué), the largest between the Congo and the Niger.

Outfitted with "a round net, three stout fishing-lines, three paddles, Dr. Günther's *Study of Fishes,* [and] some bait in an old Morton's boiled-mutton can," Kingsley would have her adventure with the catfish. As she sat reading in a canoe, presumably perusing Günther, one of her men hooked a fish and landed it in the boat. Mayhem broke out as a "3-foot long, grunting, flopping, yellow-grey slimy thing" left all but Kingsley and the fish virtually standing on their heads to avoid the creature's barbs (*West African Studies* 83). Then, in her words,

> *"Brevi spatio interjecto,"* as Caesar says, in the middle of a bad battle, over went the canoe, while the cat-fish went off home with the line and hook.

One black man went to the bank, whither, with a blind prescience of our fate, I had flung, a second before, the most valuable occupant of the canoe, *The Study of Fishes*. I went personally to investigate fluvial deposit *in situ*. When I returned to the surface—accompanied by great swirls of mud and great bubbles of the gases of decomposition I had liberated on my visit to the bottom of the river—I observed the canoe floating bottom upwards, accompanied by Morton's tin. (83–84)

What happens here, among other things, is a comic deflation of Günther, whose book is rescued at all costs, though the lives of others are made to seem gravely— or foolishly—at stake. This action both foregrounds Günther's authority as a taxonomist and, at the same time, undercuts it, a literary sleight of hand that Kingsley uses over and over again in her work. If the reader chooses, his or her mind can wander back to a real Günther, safely ensconced in South Kensington classifying specimens, while the imperiled Mary Kingsley, accompanied only by her faithful black friends and a metonymic text, risks life and limb out in the field and makes his authoritative knowledge of fish possible. In her mock-heroic plunge for Science and her stewards—doing battle with fish, for the sake of ichthyology, and with stinking muck, for the sake of geology— Mary Kingsley, who saves both canoe and apparatus, herself emerges as much the martyred heroine as the clown in this carnivalesque "circus."

Kingsley would compound the kind of backhanded compliment inherent in rescuing Günther's text when she quipped off other comments like the famous: "I can honestly and truly say that there are only two things I am proud of—one is that Doctor Günther has approved of my fishes, and the other is that I can paddle an Ogowé canoe" (*Travels in West Africa* 200). Whatever Kingsley's real feelings toward Günther, for his part, Günther believed in Kingsley, who brought home sixty-five species of fish, including three never before recorded, *Ctenopoma kingsleyae, Mormyrus kingsleyae*, and *Alestes kingsleyae*, plus eighteen species of reptile (see figure 22). The ichthyologist called her a woman with an "extraordinary gift of observation," and "indefatigable energy," who had made a "judicious selection of specimens" (qtd. in Stevenson 148). On her behalf, Günther would contribute to *Travels in West Africa* an authoritative appendix about Kingsley's collection of reptiles and fishes, a reprinted official report that gave Kingsley's work the stamp of purposeful natural science, not purposeless circus.

Kingsley was nevertheless ambivalent about her mentors, seemingly grateful or admiring but often resentful, too. Catherine Barnes Stevenson points out a similar ambivalence in Kingsley's relation to her father, George Kingsley (1827–1892), who often left his family to go off collecting and who saddled her with many of what should have been his own responsibilities. In the end, Kingsley wound up editing her father's work, her own last effort at publishing, and white-washed her earlier resentment of him by suggesting that he had inspired her to

Mormyrus Kingsleyae

Ctenopoma Kingsleyae

Figure 22. *Mormyrus kingsleyae* and *Ctenopoma kingsleyae,* fishes named for Mary Kingsley.

travel. At the peak of her powers, however, she was double-minded not only about her father and about Günther, her mentor, but also about E. B. Tylor (1832–1917), her "ju ju" in the area of fetish. As with her attitude toward the ichthyologist, her appreciation of the ethnologist cut both ways. In her preface to *West African Studies,* Kingsley remarked: "I am also under a debt of gratitude to Professor Tylor. He also is not involved in my opinions, but he kindly permits me to tell him things that I can only 'tell Tylor'" (viii). I, Mary Kingsley, she again seems to be saying, am the knowledgeable field worker, the originator of information; but through their kind permission, I offer my findings to buttress those of the already acknowledged experts. This combination of polite deference and ironic deflation in the name of self-authorization is at the heart of the contradictory discourses that have troubled Kingsley's critics.

The need to self-authorize in relation to known authority was also responsible for Kingsley's exasperation with Macmillan's scientific arbiter and editor, Henry Guillemard, who was to have been only the scientific check on Kingsley's *Travels in West Africa* but who instead attempted virtually to rewrite her book. Guillemard's Latinate prose irked Kingsley into demanding a halt to his editing: "Your corrections," she wrote him, "stand on stilts out of the swamps and give a very quaint but patchy aspect to the affair so that I do not know my way about it at all. I never meant you to take this delicate labour over the thing but only to arrange it and tell me point blank if I was lying about scientific subjects" (qtd. in Frank 224). Kingsley loved what she called her "word-swamp of a book, about the size of Norie's *Navigation*," as she dubbed the *Travels* in her preface to *West African Studies* (1). And here, again, she authorizes with a derogation—"word swamp"—followed by comparison to a well-accepted authority.

Thus despite her own frequent protestations to the contrary, Kingsley felt the firm hand of gendered science clenching at the long skirt she had so prided herself on wearing, even in the wilds of Africa. As she wrote in a letter to Mrs. Farquharson, the dauntless challenger of the Linnean Society, Kingsley did not believe that women should push for membership in the scientific societies of her day because "if we women distinguish ourselves in Science in sufficiently large numbers at a sufficiently high level, the great scientific societies . . . will admit us" or "we shall form . . . our own of equal eminence" (26 November 1895). Elsewhere, she is quoted as having said: "If I were a man, I'd have a love of a fight with the cabinet of comparative ethnologists" (qtd. in Gwynn 143). In her books, however, she battled catfish in mock-heroics, hoping that clever readers could not overlook her in favor of her more famous male colleagues. Kingsley thus worked hard to legitimate herself through her narratives but seemed to realize that for a Victorian woman, the labor of self-authorization was never really finished.

There was an arena other than books, however, that would serve to validate Mary Kingsley's science, one even less a woman's province—the lecture circuit. When Kingsley came back from Africa, the England to which she returned was not only avidly listening to men of the scientific societies but eagerly watching stagy scientific popularizers like the Reverend J. G. Wood, who often attracted huge crowds to his performances. Mary Kingsley also wanted to draw crowds, partly to promote her books, and so she too took to lecturing. Looking into private archives and reviews of Kingsley's appearances, Julie Early, in "The Spectacle of Science and Self," has reconstructed the self-created, public Kingsley of the popular lecture circuit, where gimmicks like Wood's "sketch-lectures" had become crowd pleasers. Creating a carefully devised stage persona, Kingsley would hail herself "the sea monster of the season"; she would act the part of a self-fashioned anomaly who purported to be at one and the same time every-one's long-deceased maiden aunt and a survivor of West Africa, "the White Man's Grave." Such contradictions would of course have prepared, and even in-cited, Kingsley's audiences to become readers of her contradictory written dis-courses, and, in fact, thousands of potential readers came out to watch both Kingsley's performance and her magic-lantern slides. On the podium, Kingsley could validate her own kind of fact-finding with her own kind of humor and receive immediate recompense—intellectually, emotionally, and financially—for her trouble. In effect, she invited people to watch her at work, much as she might have invited them over for dinner. The result was not only instantaneous popularity but a form of validation for her scientific work in Africa.

If Mary Kingsley constructed a set of mock-heroic situations to validate her-self as a collector and so featured a series of narrative episodes of female bravado that made her exploits figure prominently in the story of West African explo-ration, Marianne North (1830–1890) (see figure 23) had also turned to bra-vado to validate herself as a painter of plants. North was an inveterate, self-financed traveler and botanical artist who traversed the globe in search of subjects for her art. Well-connected and well-respected, especially by Sir Joseph Hooker (1817–1911) at Kew Gardens, she nevertheless was ambitious for wider recog-nition. As she was formally trained neither in art (William Holman Hunt, with whom I opened this study, refused to accept her as a pupil) nor in science, North was forever overcompensating for what she felt were inadequacies in her formal education. Wit and bravado seem to have helped her toward a sense of increased self-regard, as, for example, in an unpublished letter to Dr. Allman, a zoologist and president of the Linnean from 1874 to 1881. North opened this letter (see figure 24) with a sketch of herself perched atop a high rocky outcrop sketching a tree:

> I am sending you the above sketch of myself in the Seychelles. . . . I feel that you will better enter into the delight of the situation. How I got up and how I got down is still a mystery to me—but I know that if a cramp had seized me, you would have seen little more of your friend, for the boul-der went sheer down some 30 feet or more on all sides! (4 November 1883)

Of course the steel-nerved, skilled North survived this ordeal to write its story. Self-validation and self-presentation of the sort found in North's vignettes and Kingsley's lectures was of the utmost importance to women engaged in self-promotion for the sake of science. The patterns of self-negation that George Levine notes as characterizing the scientific writing of men like Charles Dar-win and the literary autobiographies of men like Anthony Trollope (1815–1882) and that I noted in the case of Jemima Blackburn, were inappropriate to women who, like North, were in danger of being overlooked, their efforts in

Figure 23.   Marianne North. Courtesy of Royal Botanic Gardens at Kew.

cataloging the natural world ignored. A different set of tropes was necessary for women who had to work to make their scientific discoveries known. North had collected thousands of plants for Kew Gardens and had discovered five species later named for her—*Kniphofia northiana, Areca northiana, Crinum northianum, Nepenthes northiana,* and *Northea seychellana,* a tree of the Seychelles (possibly the

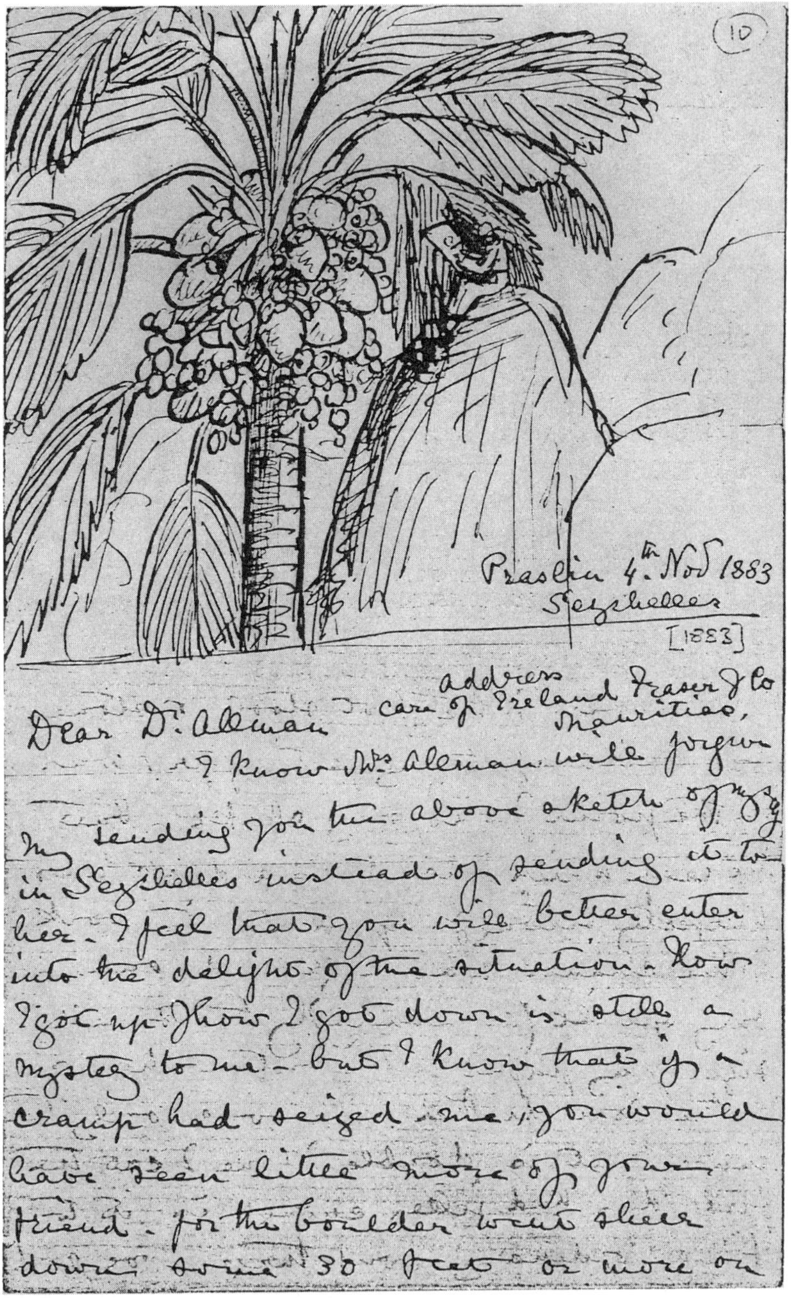

Figure 24.   Marianne North, letter to Dr. Allman (4 November 1883). Courtesy of Royal Botanic Gardens at Kew.

one she sketched for Allman), which Hooker named in her honor—but still did not win the acclaim the scientific community routinely awarded to men who had accomplished far less than she. Hooker recommended North for the Order of the Cross of Malta for her contributions to botanical study but was told that the only women who were eligible for this award were royalty and the wives of high-ranking colonial officials. Recognition through official channels was not forthcoming for Marianne North.

And so North set out to create her own recognition—and, as Mary Kingsley did, she tapped more than one source. North's *Recollections of a Happy Life* (1892–94), a three-volume autobiography drawn from her letters coupled with reminiscences, was one attempt in this direction. Never published in her lifetime—both Murray and Macmillan read and rejected the first two volumes— *Recollections* was edited by North's sister and, eventually, issued posthumously. As had Kingsley, North thought that her scientific knowledge might best be mediated through travel accounts, one literary form in which women might gain popular credibility for their knowledge of the natural world. On the whole, North's narrative reveals a woman eager to observe accurately and add to the store of scientific knowledge. Her recollection of Borneo and Java, for example, offers a useful correction to previous observations: "The mangosteen was one of the curious trees people told me never had a flower. But I watched and hunted day by day till I found one, afterwards seeing whole trees full of blossoms, with rich crimson bracts and yellow petals" (1: 240). So far as little-known plants were concerned, North was careful to remind her reader that only her own observations, tested and validated with utmost scientific care, would do.

North labored hard to be known for those observations. Despite her close connection and easy familiarity with the botanists at Kew and with collectors and scientists throughout the world, North felt that, as a talented amateur, she had to overcome considerable public prejudice. For example, when she was asked to lend her paintings of plants from the Indian subcontinent to the Kensington Museum, she was delighted at the prospect. Then she was told that, in the cab on the way to her flat, Mr. Thomson of the museum had said to his companion: "We must get out of this civilly somehow. I know what all these amateur things always are!" Her spirits rose when she was also told that, on the way back from the flat, he said: "We must have those things at any price" (*Recollections* 1: 321). North then goes on to tell her readers that before going back to seek out more plants in India, she spent the last few weeks of that stay in England "in making a catalogue as well as I could of the 500 studies I lent them, putting in as much general information about the plants as I had time to collect, as I found people in general woefully ignorant of natural history" (1: 321). North was forced to take great pains to ensure that she was known for what she did know, not stereotyped for what she did not. She not only cultivated experts but worked with and among them. During the trip to India, she would study with two professionals in Tanjore (now called Thanjavur), reading from their "valuable botanical books (including MSS)" and being presented with "all sorts of sacred plants ready for me to paint" (1: 327). Hooker himself praised her for painting a botanical world that was otherwise fading before the world's eyes:

> Such scenes can never be renewed by nature, nor when once effaced can they be pictured to the mind's eye, except by means of such records as this lady has presented to us, and to posterity. (Qtd. in *Recollections* 2: 338)

Already in North's time, species were no sooner discovered than they were discovered to be disappearing from the earth.

Today, Marianne North is best remembered for one particularly ingenious act of self-promotion and self-perpetuation. She lives for us because we can still walk through the Marianne North Gallery at Kew Gardens and see her work ranked along its walls—painting after painting (832 in all) along with 246 types of wood collected in country after country. Toward the end of her life, North insisted that the human world gaze at her remarkable paintings as she had gazed at the natural world. Over a hundred years later, these distinctive paintings hold their vividness—electric blues, brilliant reds and peaches—rendered with what seems an expressionist kind of energy. After suggesting to Hooker the idea of establishing a gallery, North employed another friend, James Fergusson, an architectural historian, to design a Greek temple-like building to house her collection. She then carefully arranged all of the pictures herself, so that they nearly covered the walls, with little space in between. She also arranged for a prime botanist, W. Botting Helmsley, to do the catalog, which was prefaced by Hooker, and paid for—at least the first two thousand copies of it—by herself. In the end, like Ormerod she kept control over her own work and had the wherewithal to effect this control.

Ironically, the acclaim North achieved for the erection and decoration of her building was gendered for a female amateur, the very role she was redefining through the installation of her work. The first newspaper reports of the opening of the gallery included these remarks from the *Times:* "Miss North, although no botanist in the strict sense of the term, has an extraordinary *flair* for a rare specimen, and great numbers of her sketches represent types which are either unknown or almost unknown in Europe, or exceedingly scarce and difficult to reproduce in the best organized gardens ("Miss North's Paintings of Plants"). For the *Times,* "*flair,*" not scientific value, was what drew éclat. Likewise, the *Daily News,* after acclaiming the prodigiousness of North's accomplishment, went on to cite her "taste" and bountifulness: "That such activity and energy should be accompanied by the taste which has presided over the arrangement of the sketches and the charming gallery which holds them, and by the generosity which hands the whole affair over as a gift to the nation, is something of which the country may truly be proud" ("A Botanical Picture Gallery"). Science as decorative personal accomplishment, bequest as Lady Bountifulness, and "charm" were encoded in the language of public appraisals of this woman's work. True to the appropriately gendered rhetoric of their time, these kinds of accolades continued for over twenty years. In 1905, the *Morning Post* offered, in a column entitled "London's Hidden Treasures," a review called "The North Gallery at Kew" that kept faith with earlier reviews of the gallery. Here North is praised as a woman traveler, not as "some intrepid explorer of the sterner sex," and cited as a "great benefactress." Her skill in art is then traced to her teachers and her dedication to painting from nature. Some twenty years after its opening in 1882, her gallery has become a "hidden treasure," and her own "intrepidness," so carefully delineated in her letters and *Recollections*, has been reattributed to others.

By exhuming the reviews of North's gallery, I am not suggesting that women like Marianne North, with her close connections to scientists whose careers she could not duplicate in her own, or like Mary Kingsley, with her offhand bravado that redraws the boundaries of scientific authority and scientific collection, were demeaned by reaching the audiences they did reach. On the contrary, they cultivated those audiences. Kingsley called them her "GP"—her general public—and North had hoped to have tea served to those who attended her gallery. These women did not allow their lives to be negatively overdetermined by their culture simply because they did not have access to museum jobs, scientific journals, or other organs of scientific dissemination. Each became a "public" figure, and each had an effect on the culture of her time, reaching a larger audience than that of most scientists. North's *Recollections* and Kingsley's *Travels in West Africa* were very well received. North's book garnered plaudits from *Nature*, the *Dial*, and the *Athenaeum*, which even suggested that "Nature revealed herself to [North] as Nature only does reveal itself to lofty souls dowered with gentleness, courage, reverence, and love" (rev. of *Recollections of a Happy Life*). Here again we might recall Barrias's famous sculpture, which I discussed in chapter 2. Far from revealing herself only to the male gaze, Nature in this case does quite the opposite, unveiling herself to those who possess qualities that were gendered female. I suggest only that the main audience these two women reached, much like the one Potter eventually gained with her fictional books about nature's creatures, was set apart from scientific authority and was related to the audience addressed by the women popularizers of science. Through Kingsley and North, travel narrative became a form of scientific narrative; their science was made accessible to an audience that included women and children and working people.

Culturally Colonized Collectors

Women like Marianne North and Elizabeth Twining, and others like Louisa Meredith (1812–1895) and Georgiana Molloy (1806–1843) in Australia and Catherine Parr Traill (1802–1899) who wrote wildflower guidebooks in Canada (Johnston, Lines, V. R. Ellis, Ainley), were, as Hooker suggested of North, invaluable in cataloging the empire with their collecting, their illustrations, and their books. Sara Mills believes that such women "produced a vision of the colonized country as a storehouse of random flora and fauna waiting for the civilizing order of the narrator with her Western science" ("Knowledge, Gender, and Empire" 41).

But I would argue that Western science was not "their" science. Gatherers they were; namers they were not. When they reached a general public hungry for news of scientific discovery, they functioned more as interpreters of science and its sites than as taxonomists or originators of scientific theory. As authors, they were still writing versions of the narrative of natural history, not the narrative of science. If, as Gillian Beer suggests, natural history was a "sub-genre" (*Open Fields* 59) in the imperialist enterprise, they belonged to an underclass of writers. But if we look at the function they played in science education, these women—again, like the women who popularized science—appear valuable to their culture. Their writing served a function quite different from that of "high" science. It made arcane or inaccessible knowledge public. Lady Eastlake (Elizabeth Rigby), writing in 1845 a review of books by women travelers, caught something of their cultural importance when she singled out Louisa Meredith's *Notes and Sketches of New South Wales* (1844) as exerting "a separate attraction of its own in the valuable store of natural history it communicates" (106). Her review is especially informative in terms of the audience it reveals:

> Birds and beasts, fishes and insects, and creeping things innumerable equally engage her [Meredith's] intelligent attention, and are described with a simplicity and precision which will give much valuable information to the professed naturalist, no additional jargon to the dabbling amateur, and involuntary interest to the most uninitiated. Not a trace of pedantry appears, nor of what is quite as bad, and too frequent when women treat such matters—not the slightest affectation of a popular tone. Not a microscope nor a herbarium is seen; but keen eyes and taper fingers, and a most active mind it is evident have been at work. (106)

These comments in the *Quarterly Review* limn the intelligent audience for which someone like the colonist Meredith or the peripatetic North might aim: the general reader who is interested in natural science in the far-flung corners of the empire and who might resent condescension. They also point to an important

Figure 25. Louisa Meredith. Courtesy of Allport State Library of Tasmania and the Museum of Fine Arts, Hobart, Tasmania, Australia.

reason why we have been slow to write these women either into the history of colonization or the history of science: in both realms, we have marginalized their media because we have underestimated their audience. Sara Mills again gives only a part of the story when she suggests that the experience of women travelers remained "eccentric" because it "could not be generalized to refer to other women" (*Discourses of Difference* 119). Other women, and men too, were hungry for new information about the world's flora and fauna and ready to read or view information from anyone who could describe this exotic world outside Britain.

Take, as an example, the work of Louisa Twamley Meredith (see figure 25), Lady Eastlake's midcentury model. Meredith began her career as an illustrator and expert on British wildflowers. Under her maiden name, Louisa Twamley, she published *The Romance of Nature; or, The Flower Seasons Illustrated* in 1836 and *Our Wildflowers Familiarly Described and Illustrated* in 1839 before she set out with her new husband as a colonist to Tasmania. There she continued to write for a British readership fascinated by the exotics of the world "down under." Meredith composed and illustrated a number of beautiful books on Tasmanian flora and fauna, describing the natural world of her new home. She became an Australian through her love of the natural world she came to know there, entitling one of her books *Our Island Home* (1879). Yet all of her work, from the 1830s to the 1880s, was published in London for a British readership with a very different "home." The preface to her first Australian work, *Notes and Sketches of New South Wales during a Residence in that Colony from 1839–1844*, the book that Lady Eastlake reviewed, offers its subject knowing that

> many persons at 'Home' are deeply interested in these distant colonies, as being the residence of dear friends and relatives, and that, as in the case of my own home-connections, they really understand very little of the general aspect of things here, I believed that a few simple sketches from nature, however devoid of scientific lore, would be a welcome addition to the present small fund of information on common every-day topics relating to these antipodean climes. (vii)

Some forty years later in the preface to one of her last works, *Tasmanian Friends and Foes: Feathered, Furred, and Finned* (1880), Meredith would still offer "bits about the live things here" to interest cousins abroad (see figure 26).

Similarly, North and the famous adventure traveler Isabella Bird (later, after her marriage, Isabella Bird Bishop) edited their reminiscences with a more popular home audience in mind. In their cases, this audience grew from one more familiar. North collaborated with her sister in the issuing of her autobiographical story, using that sister's readerly response as a testing ground. Bird, who initiated her travels to improve her health, began her travel writing by sending detailed letters to her own sister, Henrietta, who in turn read those letters to a group of women friends who waited for each installment. Bird turned professional author only after she learned of the warm reception her letters were accorded by those women. Several of the women in this chapter benefited from such a sisterly audience for their work; for example, Eleanor Ormerod's sister often served her as an illustrator, drawing the insects Ormerod studied.

In one sense, all of these women and the others in this chapter—rich and poor, married and single, early and late alike—were, as contemporary critique of travel writing has named them, colonizers. Even though, as women, they were marginalized by their culture, they nonetheless participated in imperialist science or exploration: they stared at, depicted, and dominated other species or

Figure 26.   Louisa Meredith, illustration from *Tasmanian Friends and Foes: Feathered, Furred, and Finned* (1880), by Louisa Meredith.

native peoples. In another sense, however, British though they might have been, the women we have so far visited in this chapter were all colonials in the land of science. They aimed in one way or another to enter the politicized space of British and European science—through meetings with museum personnel, through subversive bravado narratives, through the use of new technologies like cyanotypes, through advancing new scientific fields like economic entomology, through drawing nature differently and correcting others' misperceptions, through living in an exile that became a naturalist's home. If because of their different status in the symbolic order of their culture, the judgments of professionals in their desired scientific fields sent them back home to gentlewomanly rhetoric or to some other form of domestication in art, they nevertheless ventured out and created new literary and artistic forms in the process. Their exclusion from the professional ranks of scientists, their very marginalization, generated for them and their contemporaries new narratives of science and of woman. The recovery of those narratives in turn enables us to generate a more comprehensive narrative of Victorian science, one that can include women and suggest their "GP" as well.

Epilogue: Hard Science versus Popularization—
The Case of Marie Stopes

In contrast to the other women in this chapter, Marie Carmichael Stopes (1880–1958) took first-class honors at University College, London, earned her doctorate in botany in 1904, and became not only a fellow of the Linnean and Geological Societies but the first woman scientist on the faculty of the University of Manchester. A member of the generation of women educated at the turn of the century,[6] Stopes was a field and laboratory scientist who seems to have begun even her nonacademic writing with a desire to be known for her research. Her travel book, *A Journal from Japan* (1910) (see figure 27), set out to show her at work as a paleobotanist as well as a stranger in a strange land. Its subtitle, *A Daily Record of Life as Seen by a Scientist,* leaves no doubt as to Stopes's pride in her profession, nor does the string of letters following her name as author: "D.Sc., Ph.D., F.L.S." Throughout the *Journal,* Stopes juxtaposes her thoughts on Japan and the Japanese with entries about her visits to coal mines to search for specimens, her careful professional handling of them, her lectures to experts and students, and her attendance at official scientific functions. As Stopes's introduction makes clear, her successful visit to Japan was itself made in the name of science: "The scientific results," she authoritatively explains, "which most fortunately seem to be justifying the expedition, are being published in suitable places; there is no technical science in this journal" (xi). Stopes would split her accounts of her work in Japan in two: her life, opinions, and comments would appear in the *Journal,* while the scientific findings of her activities would appear in appropriate journals of another sort. Although she would go on to publish those and other articles in the area of paleobotany, would continue to lecture on that subject, and would produce a catalog of Cretaceous flora for the British Museum of Natural History, Stopes also went on to make a highly interesting literary choice, one that would land her in the ranks of popularizers rather than scientists for most of the rest of her life.

In 1918, Stopes wedded the matter-of-factness she was trained to utilize in her scientific writing with the concern she felt about the sexual inexperience of some married couples and produced her best-seller, *Married Love.* The book was a primer intended to prevent the kind of misery that greeted Stopes in her first marriage: a disastrous sexual life based on ignorance, which in Stopes's case

6. The University of London first admitted women to its degree programs in 1878, but as Carol Dyhouse has pointed out, the patterns for university admissions of women are complex and not easily defined (*No Distinction of Sex?* 12–55). Dyhouse offers the case of Mary Adamson, who was enrolled at Bedford College in the 1880s but needed the advanced training in science that was offered at University College, London, but not at Bedford. Adamson was permitted to study physics and botany at University College but was forbidden to take chemistry, since women in the chemistry laboratory might be "scarred for life and have their clothes burnt off them as the men threw chemicals around" (qtd. in *No Distinction* 33).

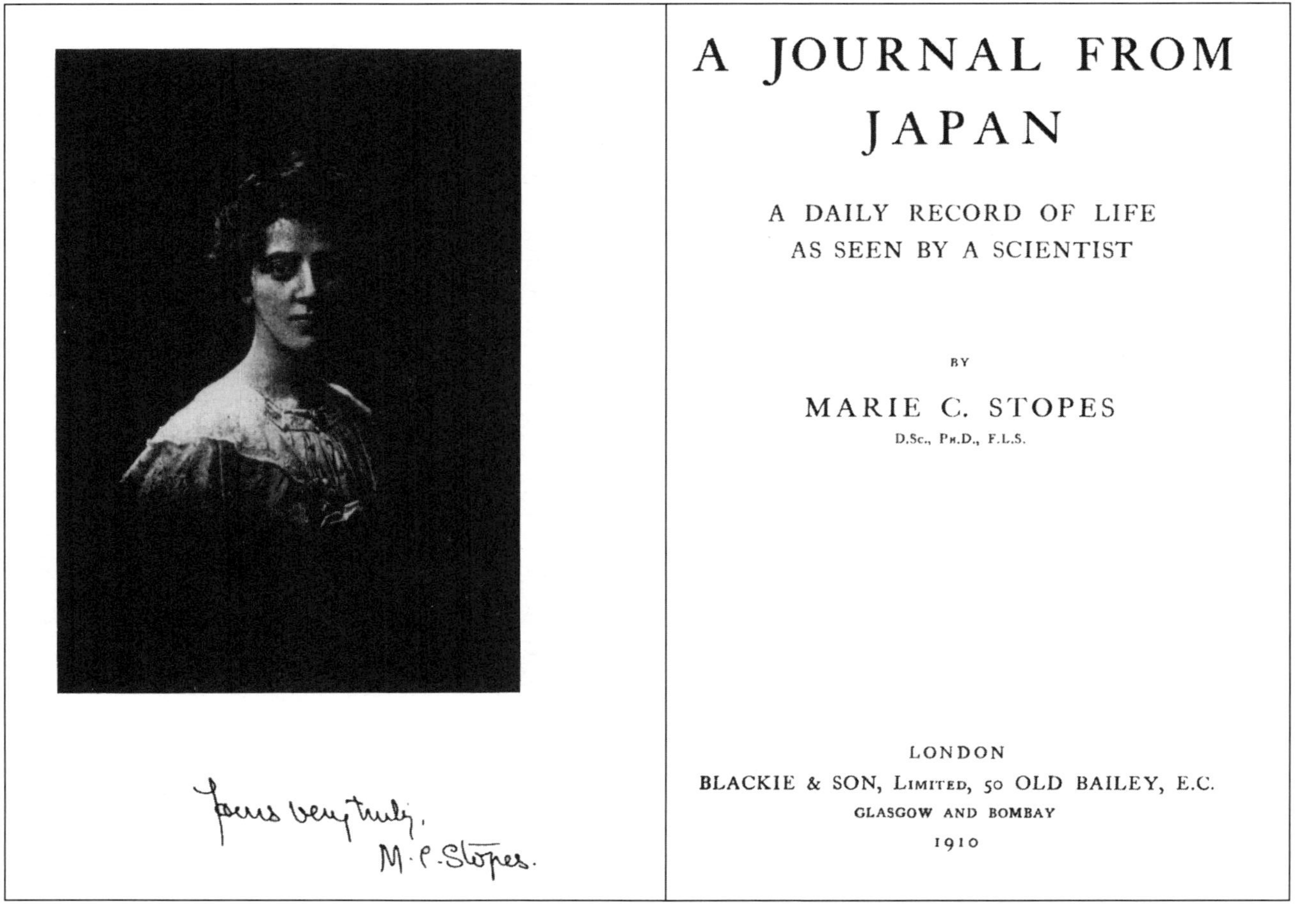

A JOURNAL FROM JAPAN

A DAILY RECORD OF LIFE
AS SEEN BY A SCIENTIST

BY

MARIE C. STOPES

D.Sc., Ph.D., F.L.S.

LONDON

BLACKIE & SON, LIMITED, 50 OLD BAILEY, E.C.

GLASGOW AND BOMBAY

1910

Yours very truly,
M. C. Stopes.

Figure 27.   Frontispiece and title page, *A Journal from Japan: A Daily Record of Life as Seen by a Scientist* (1910), by Marie Stopes.

had meant nights spent in nonconsummation and days spent in the British Library, trying to figure out what was going wrong. But the book's reception also offers evidence of the double bind that might greet an Edwardian woman who for a moment strayed from the halls of science into the marketplace of sexology, where the likes of Havelock Ellis and Edward Carpenter dwelt. For Stopes, the "detour" into this new field seemed logical. "It seems strange," she said,

> that those who search for natural law in every province of our universe should have neglected the most vital subject, the one which concerns us all infinitely more than the naming of planets or the collecting of insects. Woman is *not* essentially capricious; some of the laws of her being might have been discovered long ago had the existence of law been suspected. (*Married Love* 25–26)

Those laws, according to Stopes, were the unwritten laws of female sexuality. Women were subject to internal "tides" as persistent as the tides of the ocean. Those tides—monthly indicators of female sexual desire—needed to be felt and acted upon, to the deeper satisfaction of both women and men. Stopes was outraged by the belief that women were somehow "lowered" by sexual intercourse and wrote to explain both the beauties and necessities of sexual practice; women and men alike could only gain from increased knowledge of female sexual function. A eugenicist as well, Stopes further believed that such knowledge could also lead to a better strain of humanity. In her rewritten version of the Declaration of Independence, she advocated for men and women, "life, liberty, *knowledge*, and the pursuit of *health* and happiness, *both for themselves and to control their unborn children in the interests of the race*" (qtd. in Hall 202).

In *Married Love*, Stopes crossed both genres and fields. She utilized both clinical, sexual terms and poetic language to describe human sexuality and sex acts, a combination that caused her to be attacked on all sides. P. Chalmers Mitchell, a fellow of the Royal Society who was also secretary of the Zoological Society, refused to write a preface for the book because it seemed to him insufficiently scientific. And Dr. R. V. Wheeler, one of Stopes's respected colleagues in coal research, reflected in a letter to Stopes on his agitation at reading the book, realizing that "in nearly every instance it is the insistence on the animalism of the act of sex-relation which has aroused my anger." He went on: "It is a tribute to the power of your writing to say that you have almost convinced me that man should model himself on 'other mammalia'—and so have disgusted me with the whole idea of marriage relations." A believer in scientific language in his own work, Wheeler was shocked by "the ugliness of many of the words you have chosen (perforce?)—'orgasm,' 'intumescent,' 'ejaculation,' and so forth" (qtd. in Hall 129). The language of science when applied by a woman to men's bodies was simply unacceptable.

Despite such critiques, Stopes's book was an instant popular success, going through six editions in its first year. In the end, the number would reach eighteen editions, and the book would be published in twelve languages. Nevertheless, *Married Love* reaped bitter fruit, a combination of fame and notoriety brought on in part by the resistance of the Catholic Church to the ideas Stopes advocated. After enduring five years of protest in the form of poison-pen letters and bitter essays in church publications, Stopes wound up in a courtroom, on trial. Her opposition was a physician and Catholic convert, Dr. Halliday Sutherland, who objected to Stopes's urging her ideas of birth control—a part of her platform for granting sexual freedom to women—on the poor. Sutherland appealed to the home secretary, suggesting that Stopes was harmful to the working classes, that she had exposed them to physical dangers in her advocacy of various birth control methods, which included prophylactic devices. Stopes countered with a libel suit, but after nine days in court, the jury found for Sutherland. Stopes appealed the verdict and won, but only after months of strain and still more notoriety. In her case, the toll for popularization was high.

Securely established in an academic career in paleobotany, Stopes ventured into a dangerously different male preserve—the study of human sexuality. It would have been safer for her to have continued cataloging fossilized plants and garnering the kind of respect and admiration that she had known as a woman scientist in Japan. Despite the difficulties Beatrix Potter had in gaining recognition for her work in mycology, the time finally was ripe for Marie Stopes's acclaim in paleobotany. But it was too soon for a Dr. Ruth.

PART

II

Nature's Crusaders

CHAPTER

4

Nurturing Nature

The strong impulse to altruism that drove so many of the women who popularized the natural sciences impelled still other women passionately to crusade on behalf of nonhuman nature. Nature's crusaders tended to be well-informed, diligent, and effective amateurs who were willing to defy the speciesism, aggrandizement of science, and commercialism of their day. Their numbers grew in the last quarter of the nineteenth century, when women were freer to take up social causes publicly and when the need for conservation and the preservation of endangered species began to be recognized. Those who wrote belonged to a literary tradition dating back a hundred years to books like those of another passionate crusader, Mary Wollstonecraft, who championed not only the rights of women but also the rights of animals. In her *Original Stories from Real Life* (1783), Wollstonecraft had graphically shown the young protagonists the suffering of a bird stoned by a thoughtless boy. The bird has "one leg broke, and both its wings shattered; and its little eyes seemed starting out of their sockets, it was in such exquisite pain" (6–7). In Wollstonecraft's book, the female instructor draws a telling parallel by pointing out that the bird is in far more pain than were her pupils when they suffered from smallpox.

Conduct books like Wollstonecraft's (and Trimmer's and others discussed above, in part 1) helped lay the groundwork for the middle-class ethic of kindness toward animals which flourished during and after the 1820s. At this time—the decade of the establishment of the Royal Society for the Prevention of Cruelty to Animals (RSPCA) (1822–24)—benevolence and stewardship toward animals began to be widely seen as appropriate behavior for sensitive people. Again under the influence of women, families had begun to regard certain animals as possessing individuality and a capacity for deep feeling and to treat them accordingly. Anne Brontë's Agnes, the harried and benevolent governess-heroine of the novel *Agnes Grey* (1847), works hard to civilize the children under her care, stopping their torture of birds and defying their callous upbringing as hunters and abusers of nature. By midcentury, as James Turner shows in his *Reckoning with the Beast,* animals were believed to have "human" characteristics (71).

Benevolence, however, played only one part in the redefinition of nonhuman creatures as kin to humankind; for very different reasons, science was also pointing up the kinship between humans and other animals. Huxley, for example, in *Man's Place in Nature* (1863), supported evolutionary theory as he queried his readers:

> Is he [Man] something apart? Does he originate in a totally different way from Dog, Bird, Frog, and Fish, thus justifying those who assert him to have no place in nature and no real affinity with the lower world of animal life? Or does he originate in a similar germ, pass through the same slow and gradually progressive modifications, depend on the same contrivances for protection and nutrition, and finally enter the world by the help of the same mechanism? The reply is not doubtful for a moment, and has not been doubtful any time these thirty years. (89)

For the moment, science might seem in league with altruism. With their very different agendas, then, evolutionary science and the love of animals both led to a "creed of kinship," a belief in the interrelationship of all living creatures. According to Peter Gould, "the first essential of the kinship creed was brotherhood [*sic*] between human beings. . . . The second element was the cultivation of an empathy with sub-human beings" (46). Both of these elements would be well-represented in the work of women crusaders. If, as Gould suggests, in the later nineteenth century many men looked to nature for personal solace in an increasingly busy, industrialized world, many women looked instead to the solace they could provide to nature by working for the protection and preservation of other creatures.

Writing for the Birds

By the 1870s, women had taken the lead in animal protection and animal rights movements, and by the 1890s, they were crusading to save every type of animal. Consider, as a cameo example, the history of two unheralded women whose work affects our own lives every time we drive by or step into a marsh—the women who founded and fostered the Society for the Protection of Birds. To find these women in their own habitat, you could imagine yourself at afternoon tea in 1889. You might then be at the home of Mrs. Robert Williamson, in Didsbury, Manchester, discussing the slaughter of American egrets to satisfy the voracious popular taste in feathered millinery. You would be surrounded by acquaintances who had just formed a fledgling society to protect such birds. Or you might be in Croydon, at Mrs. Edward Phillips's, sipping your tea in the company of W. H. Hudson along with other members of the newly established Fur, Fin, and Feather Club. In either case, you would probably be headed for membership in a larger group as the two gatherings joined forces to form a larger organization that would take as its name the Society for the Protection of Birds (SPB).

That group was headquartered in London and headed by women whose long-term leadership—exclusively female—was unique in the inauguration and continuation of protective or scientific societies. By way of contrast, Frances Power Cobbe's Victoria Street Society, which protested vivisection, was founded in 1876 by five women and eight men and throughout most of its Victorian history was dominated by male presidents and vice-presidents, even though 70 percent of its members were women. And the Royal Society for the Prevention of Cruelty to Animals, although established in 1824 and always registering females as the majority of its members, prevented women from sitting on its general council until 1896.

The new Society for the Protection of Birds was different. During its first year, all of its officers were women. Eliza Phillips (b. 1823) became the organization's vice-president and publications editor, a position she held through many tempestuous years of propagandizing until her death in 1916. She wrote the annual reports as well as selecting the pamphlets to be reproduced and editing the house organ, *Bird Notes and News*. Winifred, Duchess of Portland (1863–1954), became the society's first president, holding office for sixty five years, and Margaretta Lemon (1860–1953), its first honorary secretary. Because of legal intricacies, Lemon's husband, a lawyer, took over her title when the society was incorporated by Royal Charter in 1904 and became the Royal Society for the Protection of Birds (RSPB), but Lemon herself continued virtually to run the organization for forty years. Among her duties were historianship, the general correspondence, and the secretaryship of publications. Thus until Phillips's death in 1916, Lemon and Phillips controlled the pen at the RSPB. Their remarkable skill as polemicists, writers, and editors of protest literature in defense of birds gives us an inside view of women's efforts on behalf of animal species in late Victorian Britain.

When these two women began their campaign to save wild birds, protest and concern over birds had been under way for a quarter of a century. In the 1860s, the common use of seabirds as hat decorations had led to the passage of the Sea Birds Protection Act of 1869. Unfortunately, this measure seemed only to encourage the use of other kinds of birds in millinery, particularly imported birds. In just one year in the 1880s, over 400,000 West Indian and Brazilian birds and 350,000 East Indian birds were sold on the London market. Not just feathers but parts of birds and even entire animals were used to decorate hats. In the 1880s and 1890s it was fashionable to set the heads of owls, with false glass eyes staring out into space, into the crowns of ladies' chapeaus. A cartoon from the *Westminster Gazette* (July 1901) of a fashionable lady sporting an extravagantly owled hat (see figure 28) spoofs the ends to which women were believed to go in their quest for originality. Coupled with the owl is a pair of stork legs, and coupled with the illustration, a poem:

Figure 28.   Cartoon from the *Westminster Gazette* (July 1901).
Courtesy of the Royal Society for the Protection of Birds.

I have found out a gift for my fair—
A pair of stork legs—think of that!
If they do look absurd
That's the fault of the bird,
Not to grow legs more fit for a hat.

Ten years before this spoof from 1901, Lemon and Phillips had set to work for the same cause, not in fun but in deadly earnest. In her history of the RSPB, Lemon tells us that new members of their society took a pledge and received a white membership card that enjoined them in gold letters to "discourage the wanton destruction of Birds, and interest themselves generally in their protection" and to "refrain from wearing the feathers of any bird not killed for purposes of food, the ostrich excepted" ("The Story of the R.S.P.B." 68). Ostrich feathers were taken during molts and thus considered fair game. Lemon felt so strongly about women who wore plumed hats that in the early years of the society she took note of all the ladies in her church who were wearing them. Then, early on Monday mornings, she would send each of them a letter detailing the cruelties of feather hunting. To appeal to their sentiments, she would include discussion of the plight of starving young birds whose parents, plumaged for the breeding season, had been killed for the women's gratification. Not all of the churchgoers might have been convinced, but by the end of its first year, the SPB had over five thousand members.

Nevertheless, Lemon and Phillips had a huge public relations task ahead of them. In the first two years of the society's life, they had hoped to enroll enough women to halt the trade in feathers. By 1891, they knew they were in for a long fight. For every hundred women who joined their group, hundreds of thousands continued to wear plumes. Just how Lemon and Phillips engineered their task of written protest and persuasion can be ascertained from the pages of the early pamphlets they issued, before their society was incorporated and before *Bird Notes and News* came into being in 1903. As much as is possible—since not all of the pamphlets are dated and many were reissued and reprinted—I have pieced together a rough chronology that shows the main course of the society's aims from its early years until the turn of the century.

Phillips, always the more trenchant of the two writers, set out her concerns in the 1891 leaflet *Destruction of Ornamental-Plumaged Birds*. The piece was sent to the queen that same year and was accepted with the somewhat curt notation that "Her Majesty's attention had been already directed to this subject." All the same, in an important way, the queen was a proper recipient, for Phillips was intending to prove that bird protection was a woman's question and hoping to gain the support of the most revered woman in the realm. In the pamphlet, Phillips assumed the forthright voice of a woman speaking to other women. "It is our vanity," she says, "that stimulates the greed of commerce, and our money that tempts bird-slaughterers to continue their cruel work at home and abroad." She particularly castigates those women who are mothers with nurseries at home—a reference intended to recall the nestling birds which she has just discussed—who wear bird feathers "even when engaged in public worship of the Creator of the beautiful and useful life of which they are inciting the continued destruction." And she excoriates all women who speak in public "with their heads bedecked with stuffed birds," implying that their messages must be as dead or head-stuffing as their headgear.

If Phillips's primary appeal was to women, her primary tactic was to shame them. Further appeals were made via carefully selected authorities. Buttressing her own powerful language with that of well-respected Englishmen, Phillips cites Lord Lilford (1833–1896),[1] the president of the British Ornithologist's Union, himself a very outspoken man, on the "disfigurement of women's heads" effected by the wearers of "Keeper's-Gibbets," Phillips's own loaded term for the

---

1. In addition to his duties as president of the organization, Lord Lilford published the eight-volume *Coloured Figures of the Birds of the British Islands* (London: R. H. Porter, 1881–97).

current hat style featuring birds that had been trapped and executed. Phillips's strategy shows one of the ways she chose to reinforce her arguments: she takes her own phrase and, like a ventriloquist, projects it as though it came from another, more prestigious person. In this way, she not only authenticated her own prose but validated her female outrage without seeming unfemininely harsh. After quoting Lilford, she goes on to cite the prominent writer W. H. Hudson (1841–1922), whom we encountered earlier at tea, on the horrors of bird warehouses, "where," according to Hudson, "it [was] possible for a person to walk ankle deep—literally to wade—in bright-plumaged bird skins, and see them piled shoulder high on each side of him." Next, she appeals to aesthetics and common sense: birds are beautiful and birds are useful, especially as insect eaters. Orchards and gardens need them, as agriculturalists in England and in America will attest. Her final, stirring appeal is directed to the clergy of England, whom she enjoins to speak out from their pulpits and condemn those who neglect the "duty of righteous and merciful dealing with every living creature, as inseparable from the dominion given by God to man."

This early pamphlet is typical of the society's first efforts at persuasion. The women of the SPB were hard on other women because they felt responsible for reforming their sisters. These women did not see bird preservation as a feminist issue. And because the society's spokespeople were women speaking to women, they spent less time writing about the feathered military—another favorite target of bird protectors—than they did about feathered women. For them, if women were the victims of a culture that demanded conspicuous consumption and display, they were nonetheless also people who might be exhorted and persuaded to alter their ways through intelligent and passionate address. Because men, too, aimed to protect birds, the SPB spokeswomen used the names and words of their most famous male cohorts—like Hudson—to bolster their own arguments. And they appealed to the high moral sense of the Victorian public in their quest for justice for birds.

In support of her viewpoints, Phillips arranged for pamphlets complementary to *Destruction of Ornamental-Plumaged Birds* also to be printed and disseminated. Among those early SPB leaflets were Hudson's paper *Osprey, or Egrets and Aigrettes*—"osprey" and "aigrettes" being inaccurate names for egret feathers when turned into hat materials—and his letter to the editor of the *Times* (17 October 1893) suggesting that cannibals had more respect for God-given creatures than did "Ruskin-reading" civilized persons of the nineteenth century.[2] Also among the early leaflets was one by a writer identified as the Reverend H. Greene, used to strengthen Phillips's exhortation to the clergy to severely criticize all feather wearers. If Phillips cited male authorities, Greene in his essay, entitled *As in a Mirror,* cited women, recalling that "E. V. B." (Eleanor

---

2. See W. H. Hudson, *Feathered Women,* SPB leaflet no.10. This leaflet is a May 1902 reprint of the letter to the *Times* of 17 October 1893.

Vere Gordon Boyle [1825–1926], a noteworthy writer and illustrator of children's books) once noticed that bird hats were great levelers: there were no shoddy birds killed for the trade involving the lower classes because there was "no such thing to be found as an ill-made seagull" (9). I bring in Hudson and Greene for the same reasons that Phillips did—to indicate that despite the direct appeals to women and the importance of women founders and officers to the SPB, the movement to save birds was not exclusively a women's movement. Lemon and Phillips never risked alienating powerful male allies who could serve their cause.

Lemon's hand was nearly as visible in the first pamphlets as was Phillips's. Lemon had discovered her interest in bird welfare early. After reading Eliza Brightwen's *Wild Nature Won by Kindness,* Lemon had become determined to do something about the plight of birds slaughtered during mating season, a cause she would always espouse. Like Brightwen (1830–1906), Lemon began her crusading hopefully, almost sentimentally. Not surprisingly, one of Brightwen's essays also became one of the early numbers in the SPB leaflet series. In her autobiography, *Eliza Brightwen: The Life and Thoughts of a Naturalist,* Brightwen recounts that she was ready to support efforts at bird preservation because she found the suffering of birds victimized for their feathers all but unbearable. She describes an idyllic Florida nesting site, then redescribes it "invaded by a gang of men, bang go the guns, the little tender, loving mothers cannot bear to leave their young and hover close around them. On goes the slaughter, and with regardless cruelty the skin of the back and the wings are torn off the poor birds whilst they are still alive" (135). Here Brightwen uses a strategy common in protest literature on behalf of animals: the analogy to human feelings and family structure. In the essay reprinted by the SPB, Brightwen reveals equivalent sympathy and sentiment for mother birds but also, with equivalent vividness, delineates the cruelties of electrocuting tired songbirds on traplike telegraph wires deliberately placed along the French coast to entice them in their first landfall after a longish flight over water (*A Talk about Birds).*

Lemon's early work as pamphleteer was in aid of the bird of paradise. Aware in 1895 that exceptionally large numbers of these rare birds were being killed for the plume trade and aware, too, of the enormity of the task of halting that trade, she spoke out with utter forthrightness, eschewing the Brightwen-like sentimentality she had once so admired. If the touted female sensitivity toward animals was still with Lemon, the language she would use to express her sympathy became more harsh. At this stage of Lemon's career, the facts themselves were glaring enough: living birds were no longer capable of reproducing the feathers that the trade required because most specimens were not "allowed to live long enough to reach maturity, the full plumage of the male bird requiring several years for its development!" (*The Bird of Paradise 2*). In a footnote added in 1899 to a revised edition of the 1895 pamphlet, she pointed out that "on six auction days during 1898, 34,860 single Birds of Paradise, and 45 packages were disposed of at the London Commercial Sale Rooms." Despite a decade's efforts at bird preservation, Lemon often seems to have felt that the SPB's work was losing ground.

But back to 1895. By then, Phillips, too, had changed her tone—from trenchant to angry. In that year, her pamphlet entitled *Mixed Plumes* disdainfully described the bouquetlike sprays that then adorned women's hats. Phillips would no longer mince words. "Nuptial plumage" is "torn" from parent birds, and the people wearing such plumes should be not only "feathered" but "tarred." The hats women wore might no longer be "stuffed carcasses," but a look at the newly fashionable bunched plumes indicated to Phillips that "the tar brush, suggested [by her] for the wearers, seems to have been employed upon the feathers" and that women seen in the boxes at the opera were adorned with hair ornaments "exactly like the sort of brush servants use to clean lamp-chimneys with." In *Mixed Plumes* we can also see how Phillips and Lemon collaborated. Phillips refers to Lemon when she mentions birds of paradise, to insinuate her point that the newly beloved feather sprays are drawn from the rarest of species.

Phillips concluded her essay with a direct appeal to the Princess of Wales to serve as a model for other women and desist from wearing mixed plumes. This time she was read and heeded. The *Evening Standard* (21 November 1895) reiterated her plea to the princess and cited Coleridge's moral from "Rime of the Ancient Mariner" in the bargain: "He prayeth well who loveth well, both man and bird and beast." In fact, the royals did begin to listen to the society and by the time of the Royal Charter (1904), Princess Alexandra would stop wearing feathers. Earlier, in 1899, Queen Victoria had ordered her regiments to cease wearing "ospreys."

Still, there was much left to be done. Lemon's history of the society recalls the pride with which the young SPB in 1892 welcomed Linley Sambourne's *Punch* cartoon of a female harpy, dressed in full Victorian feather regalia, about to snare a tiny songbird in her talons—a piece done in honor of the fledgling organization (see figure 29). Sambourne (1845–1910) was still at it in 1899, when he felt moved to offer another *Punch* cartoon in support of the discouraging, long-standing attempts at egret preservation, a drawing replete with images made familiar by the society's leaflets: baby egrets starving in the nest, birds plummeting from the sky, and a haughty, unheeding woman crowned in feathers and holding a new chapeau of dead birds.

The gruesome scenes that prompted that cartoon were still occurring when, in that same year, 1899, Margaretta Lemon addressed the International Congress of Women in Westminster in a speech entitled "Dress in Relation to Animal Life."[3] Lemon's title, juxtaposing the frivolities of one species over and

---

3. This speech was later printed as *Dress in Relation to Animal Life*, leaflet no. 33 in the society's series.

A BIRD OF PREY.

Figure 29.   Linley Sambourne, cartoon for *Punch* (May 1892). Courtesy of the Royal Society for the Protection of Birds.

against the very life of another, carried the message she wanted to convey. By century's end, Lemon's voice carried a tired certainty along with a ring of authority. Many women in the 1890s were interested in the question of "rational dress." Now a woman to be reckoned with, Lemon presented herself to her audience as an expert convinced that her cause was not "only a sentimental one, but a serious economic one." In this respect, she was in part countering the voice of economic entomologist Eleanor Ormerod, who was recommending that house sparrows be culled in order to save English crops. Avoiding the mention of crops or insects, Lemon took a different ecological position, noting that vermin were increasing because owls were being slaughtered and that women were not guiltless. Current laws protecting birds were virtually ignored. Seabirds and Florida egrets were dying by hordes. Birds of paradise were diminishing. Mother birds were still ripped away from their young. And then, once again practicing a kind of gendered ventriloquism when it came to real nastiness, the SPB leader would crown her argument with the words of an indignant Lord Lilford: "the fittest place for any wilful destroyer of an owl was an asylum for idiots." With all of these reminders before them, Lemon asked the women of the congress to become "citizens of the world," an epithet she put before them along with the word "extinction." Women—"good" women—had become exterminators rather than nurturers.

Throughout, Lemon's rhetoric was hyperbolic and dramatic. Toward the end of her talk, she called out the plea, "When it is too late, man (and woman) will discover what a poor, worthless, uninhabitable place this world is without the birds." And she concluded by presenting a painting produced on behalf of the society, one valorizing woman's compassion toward birds, *The Shuddering Angel* (see figure 30), by George Watts (1817–1904). As she looked at this work, Lemon recalled Watts's dedication "to all who love the beautiful and mourn over the senseless and cruel destruction of bird life and beauty." She then read a poem, which she had adapted from *Punch:*

> Feathers deck the hat and bonnet;
> Though the plumage seemeth fair,
> *Angels* as they look upon it
> See but slaughter in the air.
> Many a fashion gives employment,
> Unto thousands needing bread;
> This to add to your enjoyment,
> Means the dying and the dead.
>
> Wear the hat without the feather,
> All ye women, kind and true,
> Birds enjoy the summer weather
> And the sea as much as you.
> There's the riband, silk, or jewel;
> Fashion's whims are oft absurd,
> This is execrably cruel,
> Leave his feathers to the bird.

Dramatic though it might be, this capsule history cannot be left here, at the International Congress of Women, or, tempting as it might be, taken back full circle to the tea table. In 1899, the day for simply giving tea parties to raise support for endangered birds was over, as the stories of Lemon and Phillips have shown. The two women would work on together—with the added help, in 1900, of a new arrival, Linda Gardiner (d. 1940)—and, in consequence, the story of women writing for the RSPB went on. Politicians, rather than the hoped-for

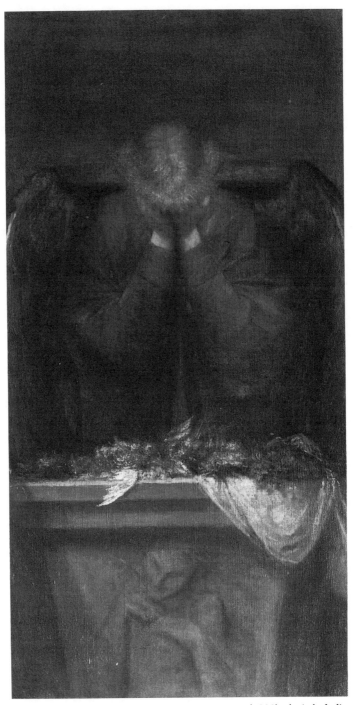

Figure 30. George Watts, *The Shuddering Angel* (1898). Artist's dedication: "To all who love the beautiful and mourn over the senseless and cruel destruction of bird life and beauty." Courtesy of the Trustees of the Watts Gallery, Guildford, Surrey, England.

clergy, became the women's primary allies in the long battle for bird preservation. Despite such events as the famous sandwich-board protests illustrating the "life of the egret" that took place in the streets of London in 1911, it would be 1921, five years after Phillips's death, before the Plumage Act would become operative. And yet another forty-three years before the indefatigable Lemon would, for her by then old companion *Bird News and Notes,* write the history of the society she had so dedicated herself to for over half a century.

Speaking for the Animals

Animal preservation implies an ecosystem in which animals with language—human beings—speak on behalf of other species. Language, for example, the polemical rhetoric of Phillips and Lemon, is a tool that helps humans conceptualize the functioning of an ecosystem and so work to protect and defend it. Gender issues can enter such an envisioned ecosystem in different ways. As we have seen, Lemon and Phillips did not blame men or patriarchal political, economic, or religious structures for inhumanities toward animals. Other crusaders on behalf of animals, however, made other assumptions. For example, *Shafts,* a feminist magazine for women and workers, ran a regular column entitled "Lives That Bless" that spoke out for animal brethren. In one installment, called "The Dog," which appeared in December 1892 (see figure 31), the column blasted the clergy as it praised the animal kingdom:

> there are to be found in the present day men who not only bear the name of Christians, but who wear the livery of the Church, and who, Sunday after Sunday, stand in surplice, vestment, or gown, and call upon a merciful God, to have mercy on sinners, and who afterwards, with composed countenance, and in *polished* language, *dare to insult* the Creator of the beautiful animal world, by the blasphemous assumption that scientific knowledge, for man's benefit, may be looked for in the living bodies of these His beloved creatures, who, He once trusted to the care of man. (67)

The essay would go on to indict a recent church congress which, it declared, should "sit and discuss the moral aspect of scientific cruelty." Better a decent atheist than such religious, the article concluded.

Other late-Victorian voices sounded very like those of our own contemporary "ecofeminist" movement. Ecofeminism is based on the premise that both women and the natural world have suffered from the domination inherent in Western patriarchal civilization, a premise that would have been shared by Frances Power Cobbe (1822–1904) (see figure 32). Cobbe crusaded on behalf of both women and animals, seeing both as victims of patriarchal control. She firmly believed that the kind of sympathy Arabella Buckley had found so typi-

Figure 31. Illustration from "Lives That Bless: The Dog," *Shafts* (December 1892).

cal of the vertebrates was often lacking in the very species—humanity—that prided itself on compassion and understanding. This she found particularly true of the males of the species, whom she would censure on a number of counts, including their greed in appropriating women's possessions through marriage. On this issue, her outspokenness helped initiate the passage of the first Married Women's Property Act in 1870.

Suspicious of the motivations of men, Cobbe exposed her culture's tacit disdain for qualities it had come to consider female, such as altruism. Brian Eastlea suggests that what he calls the "viriculture" of nineteenth-century Britain suspected the very womanly compassion it had constructed as female—and that men like Herbert Spencer actually feared the power of altruism. Eastlea argues persuasively that Spencer's alarm over a society dominated by excessive compassion led him to militate against enfranchising women since they might be in favor of an "increasing population of imbeciles and idlers and criminals" (qtd. in

Figure 32.   Frances Power Cobbe. Courtesy of the
Fawcett Library, London.

Science and Sexual Oppression 153). This statement, which Eastlea extracted from
Spencer's *Study of Sociology* (1873), may well have been a personal reaction to
Cobbe. Just five years earlier, Cobbe had brought home a portion of her strong,
feminist resentment in the now famous essay "Criminals, Idiots, Women, and
Minors," in which she suggested that men assigned women, along with other
disempowered human beings, to an underclass. It may well be that Spencer's
concern for the eugenic future of his country was stimulated by the words of an
uncanny and outspoken woman who had a way of placing her fingers on the
pulse of the feminist issues of her day.

   Cobbe was equally outspoken as a crusader on behalf of laboratory animals.
In recreating Frances Power Cobbe lecturing on vivisection to a mixed group of
men and women, Coral Lansbury reveals something of the generally negative
reaction to women's sympathy that Eastlea discerns in the dominant culture of
the day. According to Lansbury, when Cobbe described some of the experiments being performed on dogs, "the women in her audience would become
hysterical, to the delight of the jeering medical students, who saw this as another example of women's volatile sympathies" (84). Here then, in the persons

of the sneering medical students, was a more popular, masculine reaction to women's sensitivity to suffering, but one that certainly echoed Spencer's disdain. Lansbury goes on to suggest that women like those in Cobbe's audience identified with the domesticated animals. Certainly, Cobbe herself made the conceptual leap to recognizing women's analogous powerlessness at the hands of the medical profession.

In 1863, Cobbe wrote "The Rights of Man and the Claims of Brutes" for *Fraser's Magazine,* an essay she called "the first effort to deal with the moral questions involved in the torture of animals" (*Life* 562). From then on, she was fully engaged in the antivivisection movement—presenting a petition to the RSPCA with six hundred signatories, all hoping to regulate vivisection, and founding the Victoria Street Society, also known as the Society for the Protection of Animals Liable to Vivisection. This society lobbied for a passage of a government act to regulate the practice of vivisection but was disappointed when the 1876 Vivisection Act licensed vivisectors but failed to stop the scientific torture of animals.

For two decades, Cobbe wrote dozens of potent essays against vivisection, which she called the science that was no science, only cruelty. This "science," she wrote, "has achieved the creation of *agony* such as simple Nature never knew" ("The Future of the Lower Animals," *The Modern Rack* 91). Here, Cobbe was attempting to counter those disciples of Darwin who used his theories to justify vivisection. Like Arabella Buckley, Cobbe worried about the appropriate interpretation of the "struggle for existence." In her case, however, the worry was over those humans who were attempting to justify what she considered immoral behavior. Cobbe immediately foresaw the perils of Darwinism in relation to vivisection, and warned against them just after she had received a copy of *The Descent of Man* from Darwin himself. Darwin's work, Cobbe said, filled her "with deadliest alarm" (*Life* 447), and in her "New Morality," she would sardonically summarize the "Darwinian" arguments she felt were attributable to vivisectors: "'Nature is extremely cruel, but we cannot do better than to follow Nature. The law of Survival of the Fittest, applied to human agency, implies the absolute right of the Strong (*i.e.,* of those who can prove themselves Fittest) to sacrifice the Weak and Unfit, *ad libitum'*" (*Modern Rack* 66). Clearly, her analytical approach had implications for social Darwinism as well as vivisection. What troubled Cobbe here was the mistake of "gathering the grapes of Morality off the thorns of Physics and Zoology," a practice she shunned because "no such fruit grows on such trees," since "moral truths are morally discerned" and "not to be got through researches into things which are not . . . moral" (68). Such thinking was what made science "childish," to her mind (69).

What was not childish was "zoophily," an ethics she fully embraced. According to Cobbe, zoophily acknowledges that the "chasm" between the human race and nonhuman animals is "*not* sufficient to cut short the moral obligations of man at the confines of humanity" ("The Ethics of Zoophily" 503). Nevertheless, Cobbe herself was willing to relax those obligations when it came to the lower animals, like the oyster or parasite. To her way of thinking, what must be assessed was the "*sensibility of the object to pain*" (503). In her ranking of creatures' sensibilities, Cobbe was content to follow an outdated hierarchy modeled after the great chain of being, a hierarchy that proved useful for her moral attack on vivisectionists. A play on the idea of the chain of being gave her the metaphor for one of her most trenchant and original essays, "Science in Excelsis." In her epigraph to "The New Morality," Cobbe had concocted a beatitude for a fictional *New Gospel of Science:* "Blessed are the merciless, for they shall obtain useful knowledge" (*Modern Rack* 65). In "Science in Excelsis," she turned the tables on merciless scientists by making them the victims of higher beings—fictional cherubim who stood closer to God in the chain of being and therefore could have dominion over human beings as human beings did over animals.

Since Cobbe's angels first determined that science was being treated as superior to both learning and philosophy and that the physiologist-vivisectionists felt they represented the highest ranks of science, the angels then determined to experiment on vivisectionists' brains and stomachs. These might best yield the peculiar secrets of human scientific behavior. Accordingly, they licensed themselves to set to work. Put to the test in a kind of mock trial, the hubris-filled, vivisecting physiologists at first refused to justify themselves, because they believe they are self-justified. They consider themselves "philosophers, and can allow no superstitious moral considerations derived merely from the inherited prejudices of our ancestors to interfere with [their] pursuit of knowledge" (*Modern Rack* 245). In the end, however, they are reduced to vigorously pleading for mercy, though none is forthcoming; ironically, the angels have set out to use the laboratory manuals of the physiologists themselves to guide them in their incipient experiments on physiologists. As the angel Raphael points out, "PITY has fled before SCIENCE, who alone will henceforth direct our proceedings" (251).

Behind all of this satirical fun was a deadly serious woman. Cobbe found vivisection not just a cruelty but a threat to European civilization. Despite her love of animals, she shared the Victorian fear of what she called "the bestial"; her vision of the human characteristics of animals was certainly most applicable to the domesticated creatures she was trying to save. And so, for her, the civilized world and the natural world were distinct from one another, if allied. Vivisection was uncivilized and, like the bestial, predatory and therefore detrimental to Europeans. As she said in *The Modern Rack* (1889), her late compilation of her own essays on vivisection, "to help one order of sufferers is to help all, for it is to keep alive in human hearts those feelings of justice and compassion on which not only charity, but civilization itself is founded" (238). From Cobbe's perspective, "either the moral progress of Europe itself must be arrested and re-cede far back behind the point attained at the Christian era, or Vivisection must cease" (271). Civilization and vivisection were totally incompatible.

Throughout her career, Cobbe was criticized for the unwomanliness of her position; she wrote with an authority in her day more commonly associated with men. But she always showed pride in her gender, to the point of happily acknowledging her femaleness in print: "I do not in the smallest degree object to finding my appeals on behalf of animals treated as womanly. I claim, as a woman—nay, as an old woman, that climax of feebleness and futility!—to have the better right to be heard in such a cause than a man, or even than a priest. If my sex has a 'mission' of any kind, it is surely to soften this hard world" ("Ethics of Zoophily" 497). Like so many of the women represented in this book, Cobbe chose never to deny the importance of the legacy of compassion and of educa-tion in sympathy that was widely thought to be the special province of women. But unlike up-to-date popularizers such as Arabella Buckley, Cobbe was scien-tifically conservative and built alliances wherever she could to strengthen her moral position against Darwinism. Heterodox though she was, in the cause of antivivisection she aligned herself with churchmen like the Roman Catholic cardinal Henry Manning (1808–1892), sharing the podium with them to de-nounce the perceived evils of Darwinism at antivivisection meetings. Despite her convinced feminism and her very different attitudes toward men and women, Cobbe accepted male help with her work, as did Lemon and Phillips: the cause of animal preservation demanded coalition.

Cobbe also had female allies in her work to further antivivisection: Anna Kingsford (1846–1888), for one, who studied medicine and was appalled both by the work of vivisectors and by the social hypocrisy inherent in teaching the young to respect animal life when, meanwhile, live animals were being dissected every day in the name of medicine. And Mona Caird, for another, a woman who laid the blame for vivisection both on the cancerous power of the medical profession to do what it wished, when it wished and on the indifference of an amoral society that persistently looked the other way. Caird hoped for the end of patriarchy and the beginning of a civilization based upon respect for human and nonhuman creatures alike. Cobbe had another strong moral ally in the world of the humane letters, Sarah Grand (pseudonym of Frances Elizabeth McFall, née Clarke [1854–1943]), who, like Cobbe, recognized a link in male-dominated society between the treatment of animals and the treatment of women.

In 1897, Grand published *The Beth Book*, a lengthy novel about a bright, tal-ented, nature lover who marries a doctor only to suffer from his indifference and her loss of independence. Beth's husband, Dan McClure, is the embodi-ment of cruelty toward both women and animals. The medical director of a lock hospital—an institution in which women with venereal disease were kept in accordance with the Contagious Diseases Acts—McClure spends his days enforcing Contagious Diseases regulations. Both Beth and the women whose bodies he inspects during the day are subject to violation by Dr. McClure. By night, when he is not demanding a husband's rights and shaming Beth, he is busy disassembling animals like a "bonny wee" terrier he has brought home to show Beth (437). Clearly, there is no refuge for either woman or animal in Mc-Clure's Victorian home. Shocked by the discovery of her husband's cruelty, Beth puts the terrier out of its misery and herself out of harm's way, not by dying like a dog but by living as an independent woman. For Beth, McClure's white hands have come to signify death, not healing. They are "associated with torture, from which humanity instinctively shrinks; and when he touched her, her delicate skin crisped with a shudder. She used to wonder how he could eat with hands so polluted, and once, at dessert, when he handed her a piece of orange in his fingers, she was obliged to leave it on her plate, she could not swallow it" (445).

Grand saw unblinkingly the deadliness of the cultural link connecting the degradation of the female human body to that of the bodies of animals. Her Dr. McClure makes this evident when he comments on the fine lines of a female form as though he were describing cattle he might purchase. And her Beth realizes this connection more and more as the story unfolds. Like the crusaders working for the repeal of the Contagious Diseases Acts, the fictional Beth is appalled at the loss of liberty inherent for women in the inspection of their bodies by male officials for what amounted to a kind of certification—rather as meat might be certified today. But like a contemporary ecofeminist, she comes to believe that "anything we could do to the animals we could do to each other: we practiced on them first" (Margaret Atwood, *Surfacing* 143).

Nurturing through Nature: Teaching through the Plants

Discussing Victorian environments, Peter Gould notes that "being at one with the animals, other people, and the physical environment was related to the concept of 'natural' sexual relations" (*Early Green Politics* 48). "'Natural' sexual relations" had certainly been around at least since Darwin's work was read as eroticizing nature. Not just Marie Stopes in the early twentieth century but many Victorian women believed that it was utterly essential for women to understand human sexuality as natural in a positive sense of the word. Especially after the repeal of the Contagious Diseases Acts in the mid-1880s, women dedicated themselves to educating one another about their bodies. Other women became concerned that both young men and young women receive instruction about the sexual functions of their bodies in the hope that this might lead to more enlightened behavior on the parts of both. In *Cultivating Women, Cultivating Nature*, Ann B. Shteir describes what she calls "the bowdlerizing botany," a female way of talking about flowers and their reproduction without using sexual language. The necessity for this bowdlerizing arose in response to clerical condemnation of female use of Linnaean classification; it was too close to language about sex. Although such bowdlerization typifies early-nineteenth-century discussions of stamens, pistils, and botanical reproduction (Shteir 200–202), by the end of the nineteenth century this kind of bowdlerizing gave way to something like its opposite. Women used analogies to floral reproduction to teach human sexuality to children. Mrs. A. M. Longshore-Potts (d. 1912), a physician trained at the Women's Medical College in Philadelphia but living in Britain, opened her book *Discourses to Women on Medical Subjects* (1887) by counseling the appropriateness of analogies from nature:

> The study of the male and female, or the positive and negative forces, need not be eschewed as indelicate by even the most fastidious persons, when they are viewed in the light of agents known to operate in all parts of the universe, and to be essential for the consummation of Nature's great phenomenon, reproduction. (213)

Longshore-Potts would go on to suggest likenesses between people and flowers and then catapult directly from plants to genteel but graphic discussion of human reproduction.

Elizabeth Wolstenholme Elmy (1834–1918)—another foot soldier in the campaign to abolish the Contagious Diseases Acts and the influential friend who pleaded with and convinced Josephine Butler to lead the Great Crusade—had, under a second name, a different career in which she too would depict human sexuality through analogies with the plant kingdom.[4] Elmy wrote and published a number of books for young people, using the pseudonym Ellis Ethelmer.[5] While other women were nurturing nature, Elmy, as Ethelmer, was nurturing children through nature. Her *Baby Buds* (1895) was a birds-and-bees primer for small children in which a mother explains sexual reproduction to a child just over four years of age. Unlike Longshore-Potts's book intended for grown women, which leaps from plants to people, Elmy's book moves its younger readers through a kind of sexual chain of being, beginning with plant

---

4. For more information about other phases of Elizabeth Wolstenholme Elmy's varied career and life, see Sandra Stanley Holton, "Free Love and Victorian Feminism: The Divers Matrimonials of Elizabeth Wolstenholme and Ben Elmy."

5. There is considerable debate as to just who Ellis Ethelmer was, Elizabeth Wolstenholme Elmy or her husband, Ben Elmy. The two were known to collaborate frequently. Sheila Jeffreys, in *The Spinster and Her Enemies*, favors Elizabeth Wolstenholme Elmy as Ethelmer, and I am inclined to agree. Lucy Bland, however, believes that the name was either Ben Elmy's or a pseudonym he shared with his wife (see *Banishing the Beast*, 339n. 57). In any case, Elizabeth Wolstenholme Elmy was publisher of all of the works I shall discuss.

reproduction, then moving on to the story of birds and eggs, then reptiles, and finally mammals, including human beings. This chain ultimately allows Ellis Ethelmer both to show the kinship between animals and plants and to develop analogies between plants and people: "In a full grown female mammal or bird there is an ovary, somewhat as in a flower, and containing ovules which, under certain circumstances, will develope into young. There is not, however, any outward form of a flower, for the animal's flower-like organs are contained inside the lower part of her body, so as to be little exposed to chance of harm" (37). As she speaks to her own fictional youngsters and to the book's readers, preserving a soft, motherly voice akin to those of earlier popularizers of nature narratives, Elmy's narrator clings to her analogy: very young people have already developing "flower-like organs, male or female—according as you are a boy or a girl" (39).

In 1895, the year in which she published *Baby Buds,* Elmy also issued its complement, *The Human Flower: A Simple Statement of the Physiology of Birth and the Relations of the Sexes.* Again as Ethelmer, she described reproduction, but this time in a plainer, less metaphoric language intended for young adults and for those adults who might be uninformed about sex. Human male and female sexual organs, seminal emissions, and menstruation are forthrightly named as such while—much as would Marie Stopes—Elmy pleads for judicious sexuality and "psychic" love. Here, in *The Human Flower,* she maintains that the way to know nature is through sexuality and that the way to know one's sexual (animal) nature and still to remain human is to know love. These late-Victorian notions would resound through the sex manuals of the early twentieth century and culminate in Stopes's *Married Love.* In the 1890s, Elmy's work offered a groundbreaking female counterpart to the work of Edward Carpenter, her contemporary, whose very popular *Love's Coming of Age* (1896), a compendium of pamphlets recommending greater comradeship between the sexes, was written at the same time as Elmy's earlier books.[6]

Elizabeth Wolstenholme Elmy was not just a sex educator but a feminist sex educator who did not want women to be considered as the only reproductive member of a human pair. In her books for children, she took great care to describe the importance of the male parent to conception and child rearing. In *Woman Free* (1893)—a thirty-two-page poem with nearly two hundred pages of appended notes, which was written under her married name, not her pseudonym—she deplored the categorizing of women solely as childbearing vessels. This categorizing, she felt, made the childbearing years disproportionately significant in a woman's entire life span and therefore greatly constricted women's sense of long-term usefulness. *Woman Free* is a strange and fascinating potpourri. Sometimes its extensive notes are drawn from contemporary

---

6. For an interesting discussion of Carpenter and of sex manuals in general, see Roy Porter and Leslie Hall, *The Facts of Life: The Creation of Sexual Knowledge in Britain, 1650–1950.*

works, for instance, Edward Westermarck's *History of Human Marriage* (1891), suggesting that women must not be shut up in marriage like hothouse plants. But often Elmy quotes herself as Ethelmer, converting her own persona into a forceful voice equivalent to those of any of the male authorities she knows or references.

Elmy was particularly eloquent when taking on Darwin, arguing that in him "the masculine sex-bias is so ingrained and so ingenuous that he strives to disparage and contemn the notorious mental quickness of intuition of woman by saying: 'It is generally admitted with woman the powers of intuition . . . are more strongly marked than in man, but some at least, of these faculties are characteristic of the lower races, and therefore of a past and lower state of civilization' [*The Descent of Man*]. . . . His unconscious sex-bias apparently overlooked the pregnant and very pertinent caution which he had uttered in a previous work [*Origin of Species*]" (n. 5, XVI). This "sex-bias," Elmy felt, typified not just Darwin but all of Western civilization, and she said so whenever she had the chance. In the *Phases of Love* (1897), her voice rose to its highest pitch as she traced the roots of female oppression to the "bodily subjection (and hence degradation) of woman . . . even in systems where the feminine element in Nature was assumed to be of foremost dignity and sanctity" by "masculine schemes" (9) and derided the "pessimisms, nihilisms, theologic or philosophic vagaries of imperfectly begotten one-sexed thought" (12). In her desire to capture as many audiences as possible, Elmy had developed into a rhetorical ventriloquist by the time of *Phases of Love*. To children, Elmy spoke softly, issuing information she felt was appropriate to their age-group. For small children, she not only emphasized the connection of human sexuality to nature but constantly provided reassurances to them: "You may readily see how it is that a mother animal and her young are so dear to one another" (*Baby Buds* 41). With older young people, on the same subject, she was frank and direct as in *The Human Flower*. But for grown men and women—whom she felt compelled to educate about the dangers of patriarchal thinking and social structures and the ways in which these created false perceptions of sexuality—in *Phases of Love* she became downright fiery.

Saving the Land for the People

If Josephine Butler believed that her crusade was conducted on behalf of all humanity, her closest concerns were prompted by direct contact with those working-class women who felt most immediately the impact of the Contagious Diseases Acts, white slavery, and the lack of public information about human reproduction and birth control. A corresponding devotion to the well-being of working people and of the poor marked the career of yet another determined crusader, Octavia Hill (1838–1912) (see figure 33)—one of the earliest of the

Figure 33.   John Singer Sargent, *Octavia Hill* (1898). By courtesy of The National Portrait Gallery, London.

British land conservationists and the one who most carefully framed her efforts to further the cause of conservation in terms of dispossessed humanity. Both Hill's temperament and her early situation at home suited her for the tasks she would undertake. As a child, Hill filtered her perceptions through nature. She was always out-of-doors. In Finchley, which during Hill's childhood was still only a village, she and her sisters were known as "the young ladies who were always up in the hedges" (Bell, *Octavia Hill* 10). Eventually Hill's father's bankruptcy and the consequent family moves diminished her romps in hedges and put her into closer contact with the family's chief supporter, her maternal grandfather, Dr. Southwood Smith. While still a young woman, Hill began to spend hours and days listening to and copying medical extracts for Southwood Smith, a physician in the Fever Hospital in East London. From him, she learned of the overcrowded slums of the city and the minimal sanitation and rampant disease that characterized the place. Herself curtailed in the freedom she had so cherished in nature, she felt all the more the claustrophobia of the corridors of London; early in life, she determined to save or reclaim open spaces for its inhabitants. What Hill wanted to recreate were "fields reminding men and women long lost in the whirl of London, of child days and places near where they were born; fields where little children can see the wild flowers grow, as they are beginning to do once more on Hampstead Heath, but nearer their homes" (*Letters* 333).

In public in the 1870s, Hill trimmed her romantic language into a Victorian parlance that better suited the tenor of her time. If her primal motivations included a Wordsworthian nostalgia for a freer, childhood time in nature, Hill's actual arguments to promote the creation of open spaces were far more pragmatic. Hill was always politically astute and opportunistic in grasping what kind of approach might gain the most land for the most people. Speaking before the National Health Society in 1877, she warned, "Your best chance of escape [from disease and epidemic and contagion] is to make the place inhabited by the poor healthy, to let them have open space where the fresh wind may blow over them and their clothes, places where they may be less crowded and gain health" (*Our Common Land* 137). Described in such practical, epidemiological terms, land signifies space for humans; it becomes something less important than the people for whom it is intended. In the 1870s, this sociological approach to nature was more prominent and more effective than the environmental approach that marks our day. When, late in the century, Eliza Phillips made her speeches and wrote her pamphlets for the welfare of birds, stressing her realization of the importance of those species to a European ecology, she was actually expressing views that were far more forward-looking in Victorian Britain than were social libertarian views like Hill's. This may be a reason why, as Ann Ardis reminds us, issues like bird preservation and antivivisection "presented only local challenges to Victorian social conventions" (*New Women, New Novels* 15). They were ahead of their time.

By the 1870s, when Octavia Hill took leadership of the crusade for open spaces—for countryside, play areas, gardens, and walking areas for the public—an existing parks movement had already undergone two earlier phases. In the wake of discussions of the "condition of England," the 1840s had seen a period of private benevolence—but mainly in the north, where large gifts of land had been made in hopes of preventing cholera and quieting the Chartists. Then followed a period of struggle to preserve British suburban areas from the encroachment of the railroads and construction. Hill's work of the 1870s and 1880s built upon these earlier phases but introduced a new concentration of attention on the metropolitan spaces of London, which Hill had learned to know only too well in the preceding decade of her own life (Malchow 99–105). As an art student in the 1860s, Hill had come into contact with the renowned critic John Ruskin. Aware of her concern for the poor, he had offered her loans of money to use for whatever social purposes she liked. As a result, Hill bought and transformed three slumlike houses in Paradise Place, Marylebone, and wound up a reformer, not an artist. After the magic she had worked on her own properties became known, she was hailed as an expert on urban renewal.

Since prior victories had been won mainly in the northern and in suburban areas, Hill now worked tirelessly not only to improve London slums but to save large areas of city from further development. Defeated in her attempts to preserve the Swiss Cottage Fields against the encroachment of builders and to persuade the Quakers to set aside their burial ground at Bunhill Row for public use rather than to lease it to contractors, she joined forces with the Commons Preservation Society in the mid-1870s. Through that society, she urged the conversion of other disused burial grounds. Despite protests over the possible desecration of graves and further concerns that the people would misuse the spaces set aside for them, Hill prevailed. Arguing that people attach to the countries where they can be attached to the land, Hill queried, "Is all the land, so far as the people are concerned, from sea to sea, to be used for corn-growing, or building over only?" (*Our Common Land* 179). "Every atom of open space you have left to these people is needed" (5). In 1881, Hill saw the passage of the Metropolitan Open Spaces Act, for which she had arduously lobbied. The act enabled local authorities to acquire and maintain gardens and to accept the transfer of disused burial grounds for conversion and utilization as gardens. It forbade further building on those sites and, by driving down the commercial value of the lands involved, kept them safe for public use.

For Hill, the artist and romantic, beauty and utility went hand in hand. "There are two great wants in the life of the poor of our large towns," she wrote, "which ought to be realized more than they are—the want of space, and the want of beauty" (*Common Land* 106). In hopes of relieving that second want, Hill became a member and supporter of the Kyrle Society, an organization founded by her own sister, Miranda. Named after Alexander Pope's John Kyrle, who donated a park to his hometown,[7] the society sought to beautify human environments by planting and distributing flowers, erecting aviaries, providing clean running water, and otherwise improving spaces used by working people. For paving the way for beauty, as for everything, Hill had practical suggestions, as in the case of beautifying a burial ground: "Paths must be strong and wide, the drainage must be good; such a space is often very useful in affording light and air to a whole row of cottages if the high brick wall surrounding it is replaced by an iron railing" ("Colour, Space, and Music for the People" 747). Beauty, as necessary to mental health as space was to physical well-being, needed strong foundation stones.

---

7. In Pope's "Of the Use of Riches, An Epistle to Bathurst" (1723), John Kyrle, the "Man of Ross," gave a public walking place to the inhabitants of Ross, his native town, in 1706.

In the 1890s, however, Hill herself was laying other foundations as she joined Canon Hardwicke Rawnsley (1851–1920) in efforts to establish a National Trust for Historic Sites and Natural Scenery. The trust would aim to "promote the permanent preservation, for the benefit of the Nation, of land and tenements (including buildings) of beauty or historic interest; and as regards lands, to preserve (so far as practicable) their natural aspect, features and animal and plant life; and for this purpose to accept from private owners of property, gifts of places of interest or beauty, and to hold the lands, houses and other property thus acquired, in trust for the use and employment of the nation" (National Trust, *Report* 4). Despite her championing of the poor, Hill envisioned a trust managed by the landed and well-to-do, reasoning that neither land developers nor the impoverished could be sufficiently disinterested in the way land should be utilized to make consistently wise decisions. She wanted leaders "to whom historic memories loom large, who love the wild bird, butterfly, and plant, who realize the national value of hill slope lighted by sun or shadowed by cloud." "So," she continued, "the governing body [of the National Trust] is nominated by the great artistic, learned, and scientific foundations of the United Kingdom" ("Natural Beauty as a National Asset" 935). At times like this, Hill's romantic vision may have affronted those very classes whose lives she was attempting to improve. Nevertheless, Hill, like other successful crusaders, was a talented rhetorician, politically astute and politically effective. When she wanted to save the cities for the people, she appealed to them as well as to the landed, but when she wanted to save outlying or rural lands, as was the case with the Lake District and other areas of special interest to the trust, she appealed primarily to the upper classes, those who held specific parcels of land, working to persuade them that all land was in actuality held in trust.

Hill's care for the politics of crusading notwithstanding, she, like Marie Stopes and Frances Power Cobbe, was simultaneously admired and lampooned for her crusader's efforts, especially for her love of beauty. Linley Sambourne, the cartoonist so dedicated to the cause of the bird protectors of the 1890s, had drawn Hill as "Spring" for *Punch* in June 1883. In the depiction, Hill is a glamorous Primavera figure (see figure 34), dancing through the slums, bringing flowers and sunlight to impoverished children, and suggesting that "'the value of small open spaces in densely-populated districts, near the homes of working people, is increasingly recognized, year by year.'" "'Recognized!' Ay, but by whom?" the caption queries. Not by the conservative elements of the population nor by the "Lords of the Rail," the caption further suggests.

But Hill did become an example to women who followed her. Influenced early in life by Rawnsley and knowledgeable about his close association with Hill, Beatrix Potter, for example, became deeply involved with land preservation. She, too, worked with the National Trust, at times using proceeds from her books to preserve parts of the Lake District. Other women as well—sometimes

Figure 34.   Linley Sambourne, cartoon of Octavia Hill for *Punch* (June 1883).

conventionally and sometimes unconventionally—used their talents on behalf of causes espoused by Hill. Edith Nesbit's biographer describes a peculiar performance by this well-known cofounder of Fabian Socialism. Nesbit (E. N. Bland [1858–1924]) went into her garden at the end of one day in 1911, brought out cardboard models of suburban housing units and factories, and invited her friends—who included the novelist E. M. Forster—to help her "ritually set fire to these effigies of urban encroachment" (Briggs 321). Nesbit resented exploitation in all its forms and made this obvious not only in offbeat garden parties and socialist activities but in the stories she wrote for children.

Women of Nesbit's generation wrote a new kind of children's fiction that coupled the kind of moral instruction found in earlier books like Wollstonecraft's—which had aimed to promote good citizenship—with a socialist zeal to undercut established norms. Thus in "Fortunatus Rex & Co." Nesbit spun one unlikely story in her *Nine Unlikely Tales for Children* (1901)—"unlikely" because it was "subversive," in this case, of Victorian ideas of progress (Auerbach and Knoepflmacher). Nesbit's story tells of a middle-aged female proprietor of a school, who has invested all of her money in land, and a king, who brings his daughter to the school to board. To distract himself from his grief when his daughter disappears, the king becomes a speculative builder, the founder of Fortunatus & Co. According to the story's teller, King and Co. "bought all the pretty woods and fields they could get and cut them up into squares, and grubbed up the trees and the grass and put streets there and lamp-posts and ugly little yellow brick houses, in the hopes that people would want to live in them. And curiously enough people did. So the King and his Co. made quite a lot of money," and the king's new streets crawl "further and further out of the town, eating up the green country like greedy yellow caterpillars" (qtd. in Auerbach and Knoepflmacher 197).

Eventually the firm is forced to stop by an old woman who will not sell her land. And eventually the king strikes a bargain with the old lady and also finds his lost daughter. The headmistress has dispelled the power of the evil magician who has spirited the daughter away and imprisoned him in a globe of the world. Grateful, the king bestows on the teacher what she now wants most: for him to "Make the land green again, your Majesty" (qtd. in Auerbach and Knoepflmacher 204). Thus both king and teacher learn the hard lessons to be learned from investing in land as capital, not greenbelt. Anti-imperialist, with its amusing imprisonment of the magician in a globe of the world about to be sliced up by a set of princes questing for the lost princess and her cohorts, "Fortunatus Rex & Co." is a witty cautionary tale which is pro-green on both a local and an international scale. In this tale, women who collude with men in the exploitation of land must pay the same price that the men do. Unless, like the headmistress, they are willing to learn and atone by attacking even larger and more destructive imperialistic interests, they will be deprived of beauty and mired in bogs of immorality. The tale bears caveats for all; there are no benign Mother Natures here. Everyone—highborn or not, male or female—must work collectively to keep the land alive.

In her fiction, Nesbit repeatedly replayed her Hill-like plot of open spaces lost to the encroachment of developers. In a later work, *Wings and the Child* (1913), she again raised the specter of the metaphoric yellow caterpillars, this time painting a bleaker picture than she had in "Fortunatus & Co." In this case, she juxtaposed bulldozers with the kinds of people they might deprive and the vegetation they might devour:

> Now the trees are cut down and there are no more flowers. It is asphalt all the way, and here and there seats divided by iron rods so that tired tramps should not sleep on them. And the green fields by Mottingham where the kingcups used to grow, and the willows by the little stream, they are eaten up by yellow caterpillars of streets all like, all horrible. . . . And no one seems to care. (Qtd. in Briggs 323)

But a number of people did care, particularly a number of women who felt easier when speaking authoritatively on behalf of green spaces and plants than they did when holding forth on other subjects. Women had long been associated with botanical drawing, botanical writing, and with botanizing in general, earning a voice in botanical study. Thus when the green world began to be endangered by building and by industry, many felt a kind of protective engagement with wild plants.

The daughter of Margaret Gatty, Juliana Horatia Ewing (1841–1885) (see figure 35), was one of these protectors. Of both Gatty and Ewing, Ewing's sister observed that "the chief and lasting value of whatever both my sister and my mother wrote about animals, or any other object in Nature, lies in the fact that they invariably took the utmost pains to verify whatever statements they made" (qtd. in Eden 68–69). An amateur botanist, Ewing was, like Beatrix Potter, a lifelong observer of the plant kingdom who translated her knowledge into the realm of children's fiction. Ewing kept notebooks with sketches of plants which were new to her, inscribing them with their scientific names. She also watched the encroachment of industry on open land and carefully noted and recorded what flowers would return if the land were abandoned after mistreatment and what flowers might prevail in spite of it. Her sister recalled that Ewing once found a yellow mullein growing near a slag heap and utterly rejoiced at the sight (Eden 86). Remembering this in later life, Ewing would persuade a friend in the mining business to plant over his worked-out mines with appropriate plants.

In her short story "Our Field" (1870), Ewing projected a young narrator who also collected plants and held two of Ewing's own beliefs: that no one really owns land but only holds it in trust and that those who do hold it in trust

Figure 35. Juliana Horatia Ewing.

must act as its stewards. "I know," she says, "that Our Field does not really belong to us. I wonder whom it does belong to?" (*"A Great Emergency" and Other Tales* 182). "Our Field" involves four children who discover an abandoned field and both play and learn about nature there. They find that cowslips grow more thickly in the damper section of the field and that the progression of blooms throughout the season gives them as much pleasure as their former pursuits. They enter an agricultural show and compete for its prizes, bringing moss and wildflower collections drawn only from their field. Although the female narrator wins first prize for her array of wild flowers, one of her male playmates wins second with his moss tray with "Hair-moss, and the Pincushion-moss and the Scale-mosses" (182). In "Our Field"—as in Nesbit's later tale and, indeed, in the founding of the National Trust—learning about and preserving the green world must involve men as well as women. The children in Ewing's story reap two rewards for this coalition: first, they are rewarded by getting to know nature and playing in fields, not on streets, and, second, they also gain a cash prize, which enables them to save a stray dog by paying for its dog tax. Ewing sets up a small ecosystem as a learning experience for her readers. Children, domestic animals, wild plants all can materially provide for one another in different ways if the human children can see the value of other species. And the spoils of the Victorian capitalist society can, as in Nesbit's story, be plowed back into the earth to benefit its creatures. In addition to demonstrating the practical value of such an ecosystem, Ewing was also espousing the "creed of kinship" (Gould 42). Her sister relates that "one of the strongest features of Julie's character" was "her love for animals" which "enabled her almost to get inside the minds of her pets, and know how to describe their feelings" (Eden 43).

Ewing was as attracted to wild natural areas open to the sky as she was to domesticated animals. In a letter to her mother, she once wrote enthusiastically about the landscape near Stonehenge: "The charm of these unhedged, un-'cabined, cribbed, confined' *prairies* is all their own, and very perfect!" (Eden 257). Her fictional "Mary's Meadow" (1884), a tribute to one such perfect place, was serialized in 1883 in *Aunt Judy's Magazine for Children*, a publication begun in 1866 by Margaret Gatty and named after Juliana herself. "Mary's Meadow" centers around a young girl who plants flowers in waste areas. "I'll take," she determines, "seeds and cuttings, and off-shoots from our garden, and set them in waste places, and hedges, and fields, and I'll make an Earthly Paradise of Mary's Meadow" (*"Mary's Meadow" and "Letters from a Little Garden"* 35). Her chosen area is an empty field owned and ignored by Old Squire, a Scrooge-like man whom children fear. Mary's special interest in his field lies in its remoteness; it might afford protection for those rare plants which need wilder settings than gardens because they cannot be planted by well-traveled waysides. For Mary, as for Ewing, meadowlands offered such habitats by providing flower beds sufficient "to please the nightingale" (54). But when Mary enters the old man's meadow to plant her rare hose-in-hose flowers, the squire sets his dog against her, believing she is stealing, not planting, the flowers. Ultimately he learns of his error in judgment, softens toward children, and atones by legally bestowing the entire field on Mary.

Mary's pretend success had real implications that moved beyond the fictional boundaries of "Mary's Meadow." In the preface to the story, Ewing's sister recalls that entire families took to what they called "Mary meadowing"—beautifying "hedges and bare places." The immense popularity of Ewing's tale also led to the establishment in 1884 of the Parkinson Society for Lovers of Hardy Flowers, a society that long survived Ewing. This society was named after a Renaissance botanist whose work the fictional Mary sought out in a library and revered. It had a number of aims, all allied to Mary and her beloved Parkinson: "To search out and cultivate old garden flowers that have become scarce; to exchange seeds and plants; to plant waste places with hardy flowers; to circulate books on gardening amongst the Members; to try to prevent the extermination of wild flowers, as well as of garden treasures" (preface, "Mary's Meadow").

Like the Parkinsonians, the women who worked to preserve open spaces wrote in hope of influencing people to conserve the natural world. In the words of Octavia Hill, "buttercups [are] more abidingly beautiful and blessed than . . . sovereigns" (*Letters* 333). But if their personal sense of the earth and its species was often sacramental, their political targets were often utilitarians who saw nature as material, inferior, and exploitable. To convince such people of the need for preservation, women crusaders thus needed to stress nature's value in economic terms. This strategy was employed by Lemon in discussing birds primarily as insect eaters late in her career as effectively as it was by Hill trying to preserve greenery throughout hers. And though Ewing wanted to save the earth simply for its own sake, she, too, became adept at convincing others of its value for human well-being. "I think the smell of *earth* and *plants* has a physical anodyne about it somehow," she wrote in another letter (qtd. in Eden 183). The earth and her creatures—the living world—were not just beautiful but useful; they were instruments for humanity's physical and, more rarely, spiritual invigoration. To save them, those who loved them needed to represent them as such.

5

"Tongues of Fire": Womanist Visions of Nature

As surely as myths helped make womanhood what it was in the nineteenth and early twentieth centuries, there were women who deliberately set out to remake those myths. They were vatic-voiced women more keen on reenvisioning the entire cultural context than on effecting practical reforms to benefit particular plants, animals, or oppressed sectors of contemporary society. Octavia Hill can serve as an example of the latter, more practical kind of reformer. At the conclusion to "Colour, Space, and Music for the People," she exhorted both herself and others to "continue to set our desires on trying to heal, and lose thought of ourselves in others [so that] our mistakes and failings seem to sink into insignificance, and the great purpose we have at heart prospers, and little by little, as the years go on, steady progress is made" (752). Hill, then, was a progressive. Although convinced of the rightness of her efforts to foster green spaces and the working-class people who might enjoy them and determined to take great leaps of faith on behalf of her cause, she was also willing to relinquish the ideal for the doable. On the other hand, the more radically minded women—the first type of reformer and the subject of this chapter—needed messianically to rechart the very boundaries of their society. Anna Kingsford, Frances Swiney, and Florence Dixie worked for causes by now familiar to us: antivivisection, social purity, compassionate treatment of animals, and women's rights. In these movements, these three would to some extent make common cause with women like Frances Power Cobbe and Elizabeth Wolstenholme Elmy and attempt to achieve tangible results. But each of these three women was primarily a visionary, a utopian who wanted to revamp the male-driven world by picturing a world in textures and colors that better suited women and nonhuman species. And so each projected inward as well as outward, hoping to explode patriarchal cultural and religious myths by imagining new heavens and new earths in which New Women might function. Impatient with gradual social change, they donned seers' robes and dauntlessly projected both the transgressive power of female magic, long associated with witchcraft, and the moral authority of the biblical prophets, then associated with nineteenth-century religious discourse. Kindled by anger, they spoke with tongues of fire.

As was true of the popularizers of science, these three late-century reinterpreters of nature cannot be fully understood without reference to their precursors in the early part of the nineteenth century. In the 1830s and 1840s, a doctrine of female messianism, once a part of Civil War rhetoric about spiritual democracy, was resurrected and installed as part of the first English socialist movement. Both Owenites and Saint-Simonians linked the future of the working class to a remodeled equality between the sexes, and both groups authorized female preaching and lecturing. In a series of articles in which he described his "universalist cosmology," Owenite James Elishma Smith put forth what he called his "Doctrine of the Woman." For Smith, nature was composed of male and female principles and was self-transforming through the female, since "woman is a refinement of man[:] . . . she is the end of the old world[,] and the new can only begin with her complete emancipation from the curse of the first" (qtd. in B. Taylor 126–27). A manifesto of the Saint-Simonians published in 1834 would further proclaim "the advent of the Mother . . . wherein the spirit of emancipated women will unfold its germs of moral feelings and be instrumental in building up the new heaven and the new earth" (qtd. in B. Taylor 127).

All of this rhetoric paved the way for socialist women to try to ring out the old and ring in the new. Writing for the Owenite newspaper the *New Moral World* in the late 1830s, a colleague of Smith's, simply called "Kate," hoped to carry socialist philosophical platforms into the realm of the practical. Kate wanted education for women, marriage reform, and a better life for the working class, and she couched her demands in the language of Scripture, rightly assuming that here was a primary source of female empowerment in her society. Yet fervid religious feminism like Kate's bore the seeds of its own demise; by the 1840s, Kate and her colleagues felt a backlash that physically imperiled them. They were stoned and denounced as "whores," "libidinous in mind and body" (B. Taylor 133). With Kate and her colleagues, one confronts the sobering and ironic fact that if and when earlier-nineteenth-century women became too good at fulfilling their socially mandated roles as saints, they could still be slotted firmly into another ready-to-hand category—that of bestial sinners.

Nevertheless, by midcentury many Anglicans and Nonconformists alike accepted the idea of female morality as spiritually efficacious. Churchwomen began to influence the practice of benevolence and in general helped feminize organized religion over the course of the century. Middle-class women, in particular, were encouraged to impart moral instruction, and not just to children. Deemed appropriate civilizers of men, women in the domestic sphere functioned as counterbalances to the dog-eat-dog world of public life in which men ordinarily moved. Thus the nineteenth-century gender system handed a degree of religious authority to its women, expecting that women would work to sanctify domestication, converting conventional middle-class gender arrangements into a cultural and religious orthodoxy, in return. But by the 1860s, a number of women moved beyond these traditionally accepted roles to emerge as preachers and spiritual leaders. A vogue for postmillennialism, the belief that the Second Coming of Christ would come before the millennium, encouraged the spread of female preaching, based upon the Old Testament passage of Joel 2: 28–29: "Your sons and your daughters shall prophesy . . . and upon the handmaids in those days will I pour out my spirit" (Anderson 479). Women such as Jessie MacFarlane and Geraldine Hooper achieved what Olive Anderson calls "star status in the revivalist firmament" (Anderson 470); they indeed were perceived as handmaids of the Lord.

Not all of female culture was involved in, or even aware of, this powerful strain in the evangelical religious world. In 1859, Florence Nightingale (1820–1910) would utter her now famous, desolate harangue, "Jesus Christ raised women above the condition of mere slaves, mere ministers to the passions of the man, raised them by His sympathy, to be ministers of God. He gave them moral activity. But the Age, the World, Humanity, must give them the means to exercise this moral activity, must give them intellectual cultivation, spheres of action" (Nightingale 227). And more than a decade later, Josephine Butler would complain that woman, "God's minister upon earth in matters spiritual" was kept from her rightful place as God's messenger in the pulpit. She would go on to praise the Salvation Army—from its inception in 1878 a body rich in female publishers of salvation—for its promotion of gender equality ("Woman's Place" 30–32).

In spite of the lingering limitations that offered the majority of women spiritual authority but simultaneously tended to deny most of them actual institutional power, the three women I am about to discuss not only donned the mantle of the prophetess; they ran with it streaming as they rushed into realms of heterodoxy. Late in the nineteenth century and early in the twentieth, their roles exceeded those of working-class women like Kate some half a century earlier. Authorized by their missionary status as prescient women, they went so far, through impassioned writing, as to deeply challenge the balance of power inherent in the gender system of their day. They are perfect examples of a determination that Christine L. Krueger suggests might earlier have freed mid-Victorian women: determination built on a religious discourse already considered to be their right. Even more than women like Charlotte Elizabeth Tona and Hannah More—two of the figures discussed by Krueger—Kingsford, Swiney, and Dixie set about "'feminising' social discourse by representing female authority in terms of spiritual gifts, prophesying against the exploitation of women as sinfulness, and calling on their readers to repent of their misogynistic practices" (5). Broadcasting unfamiliar ideas in a familiar evangelical discourse, they drafted a magical cartography that might reform society and reach beyond it toward redemption outside of the boundaries of traditional space and time. Fearless in their spiritual righteousness and knowledgeable about science as well as philosophy and religion, they delivered radically revised messages not only

Figure 36. Anna Bonus Kingsford.

about womanhood, as had their precursors, but also about nature. For them, it felt as though time was running out; women were still second-class citizens, and the socialism of the 1880s and 1890s was supplanting religious authority just as the suburbs had supplanted green open spaces. Kingsford's, Swiney's, and Dixie's messages about women, nature, and woman-nature assumed the utmost urgency. Reform needed to be radical, and it needed to be immediate.

Anna Bonus Kingsford (Alias Mary, Alias Hermes)

From an early age, Anna Bonus Kingsford (1846–1888) was prone to visions and sensitive to nonhuman nature (see figure 36). Given unrestricted use of her father's library as a child, she devoured legends and myths, which she would dramatically reenact, happily and easily conversing with flowers and fairies. What most of us would call material objects—things like the flowers, for instance—were no more real to her than were things immaterial. Early and late, Kingsford would apprehend matter and spirit as one. Her twin adult occupations, as practicing physician and as mystical lecturer and writer, were never at odds in her own mind, for she resolved all to the realm of spirit, properly understood.

Kingsford began her adult life as a feminist. In the late 1860s, when Frances Power Cobbe was writing to push the Married Women's Property Act, Kingsford was canvassing for signatures on a petition to enable its passage. She also edited the *Lady's Own Paper: A Journal of Progress, Taste, and Art,* whose contributors included women such as Cobbe, Sophia Jex-Blake, and Elizabeth Wolstenholme Elmy. But in the course of a few years, Kingsford also felt a personal need for medical education more strongly than she felt the world's need for one more dedicated feminist. Deeply troubled over experimentation on animals and desiring to promote vegetarianism, she wanted to acquire the scientific know-how to argue intelligently against vivisection and in favor of a vegetable diet. At one time drawn to hunt alongside her young husband, she turned her back on meat eating and all bloody pursuits, refusing even to wear animal hides. She then went on to pass the examinations at the Apothecaries Hall, and, as women were still barred from attending English medical schools, she enrolled for medical study in 1873 in Paris, where she determined to write a thesis on vegetarianism.

In Paris, much to her horror, Kingsford got to know the business of vivisection firsthand. Appalled by the screams of vivisected animals resounding through the corridors of the school, she arranged to be tutored rather than have to stomach such lectures involving vivisection and vowed to "do at least what one heart and one voice might to root this curse of torture from the land" (qtd. in Maitland's *Anna Kingsford* 1: 79). To get her point across to fellow students and professors, she even proposed herself for vivisection, hoping to shock them with her offer and force them to see both the passion of her concern and the folly of their unhallowed art. In her essay "Unscientific Science: Moral Aspects of Vivisection," Kingsford would later trace the source of vivisection to the heartlessness of a science that misunderstood nature. How, she wondered, could physiologists who believed in evolution and humanity's common origin with the other animals claim the right to torture them? If evolution were properly understood, the human race would realize that it had "no claim to royalty over the animals" (297). "We have," she insisted, "no right to inflict upon innocent animals torments to which pity forbids us to subject guilty men" (298).

Such grisly, arrogant activity in the name of "science" needed to be stopped, for it was not science at all but a materialism that misapprehended the nature of things and believed itself self-justified. "The materialist," Kingsford insisted in a point she would reiterate time and again,

> does not understand that the Source and Substance of every series of phenomena, material and physical, the origin of which he seeks so eagerly to interpret, is equally the necessary Cause of the evolution which has produced humanity, whose distinctive appanage is the *moral nature.* To think

otherwise would be to create illogical and absurd confusion between science and morality, by opposing intellect and intellectual interests to justice and the interests of the psychic being. (295)

Thus science was not something apart from morality, just as animals were not something apart from humanity. A "science based upon torture can no more be true science than a religion based upon torture can be true religion," said Kingsford (301). Neither ecclesiastical nor scientific authority could be considered infallible in "matters of public conscience" (305) if, as they should be, their endemic limitations were discerned by members of the public. To Kingsford's mind, both forms of authority were subject to grievous errors in morality.

Up to this point in her thinking, Kingsford could have been followed, or led, or joined by Frances Power Cobbe, as she often was. She might even have been joined by Arabella Buckley, who in the 1870s explored spiritualism and refined her definition of Life (her term for the personified life force of the universe) to suggest that Life could not "be explained by mere molecular action" ("The Soul" 8). In 1879, Buckley would have called herself a spiritual evolutionist, one who believed in the immortality of Life itself. Kingsford similarly continued to extend her discussion of science and morality until she breached the boundaries of spiritualism, which Cobbe thought ridiculous. Kingsford believed that the reason both ecclesiastical authority and scientific authority failed was that neither one considered the higher "science of Heaven," which "encompasses all lower knowledges" (307). When she set out to describe that science for all humankind, she and Cobbe parted company.

Raised an Evangelical but discouraged by its "hardness, coldness, and meagreness" (*Anna Kingsford* 1: 15), Kingsford first became interested in the spirit life when she met a medium while canvassing for the Married Women's Property Act in the late 1860s. From then on, she explored religion and spiritualism with the same gusto she would bring to developing her knowledge of science. She worked with the medium she had met; believed herself to have been contacted by her supposed ancestor, Anne Boleyn; and eventually, after a dream visit by Mary Magdalene, converted to Roman Catholicism in 1870, taking the additional prophetic names of Maria and Johanna at her confirmation. Ultimately, she was disillusioned by Catholicism, not because she felt Catholic Christianity did not encompass the truth but because it misinterpreted it. She also explored theosophy, which offered her a more theoretical approach to the spirit life than anything she had previously known through her medium. Because theosophy appeared to promote gender equality, it was of interest to the feminist Kingsford, aiming as it did:

1. To form a nucleus of the universal brotherhood of humanity, without distinction of race, creed, sex, caste, or colour.

2. To encourage the study of comparative religion, philosophy, and science.
3. To investigate unexplained laws of nature and the powers latent in man.
(Burfield 32)

For Kingsford, not just the first but all of these aims were desirable, particularly the last of the three. She was attracted to theosophy's emphasis on the importance of eternal spirit, which reincarnates numberless times in the bodies of men, women, and animals, since this idea reinforced her belief in the intimate relationship between the human and animal worlds.

But Kingsford was too much of an original to follow Madame Blavatsky into the ranks of theosophical orthodoxy. She would create a Hermetic Society of her own, joined by her distant relative and spirit mate, Edward Maitland, an older man and widower whom Kingsford called her "co-religionist" and who called Kingsford "Mary," after the Virgin. Throughout the remaining years of her life, Kingsford and Maitland shared an interest in mystical experiences and jointly wrote *The Perfect Way; or, The Finding of Christ* in 1881. Widely acclaimed in theosophical circles, their book went through edition after edition and garnered for its two authors an invitation to join and to address the Theosophical Society. Speak they would, but they would not long remain in the fold. Kingsford's cabalistic gnosticism, although it shared elements with theosophy, was a thing apart.

What Kingsford's own version of gnosticism did, among other things, was to enable its author wholly to revision women and nature in an elaborate, hybrid context that defied Victorian cultural norms. Kingsford first evolved this belief system, as she had first turned to medical education, in order to validate what Maitland would call her fourfold charter: "purity of diet, compassion for animals, the exaltation of womanhood, and mental and moral unfoldment through purification of the organism" (*Anna Kingsford* 1: 21). She had based this charter on her conviction that what was needed in the world was "justice as between men and women, human and animal" (*Anna Kingsford* 1: 33). What was needed spiritually, therefore, was a system that mandated this kind of justice worldwide. And what emerged from Kingsford's imagination was her "Perfect Way," "the science of Heaven." She chose *The Finding of Christ* as the subtitle of her book *The Perfect Way* because, properly understood, Christianity could, to Kingsford's mind, be viewed as a science as well as a religion. Victorian Kingsford felt a need to reconcile faith with science and did so by positing that all existence was essentially spiritual. Thus for her the soul was "the true ego" and "the multiple rebirths of this ego into material conditions; its persistence through all changes of form and state; and its ability, while yet in the body, to recover and communicate of the knowledges which, in the long ages of its past as an individualised entity, it had acquired concerning God, the universe and itself" became the essence of her spiritual writing (*The Perfect Way* lxxi). For Kingsford, who was a reincarnationist, bodies became vessels for souls. This did not, however, deter her from being passionately interested in the social and religious role of the physical body or compel her to turn her back on either nature or gender.

Like the mystical writer William Blake, Kingsford developed a complex system of mythologies and philosophies through which to articulate her beliefs. For Kingsford (and Maitland), "all creatures whatsoever represent incarnations, though in different conditions, of one and the same universal soul" (*The Perfect Way* 24). As such, all living things are related and simply different "steps either of development or of degradation" of that soul (24). In such a philosophy, animals are not placed on earth primarily for human use but are viewed as evolutionary precursors to humankind. The soul is "first engendered in the lowest forms of organic life, from which it works upwards, through plants and animals, to man" and continues passing through many bodies until it finally dissipates (44). Kingsford's philosophy is, then, in direct contrast to Thomas Henry Huxley's belief in a "physical basis for life"—that is, protoplasm. In his discussion of protoplasm, Huxley lays spirit to rest and suggests that all life is built of one material, not spiritual substance.[1]

If, as soul-substance, Kingsford's godhead is one, as physical life it is two: a He, the life, and a She, the substance. Kingsford is careful to tell us that She, the substance, "is not 'Nature,'" nor matter, but the *essence* of matter, a kind of substrate, like the "Great Deep," or ether, like the "Infinitude" that "encircles and embraces all things" (55). Thus plants, animals, and women are not entities lower than man, nor even lower than the godhead, but are a part of the godhead and, as such, wholly deserving of the utmost respect. "Let us suppose," Kingsford says by way of illustration, "we are in a meadow covered with grass and flowers. It is early morning, and everything is bespangled with dew. And in each dew-drop is everything reflected, from the sun itself down to the minutest object. All reflect God. All is in every dew-drop. And God is in each individual according to his capacity for reflecting God" (61–62). In such a world, it would be difficult to despise or destroy anything, since—as in Hinduism—the destroyer is inescapably one with the destroyed.

Thus Kingsford's "Nature" does not create natural abominations; men fabricate and then seek to destroy them through their misapprehension of otherness. In this, they are influenced by astral spirits which abet humankind in promoting atrocities and injustices. Here, Kingsford soars far into the realms of her beloved spiritualism and overcasts her argument with shades of black magic. Her astral spirits are especially hostile to women, because they see in womanhood a kind of deeper spiritual intuition that would undermine their power. In this hostility, they reflect "the evil which men harbour and encourage in themselves" (82).

1. Huxley discusses protoplasm in "On the Physical Basis of Life," a lecture he delivered in Edinburgh on 8 November 1868, which was later reprinted and included in his *Lay Sermons* (1871).

Consequently, "whenever we find a systematic depreciation of woman, advocacy of bloodshed, and materialism of things spiritual, there, we may be confident, does astral influence prevail" (84). Of course, such spirits also lay to rest Kingsford's monism and replace it with a Manichaeanism more typical of her day, but this did not trouble Kingsford's followers.

Kingsford's very presence—beautiful, commanding, well-educated, and inspired—advertised the right of women to be seen and heard, to pronounce not just traditional religions but to announce whole new religions. Moreover, her attitudes toward the clergy and formalized religion were particularly influential in challenging the moral authority of the church, especially its stance on animal rights. As we saw in the case of Lemon's and Phillips's work with bird protection, women who had hoped through alliance and appeasement to enlist the clergy in their protests against cruelty to animals had often failed in getting them to take the lead in this crusade. Like the writing for *Shafts*, Kingsford's writing hit hard against this clerical indifference, linking clergymen to scientists in their blindness to animal suffering and opening the way for women to be vocal where men had been silent. In her explosion of the ideas of gender and species hierarchies and her abhorrence of the violence of vivisection—coefficients of her conception that there is but one spirit common to animals and humankind—Kingsford extended the women's crusade on behalf of nonmale nature as far theoretically as any antivivisectionist could. Another woman, equally visionary if not interested in the hermetic, and equally radical, would take the movement for social purity to similar heights and lengths.

Rosa Frances Swiney

> On to the dust-heap of obsolete dogmas, theories and hypotheses, are thrown, by the merciless logic of the Cosmic Law of Life, Darwin's man, a super-evolved woman, and Spencer's woman, an arrested man! (*Woman and Natural Law* 400)

Here is Frances Swiney (1847–1922) at her fanatical best, clearing the Darwinian decks and preparing to use what she believed were the latest facts about genetic coding of maleness and femaleness to prove the innate superiority of women (see figure 37). Harking back to what she felt were the muddy fountains of muddled Victorian analysis, Swiney would purify social thought by wedding early-nineteenth-century biology to a personal philosophy of the cosmos. She would teach the world how to wait for a Cosmic Virgin Mother who would signify the true culmination of human evolution. Swiney is the perfect example of Krueger's female evangelical preacher calling on male readers to repent. But her glad tidings were anything but conventional and were especially bad news for men. Swiney was what Olive Anderson has called a "hyper-feminist" (480), a preacher of the superiority of women.

Figure 37.   Frances Swiney.

Swiney attributed men's misapprehension of womanhood to their substitution of woman's sexual selves for womanhood itself:

> Men have sought in women only a body. They have possessed that body. They have made it the refuse heap of sexual pathology, when they should have reverenced it as the Temple of God, the Holy Fane of Life, the Fountain of Health to the human race. (*Bar of Isis* 43)

What Swiney wanted to do was to turn this construction completely around, to leap from refuse heap to holiness, raising woman to what she believed was her proper status—something a little below the angels. Her language here helps us position her vis-à-vis other women crusaders we have encountered. Like Frances Power Cobbe and Josephine Butler, Swiney became enraged over the prevalence of sexual disease, seeing it as a manifestation of misused power. Writing at the height of the eugenics movement, she also sensed the wisdom of Butler's and Alice Drysdale Vickery's concerns about the dangers of eugenic policies for women. This placed her on the opposite side of the fence from eugenicist physicians like Elizabeth Sloan Chesser and Mary Scharlieb, who believed in eugenic practices that would ostensibly keep the female body physically sound and therefore a better reproductive vessel, and educators like Marie Stopes, who would link female health to frequent recreational, albeit marital, sex. And, certainly, Swiney was at odds with men like the writer Grant Allen (1848–1899), who described one of his characters in *The Woman Who Did* as despising "those unhealthy souls who would make of celibacy, wedded or unwedded, a sort of antinatural religion for women" (138).

Like Kingsford, Swiney had started out as a feminist activist. She was the president of the Women's Suffrage Society in Cheltenham, founder of the League of Isis for the protection of motherhood, and a frequent contributor to the pages of the *Awakener,* an anti–white slavery paper. Her own feminist call to action, *The Awakening of Women,* was favorably reviewed by "Ignota" (Elizabeth Wolstenholme Elmy using yet another pseudonym) in the *Westminster Review* (1899), and her books were advertised in the *Suffragette.* In all of her feminist activities, Swiney claimed to put nature first—which meant, for her, putting natural law first, a law based upon female supremacy, a law constantly transgressed by the human male. "Man law and male-morality has been false to woman and to Nature," she would state in her essay "The Tender Mercies of the Vicious" (1913), printed in the *Awakener* (5). In their social analysis, men endlessly tried to circumvent nature but succeeded only to the detriment of the species. They needed to learn political humility and sexual self-restraint, and Swiney set out to teach them both of these virtues.

This she did by calling attention to the latest scientific discoveries, filtered through the crystalline lens of Frances Swiney's intelligence and experience. Reading far and wide in scientific and medical journals, she culled all the findings that would help her restore women to what she felt was their rightfully elevated place in society. Much as Victorian men had minimized female capacity by referring to what they believed was women's diminished cranial size, Swiney minimized maleness in light of the new, post-Darwinian science of genetics. In *Science and Women: The Missing Factor,* she happily quoted an issue of the *Mendel Journal* (October 1909) which had explained that "femaleness is due to the presence of a chromosome absent in the male" which makes the female a "more complex organization than the male" and the male a "defective variation from the female."[2] Seizing upon this idea, she grafted it to her own version of

2. Swiney's *Science and Women: The Missing Factor* appeared as an undated, unpaginated pamphlet issued by the National Union of Women's Suffrage Societies, now available through the courtesy of the Fawcett Library, Guildhall University, London.

evolution: all matter is evolving toward femaleness through "divine mother-hood," "the secret motive power of Evolution" (*The Ancient Road* 37). Maleness represents "a deficiency or a failure to develop to the standard of type, being a stage of evolution behind the female" (37)—as attested by the missing chromosome.

Using research from cellular biology to buttress her interpretation of genetics and evolution, Swiney believed that male deficiency is also demonstrated in the protoplasm of the male and female sex cells. Male sex cells, she first discovered via the work of Geddes and Thomson, are catabolic, female sex cells anabolic. Then, reading the biologist Rolph, she learned that male sex cells are "starving" and need union with a female ovum to survive (*The Ancient Road* 38). Putting the two together, she synthesized that in mating

> the more anabolic or female cells are fertilized by the more catabolic or male cells, which have now gone too far in expenditure of force or energy for the possibility of independent development. The fast disintegrating protoplasm is returned to the mother organism as a waste product, which must be reconstructed and transmuted into higher forms. (38)

Her conclusion: mother-substance is all, since into it all resolves—or dissolves.

Since men's sexual incontinence was harmful both to themselves and to women, men needed to "conserve the vital forces [sperm] for self-development, for growth of brain-power, and for the building up of the Higher [more womanly] Self." This belief led Swiney to found the League of Isis, whose rules encoded a pledge men were to make to observe "the Natural Law of reproduction."[3] Men also needed to "preserve in the woman during the creative periods of gestation and lactation absolute continence, so as to assure full, healthy development in the child, and no pathological symptoms in the mother during pregnancy, parturition, and nursing." Swiney believed that spontaneous abortions and innumerable other female ills resulted from intercourse during pregnancy and that the cheesy layer of *vernix caseosa* was not a natural protective material over fetuses but the result of the accumulation of decomposed sperm. If the league's rules were followed, however, such pathologies could not occur; moreover, man would regard woman as the "creatrix of the Race" and woman would see man as "the appointed coadjutor in the supreme task of race-building." Thus the league fostered a Swineyite brand of eugenics: men (and women) were to give up all sexual activity except during fertile times in the female menstrual and childbirth cycle, all for the betterment of humankind and their own

---

3. This quotation and the quotations immediately following are from an undated pamphlet from the Fawcett Collection, London, entitled "The League of Isis. Rules (of Observance)," printed by the League of Isis.

spiritual evolution. It went without saying that men were also to relinquish all forms of nonmarital sexual activity. Swiney and her league crusaded almost as diligently against "illegitimate" sexual activity—prostitution, sexual abuse, incest, and white slavery—as on behalf of sexual purity. All of this sexual restraint might then promote racial superiority by limiting the numbers of children born and improving the health of those three to four children recommended for each "pure" family. Ironically, although Swiney disliked Darwin, she was drawn to Darwin's emphasis on female choice. Possibly she conflated Darwin's emphasis on female choice in his theory of sexual selection with his theory of natural selection. In any case, she became a propagandist on behalf of human natural selection, counseling sex for breeding purposes, not for recreation.[4]

But physical improvement of the species was never enough for Swiney. For her the physical, mental, and spiritual were interconnected. The results one saw in science, one knew, could be profitably applied to religion, and so on. "I would," she said, "lay stress upon the Unity, Harmony, and Oneness of Cause and Effect, of Spirit and Matter, of Nature and Divinity" (*The Cosmic Procession* vii). If men were an "afterthought of Nature" (*Woman and Natural Law* 11), they nevertheless needed to be brought up to par not only physically, through eugenics and continence, but spiritually as well, since in both areas they were "undeveloped women" (*The Cosmic Procession* 221). Reversing male arguments about atavistic femaleness by attributing atavism to men instead of women, Swiney suggested that to humanize and to spiritualize the primitive in men would mean to feminize them. If, biologically, men need to evolve to become as resistant to pain as women are—another of Swiney's beliefs—spiritually, they need to evolve toward deeper intuition and greater harmony with the more advanced feminine phase of universal knowledge. At present, however, without intervention, they were stranded in the masculine phase, "the kindergarten of humanity" (*Ancient Road* 77), stuck there by their own defiance of Nature.

Thus Nature, for Swiney, becomes the summum bonum, and "woman," according to her, "is akin to Nature. Man has striven to live apart from nature, and has thus missed the greatest gifts of life and the higher development of himself. He has made social life entirely artificial and divorced from natural simplicity" (*Ancient Road* 144). His only path to salvation therefore lies in the ministrations of woman, who can lead him on to the Cosmic Mother. Then men can become like the statues of Buddha, "with smooth faces, Madonna features and expression, developed busts and all the characteristics of women" (*The Cosmic Procession* 237). This will allow the female messiah to come and, with her, "the supremacy of the Divine Feminine—the Living Spirit of God; with Her are ended the birth-pangs of the ages" (238).

4. For a very informative discussion of the complicated reasons for Darwin's advocacy of female choice, see Rosemary Jann, "Darwin and the Anthropologists: Sexual Selection and Its Discontents."

Womanist to the core, Swiney envisioned no yin-yang type of unified mas-culine and feminine principles as in the theories of Anna Kingsford or the Owen-ite and Saint-Simonian preachers. Hers was an evolutionary teleology that never wavered in its essentialist feminism. Woman-nature, which for Swiney was na-ture in every sense of the word, became the key to right living in a perfectible universe that, once perfected, would have no need for a world to come. The key oversight in this social philosophy is immediately obvious to the twentieth-century reader. In her efforts to ensure social survival and moral superiority for women, Swiney neglected the power of female sexuality. But this was not her point. Swiney wanted to set about reinventing the principle of womanhood as a primary source of power. For her, woman was the supreme artificer, a purified witch who could transform the universe. Living well into the Edwardian period in England, she left female sexuality to the Marie Stopeses and Havelock El-lises of her generation.

Florence Douglas Dixie

Like so many of the women in this book, Florence Dixie (1857–1905) was a nature lover from childhood to her dying day, and that love of nature in many ways determined the course of her writing. In a book of poems written when she was between the ages of ten and nineteen under the pseudonym of "Dar-ling" (see figure 38), Dixie showed an early understanding of a girl's bond with nature:

> Where Nature is, 'tis there I love to be,
> I loathe those man-made buildings men call towns,
> With all their suff'ring and their cruelty,
> Their unwashed features and their ugly frowns.
> Where Nature is unfettered she is fair,
> Be it in sunlight or in rugged storm,
> Her ev'ry breath casts fragrance on the air;
> She is a being of divinest form.
> ("With Nature," *Songs of a Child* 46)

Even as a child, Dixie coupled a Wordsworthian sense of nature with a femi-nist sense of the liberation women could find there, a desire for freedom pos-sible only in this allied, female space. A believer, like Swiney, in the dangers of the "unnatural" laws of men, Dixie was another progenitrix of ecofeminism who, like Cobbe, for most of her life bore a twin concern for the fates of women and of nonhuman creatures in patriarchal society. "Child as I was," she is quoted as saying later in life, "[I was] resolved to defy . . . unnatural laws" (qtd. in Ste-venson 41). Although as a young aristocrat, Lady Florence was expected to go hunting, from an early age she strongly defended other species:

Figure 38.   Lady Florence Dixie, age nineteen.

> Then I like to see the trout
> Basking in a shallow pool,
> And I hate to see the lout
> Drag them from their waters cool,
> With a writhing worm impaled
> On that base and brutal thing
> Called a hook. All words have failed
> To describe that fatal sting.
>   ("There Are Things I Like to See," *Songs of a Child* 78)

This passage to the contrary, words rarely failed Florence Dixie, early or late, especially when it came to other species. She would later write "A Prayer for Dogs" to beg people to realize the necessity for proper treatment of domestic animals and "The Union of Mercy" to teach children to stop tormenting birds and persuade adults to quit wearing furs. A staunch convert from hunting, she would herself become a vegetarian.

Ever free-spirited and original, seeing herself more as a literary figure than as a polemical crusader, Dixie hoped to wield her influence not through educational books and tracts, as did Kingsford and Swiney, but through utopian poems and novels. In her prefatory pages to *Isola,* a blank verse tragedy, Dixie offered a literary credo based on a cosmic vision:

> Let us in imagination soar above our Earth and look down on it revolving in space, and then look round on that infinite space, in which myriads of other worlds are also revolving. As we look down on our Earth, shall we not see upon its surface the glories of Nature's beauty and the hideous scars inflicted thereon by Man? As we look down on these unsavory sights, and realise how contemptible they are, shall we not resolve to eradicate them and make the picture one of peace, contentment and joy? (*Isola* viii)

Written when Dixie was just twenty, in 1877, *Isola* was not published until 1903, when it was also prefaced with the words: "Nothing Natural can be aught but right, for it is the offspring of Nature, the only true God. *'Isola' demands the practice of the true laws of the only true God*" (*Isola* ix).

The complex plot of this long poem centers on its title character, an independent and warrior-like revolutionary who represents Dixie's views of nature and natural law. Isola is a pantheist with a deep respect for the life of animals and disenfranchised humans and a deep disrespect for man-made law and institutions. Among the disenfranchised for whose rights Isola fights is Vergli, the illegitimate son of her husband, Hector, whom she leaves because he refuses to treat her as an equal. Together, Isola and Vergli are Dixie's politically ideal couple—two people aware of the human value of the opposite sex, champions of a classless society, good legislation, and fair taxation, and both vegetarians in the bargain. But their union is not to be. Isola in male guise saves Vergli from imprisonment but is captured and killed. Her death nevertheless brings about what she could not effect in life: a Magna Carta of Human Rights, passed in her memory, and the conversion of her husband to beliefs like hers and Vergli's, including relinquishment of the throne to this once disinherited son.

Throughout all of its swashbuckling and cross-dressing and complexities of plot, *Isola* resounds with Dixie's philosophy: all beings are disinherited because man-made law has supplanted the divine law of nature. This broad conception allows Dixie to incorporate into one long poem nearly all of the feminist thinking of her time on women and nature. Isola assimilates ideas about evolution into her philosophy, suggesting, like Swiney, that divinized nature will perfect humankind. What is wrong with man-made religion is what is wrong with man-made law: women are not present from its origin. No perfection can come from such laws, as Isola tells Hector:

> I tell you *they are rotten to the core,*
> Fruits of a tree *planted by priests* and men

Without the aid of Woman's guiding hand.
Small wonder they are false and trample down
The heads of Justice, Mercy and Great Truth.
As well might Man attempt alone the task
Of making Life without the Woman's aid.
                    (*Isola* 5)

In the end, Hector understands. In his final speech, he becomes a feminist eugenicist, a Swineyite of sorts. He will not permit men to force motherhood on women, for they will then breed "*the puny Man*" (*Isola* 148). Nor will he allow his society to raise its young men and women to disrespect each other; nor will he fail to have the laws of nature taught to youngsters; nor will he fail to instill altruism. "*Love to all things that feel* and, like ourselves, / Are sentient and possess the gift of life" (149), he mandates. In the very act of mandating, he of course exercises masculine power to the *n*th degree, but in the end he appears to be a benign male despot, ready to "raise the flag of [Dixieite] Evolution" (153).

Dixie's revisionist evolution is explained earlier in the poem by Vergli's dispossessed (that is, unwed) mother. She speaks both as a Mother Nature figure, unconcerned with questions of legitimacy, and as a progenitrix of socialist ecofeminism. For her, the dispossessed must reform the patriarchy and help nature to evolve a new earth (Erth):

It is not perfect to oppress the weak,
Or to deny to all and everything
The rights which Nature gives them as their own.
The perfect man will not delight in war,
Nor crave to make his food of bleeding flesh,
The *Vivisection Hall* and Slaughter House,
The pastime known as 'Sport' and other crimes,
Which Superstition and imperfect Man,
Have hitherto upheld and countenanced,
Will cease to be and our fair Erth become
That which Perfection shall attain for Man,
An Eden Garden, one in fact, not myth,
A world where love and kindness shall hold sway.
                    (*Isola* 29)

By now, this is a familiar Eden, as is the means to effect it—a female messiah—an Anna Kingsford, or a Frances Swiney, or a Florence Douglas Dixie:

A woman who has buried Superstition
And scorned to make herself the slave of Man,
Albeit she is his loving friend and mate,
Can lead and will lead on Humanity
To win its freedom, and to recreate

Noble conditions, elevating all
By evolutionary principles.
(64)

In 1890, in *Gloriana; or, The Revolution of 1900,* Dixie found a truer and genuinely female hero and revised not only her heroine's destiny but her art form
as well. This book was written in prose, conceived as the dream vision of a young
girl on a heath. In defense of her choice of form, Dixie immodestly claimed
prophetic powers: "*Gloriana* may be a romance, a dream; but in the first instance,
it is inextricably interwoven with truth, in the second instance, dreams the work
of the brain are species of thought, and thought is an attribute of God. Therefore it is God's creation" (*Gloriana* viii). Here, once again, read "God" as nature,
unbounded by human law, a nature that has declared the equality of the sexes.
But Dixie is more pragmatic and less romantic in her address to "Nature" in
Gloriana than she had been in the earlier *Isola.* In a kind of backhanded slap at
the female theosophists and sexual purists, Dixie suggests that if Nature is not
seen as encoding the law of evolutions and is, instead, elaborately elevated to "a
mystery," one that conceals the nature of sexuality from women and children,
it can become the "greatest incitement to sensuality and immorality" (132).

In *Gloriana,* woman becomes not just equal to man but superior, since "Nature has unmistakably given to woman a greater amount of brain power" which
"is at once perceivable in childhood" (129). This brainpower is intensified in
Gloriana, which boasts multiple heroines. Like Isola, *Gloriana*'s first heroine,
Speranza de Lara, flees a bad marriage but, unlike Isola, bears her own daughter rather than rescuing another's son. The daughter is Gloria (Gloriana), a second female hero, who disguises herself as a man, Hector D'Estrange. She/he at-
tends Eton, becomes a politician, makes a stunning feminist-naturalist speech in
Parliament (just quoted [132, 129]); Elizabeth Wolstenholme Elmy, in *Woman
Free,* also quotes from this speech [bk.8, 49–50n.8]), and is accused of murder-
ing Speranza's husband, who has disappeared—as does Hector/Gloria in short
order. The husband, Lord Westray, is not really dead but has gone underground
to wreak revenge on Speranza. Meanwhile, a man with a female-sounding name,
Evie Ravensdale, has fallen strangely in love with Hector/Gloria, finds out
Gloria/Hector is really a woman, and enlists the help of Flora Desmond, a
dauntless Scotswoman, to help find the missing Gloria. Gloria/Hector, double-
crossed and spirited off on a ship with Westray, has been shipwrecked and, in
trying to save one of the other passengers—her betrayer, Leonie—she apparently drowns. In the meantime, Ravensdale wins the day for women's suffrage,
inspired by Gloria, who, conveniently, emerges gloriously alive just in time to
join him in the triumphal march. A close call nearly finishes the newly emerged
Gloria, but she is saved from assassination by Leonie, who now is loyal to Gloria, her savior, and who becomes prime minister. Eventually, both Leonie and

Gloria die, but Lady Flora Desmond, who had helped Ravensdale find the abducted Gloria, eventually becomes the prime minister. She carries out Gloria's work and, ultimately, is buried at her feet.

What Dixie seems to be encapsulating in the complex plot of this dream vision is the platform of militant suffragettes: when one good woman is down, there is always another to take her place. If, like Dixie, one is visionary enough, one can foresee the political triumph of women, nature philosophy, and even dispossessed Celts like Flora Desmond (and possibly that other fictional persona, William Sharp's Fiona Macleod), a triumph possible only after many sacrifices. In this utopianism, Dixie offers a version of socialist feminism that, as Ann Ardis has suggested, is unique in a number of aspects. Dixie's work challenges the assumptions of Stanley Pierson, who, writing primarily about men in *British Socialism: The Journey from Fantasy to Politics* (1979), posited that British socialism between 1880 and 1910 was transformed from a utopianism like William Morris's to a form of realpolitik that marked the Independent Labour Party in the early twentieth century (Ardis, "'Journey'" 43–44). Dixie remained a utopian in this era of transformation because she continued to envision a fantasy coalition of workers and educated women who might attain power sufficient to put forth a candidate for prime minister. In contrast to Beatrice Webb (1855–1943) and Eleanor Marx (1855–1898), Dixie did not believe that women's rights could be subsumed under workers' rights (Ardis, "'Journey'"45). Ardis also effectively traces Dixie's utopianism back to the Owenites (46). I extend her argument to include the women mentioned in the introductory section of this chapter—Kate and the early Saint-Simonians. To my mind, Dixie continued to write a kind of socialist utopian literature, a genre that for men had fallen out of vogue, not because she was retrograde but because, as a woman, she knew she had more authority as a voice spiritual than as a voice secular. She had heard the voices of her women forebears.

If women like Dixie—and Kingsford and Swiney—were capable of womaning the barricades, they were characteristically more moved to transform the idea of women's role in society by creating utopias, and feminist hermetics, and "hyper-feminist" philosophies and infusing them with the power already culturally awarded to women as spiritual agents. Unlike the utopian women writers whom Nan Bowman Albinski discusses in *Women's Utopias in British and American Fiction,* they were unafraid of identifying themselves with the nature they loved because they felt protected by the mantle of spirituality. Absorbed in generating a new social fabric woven by themselves and by the women preachers who went before them, they were believers in words like those of Mary Haweis, meant in 1900 to rouse women writers to the zeal found in the visionary company of this chapter:

> In women's hands—in women writers' hands—lies the regeneration of
> the world. Let us go on with our tongues of fire, consecrated to an entirely

holy work, cleansing, repairing, beautifying as we go, the page of the world's history which lies before us now. (Haweis 71)

The self-ordained visionaries of this chapter wrote passionately toward the "re-generation" of their world. In creating their counterideology, their mythos of womanhood and nature that lay far beyond the thinking of male scientists, social scientists, poets, anthropologists and sexologists, they were not only "hyper-feminists" but hyper-ideologues. Driven to envision worlds of their own making, they demanded apocalypse now.

CHAPTER

6

Aestheticizing Nature

One way or another, nature's beauty captured most of the women in this book. Mystics like Anna Kingsford, preservers of green spaces like Octavia Hill, and collectors like Mary Kingsley were all taken by what they saw in nature. Nor were their various enterprises necessarily mutually exclusive. Kingsley can serve as an example: she could catch, classify, and catalog fish, and she could write paeans to the beauty of rivers. In her West African books, Kingsley for the most part favored the model of observation used by the empirical sciences, with their harvesting of specimens in order to scrutinize, rank, and interrelate. According to this model, the pleasing externals of the objects cataloged—the beauties of the form and color of Kingsley's fish, for example—were of secondary importance. She was engaged in the hot business of fumbling for fish in murky lowland waters; she was sorting out the species.

Transforming Nature's Beauty: The Victorian Female Sublime

On rarer occasions, however, Mary Kingsley opted for a second Victorian model of vision that would deliberately reverse this order, one that offered a different kind of questing in nature. It amounted to a conscious quest for beauty, not for fish or fetish, and it was based in nature and its literary representations as sites of wonderment, as in this passage about Kingsley's beloved Ogowé River:

> Do not imagine it [the Ogowé] gave rise in what I am pleased to call my mind, to those complicated, poetical reflections natural beauty seems to bring out in other people's minds. It never works that way with me; I just lose all sense of human individuality, all memory of human life, with its grief and worry and doubt, and become a part of the atmosphere. If I have a heaven, that will be mine. (*Travels in West Africa* 177)

The "complicated, poetical reflections of natural beauty" that Kingsley refers to are in some ways similar to what one finds in the work of travel writers like Mary De la Beche Nicholl (1839–1922), a mountaineer and butterfly expert. Nicholl's journal for 10 August 1889 describes a break in the mists of the mountains of Dauphiné in the French Alps:

Suddenly came the transformation scene, that which those who have once seen it never forget, the finest of all that Nature provides for those who worship her in high places—and the cold mountains flamed into gold and rose colour, as the sun touched them with his earliest rays. (Qtd. in Thomas 77)

Here are cool mountains aestheticized, something close to what Sara Suleri calls the "feminine picturesque." Researching the peripheralization of women in English India, Suleri noticed that women's writing and sketching were seen as harmless enterprises that kept women busy and kept the representations of India domesticated—in word and picture, if not in fact (75–76). Nicholl's work belongs to such a domesticating genre. Her language is a form of picture writing, an excess in yellow and rose. She paints a watercolor in words, tinted with the pathetic fallacy and hued by a sweet, often clichéd, literary palette. The scene itself may be something new, but the picturesque language used to describe it would have been familiar to British readers.

Earlier, at midcentury, Fanny Parks had traveled in India quite deliberately in search of the "picturesque." What Parks wanted to find was an India whose nature was already familiarized by art and legend but whose wilderness was still available for further domestication, English-style. Since this is what she was looking for, this is what she found. Here is how she recreates a dangerous incident in a rushing mountain stream:

We descended into the khud, and I was amusing myself jumping from rock to rock, and thus passing up the centre of the brawling mountain stream, aided by my long *pahari* pole of *rous* wood, and looking for the picturesque, when my fair friend, attempting to follow me, fell from the rocks into the water, —and very picturesque and very Undine-like she looked in the stream! (2: 241)

If Parks authorizes herself as in-the-know about things Indian by dotting her picturesque description with Indian words, she domesticates the danger to her friend and herself by suggesting that they were simply frolicking on the rocks like water nymphs. Parks's work was prepared for by romantic writers like Ann Radcliffe (1764–1823) and Lady Morgan (1783–1859) who, as Anne Mellor has shown, "domesticated" the sublime (Mellor ch. 5).

As Mellor also points out, in the gendering of the Burkean categories of the beautiful and the sublime, the beautiful is usually associated with women, since it betokens pleasure, affection, and tenderness, and the sublime with men, since it bodes danger and a possible annihilation of the self, which in turn demands bravery. As Edmund Burke (1729–1797) himself pointed out about women:

[Beauty], where it is highest in the female sex, almost always carries with it an idea of weakness and imperfection. Women are very sensible of this;

for which reason, they learn to lisp, to totter in their walk, to counterfeit weakness, and even sickness. In all this, they are guided by nature. Beauty in distress is much the most affecting beauty. (203–4)

Gender stereotyping like Burke's fed romantic culture. Yet women writers like Ann Radcliffe effected a shift, particularly in terms of the sublime. For them, patriarchal authority in the home came to represent the unmitigated power and corresponding horror of nature—like the rugged mountainscape or the storm. In gothic fiction, they altered the subject of the sublime: it was domesticated to include the potential dangers of the male-controlled home (Mellor 91–94). Other romantic women writers, like Lady Morgan, offered a second sort of domestication of the romantic sublime—the sublime landscape as mountain home, a tradition favored primarily by women writers in Scotland, Ireland, and Wales. In this kind of sublime, the fear and ecstasy aroused by mountains are literally based in mountain "homes," the locales where women in the sublime novels actually live. These mountainous places are shared with other females and thus doubly "domesticated" (97–103).

In the passage about the effect that the Ogowé had on her, Kingsley emphasizes something quite different from these romantic feminine domestications and from Parks's and Nicholls's remarks as well. She briefly favors a literary landscape which I call the "Victorian female sublime" in order to distinguish it both from Suleri's "feminine picturesque" and from Mellor's "domesticated sublime." This distinctively Victorian form of literature about the individual encounter with the sublime offers a later-day, regendered, international Wordsworthianism in which language ventures out and tries to envelop the vastness of space. In this type of literature, there is always an attempt to capture nature's sublimity— in both its beauty and its terror—but the true experience of the sublime moment is felt to escape the pen. It resists literary aestheticization first because of its incommensurablity and then because of a corresponding sense of the ineffable that arises in the beholder. Because the sublime experience transcends normative human life, its experiencer is beset by what Kingsley described as a loss of human distinctiveness, a sense of infinitude—Kingsley becomes "part of the atmosphere."

This kind of female sublime can also be distinguished from a Victorian male mode of seeing—"the-monarch-of-all-I-survey" mode—that Mary Louise Pratt includes in her analysis of imperialism and travel literature (201). Pratt's monarch employs a panoramic gaze in order to aesthetically appropriate what he sees; he then invokes a "rhetoric of presence" (205) to represent his imperial authority over landscape, much as Wordsworth had represented his emotional authority over the British landscape. Pratt's category works well in describing male, imperialist travel writers and helps highlight the connections between expansionism and appropriative aestheticism. And in several ways the texts of the Victorian female sublime resemble the works of "the-monarch-of-all-I-survey."

Both are products of the international travel made possible by British empire building, and both attempt to aestheticize the landscape by packing its representations with a density of meaning, including a large number of adjectival modifiers (Pratt 204)—although such accretions of adjectives might better describe the "feminine picturesque." But the two oeuvres do differ substantially: the Victorian female sublime emphasized not power *over* nature but the power *of* nature in a given place, and not a rhetoric of presence so much as a rhetoric based in absence, especially absence of the self. The women who engaged this female sublime featured themselves as witnesses or participants, not monarchs. Sometimes—in a self-styled appropriation of the stereotype of woman as nature—they even described themselves as nature itself, utterly indistinguishable from what they believed they apprehended.

When freed by distance from the mental and physical confines of Victorian society, a number of women travelers were moved to take upon themselves the business of trying to interpret nature in terms of this awe-inspiring but fearful sublimity. They must have felt particularly fit for this work because their culture had already deputized them as interpreters of things both beautiful and religious. Kingsley was reacting to the first of these roles when she undermined "complicated, poetical reflections of natural beauty," but she was tentatively embracing the second when she suggested that "if" a "heaven" were in her future, beholding the Ogowé would provide it.

Because Victorian women bore the charge of moral interpreters, they could easily, even late in the nineteenth century, take on the role that Wordsworth had earlier adopted when he experienced in nature a "sense sublime / Of something far more deeply interfused" ("Lines Composed a Few Miles above Tintern Abbey" 2: 262). Slow to give up natural theology, many women still quite willingly invested nature with spirit, as did Nicholls in her search for "transformation scenes." If mainstream writers like Matthew Arnold and George Eliot ruefully or grudgingly abandoned the project of reconstituting Wordsworth for their time, the more marginalized women travelers, away from "home" culture and impressed with massive mountains and seas, might more easily embrace his kind of sublimity. Counterparts to the women who wrote popularizations of science—insofar as they worked within a genre they helped to transform—women travel writers accepted the freedom to reexplore early romanticism.

This was one reason why so many women's travel accounts became deeply nostalgic. Women's journeys were reconstructed as retrospective narratives, written as though the times they described were these women's finest hour, their own "spots of time" (to borrow Wordsworth's term). Women's contact with nature in their travels, like Wordsworth's contact with nature in his younger years, comprised the moments of life that seemed most meaningful, most memorable. Back in London after her trip to West Africa, Kingsley described her own nostalgia for her lost continent as downright discomforting:

> The charm of West Africa is a painful one. It gives you pleasure to fall un-
> der its sway when you are out there, but when you are back here it gives you
> pain by calling you. It sends up before our eyes a vision of dancing, white,
> rainbow-gemmed surf playing on a shore of yellow sand before an audi-
> ence of stately cocoa palms, or of a great mangrove walled bronze river, or
> of a vast forest cathedral. ("West Africa from an Ethnologist's Point of
> View," *West African Studies* 72)

As a Londoner, Kingsley seems for the moment to have lost an Eden. But
through the landscape of memory, she recovers a world of nature now quite absent. In this way, Kingsley and various other Victorian women travel writers represented a condition whereby the sense of nature becomes a void—a loss even of
the original sense of loss—and one that needs reconstitution through the word.
Their version of the sublime supplied Victorian culture with a remote landscape which could never be experienced by most readers as anything more than
a text. But what might become for the writer a source of pain, a void, could become for the reader a renewable sense of wonder, available whenever she or he
wished to return to the text. This accounts for some of the popularity of this
sublime travel writing.

Beauty, nostalgia, and religiosity were only part of the Victorian female sublime; the "horror" of nature provided the lion's share of it. Victorian fear of nature in its fiercest guises stimulated the bravado narratives of Mary Kingsley,
who endangered life and limb to find fish, and Marianne North, who risked the
fatal tumble to paint trees in the Seychelles (see figure 24). Women travelers
liked to represent themselves as directly encountering the "horrid," possibly because it reversed conventional stereotypes of the Victorian woman. It fed the
same part of their own nature as did their love of things gothic, long the staple
of women's reading and, as Mellor suggests, of the romantic feminine sublime.
In her *Recollections*, Marianne North tells of watching with fascination as Lucie Austin (later Duff Gordon, 1821–1869) played with a snake during her va-
cation times with the Norths. "Her entire fearlessness and contempt for what
people thought of her charmed me," said North (*Recollections* 1:6). Lucie "would
twist the pretty bronze creature in the great plait of hair she wore round her
neck, and once she threatened to come down to a dinner-party of rather stiff
people thus decorated, and only gave up when my mother entreated her, with
tears in her eyes, not to do so" (6). Rapt fascination, tears in the eyes, shock at
derring-do—these were powerful responses that writers of the female sublime
might also draw from their audiences. And one way of doing so was by stressing
their intimate, physical contact with nature—touching mountains and their
denizens much as Lucie Duff Gordon touched her snake.

Places wild enough to evoke sublime reactions could be found in most corners of the British empire, but nothing would surpass the Himalayas as stimu-
lants of the Victorian sublime. What the Lake District was to Wordsworth and

the Alps were to Lord Byron and the Shelleys, the Himalayas were to writers of the Victorian female sublime. Women who confronted these titanic mountains could try to represent beauty and danger at their most majestic and most extreme. In the face of the Himalayas, for example, even Fanny Parks's feminine picturesque is modified, although it still preserves sweetness:

> Look on those mountains of eternal snow,—the rose-tints linger on them, the white clouds roll below, and their peaks are sharply set upon a sky of the brightest, clearest, and deepest blue. The rushing wing of the black eagle— that "winged and cloud-cleaving minister, whose happy flight is highest into heaven,"—may be heard above. The golden eagle may be seen below, poised on his wing of might, or swooping over a precipice, while his keen eye pierces downward, seeking his prey, into the depth of the narrow valley between the mountains. (2: 273)

Here Parks colorized and beautified, but she did not minimize—yet she only edged toward the female sublime. "Loveliness," as she herself says, marks her representation of her experience (273). It would take a more experienced Himalayan traveler, Nina Mazuchelli (1832–1914), in her book *The Indian Alps and How We Crossed Them, by a Lady Pioneer, Illustrated by Herself* (1876), to offer the essence of the Victorian female sublime (see figure 39). Unlike Kingsley, Mazuchelli disclaims any pretension to "scientific character" right from the start, in her preface (vii). Mazuchelli will not represent herself as collecting plants or animals but, rather, as collecting feeling arising from her sense of natural beauty and awe. She equally disclaims the picturesque, although her book does open with a colorful paean in the style of the "feminine picturesque": "O scarlet poppies in the rich ripe corn! O sunny uplands striped with golden sheaves! O darkling heather on the distant hills, stretching away, away to the far-off sea, where little boats with white sails, vague and indistinct in the misty horizon, lie floating dreamily!" (1). But enough of this! Mazuchelli begins this way precisely to show us how she will *not* be proceeding. Refusing to reinscribe the feminine picturesque, she directs our eye elsewhere, to the "upland there to westward, bathed in a flood of ambient light an instant ago" and now "immersed in sombre shade"—to the sublime Himalayas (2). The picturesque, with its quaintness and pastoral shelter repeats the visions of a childhood spent on British shores. The Himalayas, for which she was never properly prepared by her British geography-teaching governess, will dictate the reaches of her book. Even the highest of the European mountains, the Alps, are nothing next to the "stupendous Himalaya—in their great loneliness and vast magnificence impossible alike to pen and pencil adequately to portray, their height, and depth, and length, and breadth of snow appealing to the emotions." These "impress one as nothing else can, and seem to expand one's very soul" (6). Mazuchelli authorizes herself as a

THE

INDIAN ALPS

AND

HOW WE CROSSED THEM

BEING A NARRATIVE OF

TWO YEARS' RESIDENCE IN THE EASTERN HIMALAYA
AND TWO MONTHS' TOUR INTO THE INTERIOR

BY

A LADY PIONEER

ILLUSTRATED BY HERSELF

NEW YORK

DODD, MEAD, AND COMPANY

PUBLISHERS

Figure 39.   Title page, *The Indian Alps and How We Crossed Them* (1876),
by Nina Mazuchelli.

writer of the sublime, no painter of genteel word pictures but an eyewitness to majesty. People in England know as little about the sublimities of the Himalayas as they do "about the mountains in the moon" (8). They need her as a guide.

These introductory passages serve as Mazuchelli's prelude to the sublime. Mazuchelli lifts her readers out of the pastoral landscape, out of the beautiful/horrible Alps of Byron and the Shelleys, and lands them in a place where none of the romanticists—male or female—has gone before her. This is her own literary turf; she knows it as no one else can. "Few Europeans, and no lady, had hitherto attempted to explore the Eastern Himalaya," she tells us (80). In these remote places, she does not just describe eagles, as did Parks. She becomes an eagle:

> How often from my mountain eyrie have I watched the clouds, and their marvellous and ever-changing effects, when a tempest, which has raged throughout the livelong night, has lulled and sobbed itself to rest, with the rising of the sun. (65)

The self, and not an objectified nature, assumes the subject position. Here there is no voice-over as in our contemporary version of the "monarch-of-all-I-survey"—the nature special on television—dominated by an all-knowing, usually male voice of science and nature-lore combined. Taking hold of the stereotype of the natural woman who signifies nature and turning it to her own advantage, Mazuchelli becomes nature witnessing nature. She is in harmony with domesticated as well as wild nature, as in this description of a mountain descent:

> In one place the path is almost perpendicular, but my brave little steed takes me down without stumbling in the least, pausing now and again over the most dangerous bits of the road with a sagacity that seems something more than mere instinct. . . . Presently I become conscious of the absence of the clattering hoofs of F——'s pony, and looking back, or rather upwards, for they seem to be impaled on the very sky, I behold him using every persuasion to induce his steed to follow the example of mine; but nothing is evidently further from its intentions. (96)

Her description of the trip through the Himalayas also recalls, in order to alter them, several Wordsworthian moments, his most famous "spots of time." Anticipating the trip through the high mountains, Mazuchelli invents something grander than Wordsworth's travel through the Simplon Pass: "Yonder," she exclaims, "lay the whole vast expanse of the Sub-Himalaya, Alp upon Alp, and wave upon wave of blue mountain, varying in height from eight to fourteen thousand feet, all of which we must cross before reaching even the *base* of the snowy range" (183). She is prepared for what she will witness and therefore will witness it without question, with no passing through and not grasping what she has wanted to behold, as did Wordsworth. If this witnessing comes when she is alone and bathed in moonlight, as was Wordsworth on Mount Snowden, hers is nevertheless a distinctly female quest: she will go sketching in the moonlight, not climbing, although her perch lies above her and the entire way is marked with danger:

> I was about halfway through, when something rose at my feet with a whr-r-r, which startled me greatly. I had no doubt flushed a bird, a moonāl (hill pheasant), probably. On I went, the thick rhododendron leaves through which I brushed covering me with a shower of hoar frost. Then arriving at the rock I before mentioned, which I climbed on hands and knees, throwing my block before me at every few steps, I succeeded in reaching the top. (278)

Then comes the sublime view:

> To the right, rocky mountains, shattered and riven . . . whilst to the left were the beetling crags and swelling buttresses of the Singaleelah range. Dotted about the lesser and unsnow-clad mountains, where the moonlight fell, were portions of 'mica schist,' which, sparkling brilliantly, looked like stars fallen to earth. Stars seemed not only twinkling above, but below me, and this glittering 'mica' produced the most extraordinary effect imaginable; whilst the dead pines standing with their trunks blanched, looked like phantom guardians of the whole. (279)

This prelude to Mazuchelli's visionary experience draws heavily upon two female traditions rarely present in the same way in more conventional, romantic renderings of the feminine sublime. The first, the gothic, is employed, then deflated, much as it is in Jane Austen's *Northanger Abbey* (pub. 1818). Mazuchelli is startled by the probable pheasant but then is able to explain it away. Still, the tension remains with the reader as she brushes her way past frost and crawls her way to the top, testing for solid ground before every movement, engaging her body directly so that she is physically in touch with her environment. The second tradition is that of scientific popularization. The pheasant is, we are carefully told, again "probably"—she can't see to be sure, so the gothic reemerges—a "moonāl (hill pheasant)," the rock, a "mica schist." Mazuchelli wants the sublime moment to come, but she wants every sort of reader to accompany her—including both those accustomed to gothic novels and those who prefer scientific discourse.

When the moment does come, it is too overwhelming to capture, either in sketch or word. Mazuchelli stands simply "entranced, losing for awhile even my own individuality, feeling that I had almost entered some new world" (279). Her loss of selfhood is, of course, a hallmark of the experience of the sublime. As Thomas Weiskel has pointed out, a "humanistic sublime is an oxymoron" (3). The sublime implies some sort of transcendence. On her "return" from this state, Mazuchelli startles at her own shadow, a moment that Sara Mills takes to signify her return to a feminine weakness, an instance of the fear of accidents described by Campbell Davidson in his advice book for women—something Mills believes typifies Mazuchelli's writing (*Discourses of Difference* 180). But one could instead read Mazuchelli's jumpiness as a concomitant of the mystical aspects of any sublime experience, female or male. A return to another state of mind or being is essential, whether it comes through comic self-parody, like Mazuchelli's, or through a temporary aphasia, as when Isabella Bird said that after her ascent of Long's Peak in the Colorado Rockies "no sort of description within my powers could enable another to realise the glorious sublimity, the majestic solitude, and the unspeakable awfulness and fascination of the scene in which I spent Monday, Tuesday and Wednesday" (59).

Mazuchelli always writes with a keen awareness of other artists, but most especially when she wishes to convey the essence of the sublime experience. "Why," she wonders, "do we often feel such kinship with Nature? Is it not that the Great Unseen, revealing Himself though this pure medium . . . the glorious embodiment of Himself—is making us realise more fully that we are one with Him, and them, and He with us?" (363). And then she goes on to quote from Byron's *Childe Harold:*

> "Are not the mountains, waves, and skies a part
> Of me, and of my soul, and I of them?"
> (363)

Or she thinks of the painter Joseph Mallord Turner, and his feeling about nature, reflecting on both of their affinities for "sublime sanctuaries" (368). "As I sit gazing on this magnificent mountain, so earnest and pathetic in its great loneliness, a passion of sunlight bursts over it," she writes, "and I feel more than ever how feeble is Art in its power of reproducing Nature, and I close my easel with a humbled and broken spirit" (368).

But throughout all of these musings in what she calls "sublime sanctuaries," Mazuchelli is never monarch-of-all-she-surveys. Quite to the contrary, she stresses her love of aloneness in such sanctuaries but worries about populating them at all, even with her self: "We sometimes ask ourselves what right we have to intrude upon this great lonely land, left unpeopled since the creation of man, a loneliness which our presence almost seems to desecrate" (383). In this expression of humility before the greatness of nature, Mazuchelli's writing offers a prime example of the Victorian female sublime. Mazuchelli is not beckoning

others to come to herald her vision, to follow in her footsteps, to open the remote world for commerce or for further adventure. She is inscribing aloneness
for them so that they will not need to trek over the snowfields of the Himalayas
to find it. She writes herself physically out of the landscape just as she had written herself in, and she writes like a conservationist. She is recreating a time in
order to save a space.

Other women had similar reactions to the power of the Indian mountains.
Marianne North chose to paint them by leaving out the middle distance, to better render the sense of their vastness (see figure 40). At Darjeeling, she found
she "had never seen so complete a mountain, with its two supporters, one on
each side. It formed the most graceful snow curves, and no painting could give
an idea of its size" (*Recollections of a Happy Life* 2: 28). She, too, felt that the Himalayas "would certainly have hidden any European line of snow peaks (such
as that which one sees from Berne, for instance)" (2: 1). North was transported
by her experiences in these towering mountains. When she came down to Jon-
boo from painting Mount Everest, she apprehended "a most curious reflection
of self in the sun's disc in the mist, opposite the setting sun, with a gold halo
and rainbow tints round it" (2: 33). Like Kingsley's, North's visual experiences
could become visionary; the sublime experience would transform the human
being into "a part of the atmosphere."

Other women painters had similar experiences. Earlier, in 1860, Lady Charlotte Canning (1817–1861), landscape and flower painter and wife of the gov-
ernor general of India, wrote to Queen Victoria, remarking of the Himalayas
that "the absence of Lakes and Glaciers makes this scenery far less beautiful
than Switzerland, but I think the precipices and the enormous peaks are on a
far grander scale" (qtd. in Charles Allen 141). Like Mazuchelli, Lady Canning
claimed often to have become all eye, to have laid down her paints in the presence of these sublime mountains. Nevertheless, she too returned to England
with some of their most subtly painted renderings.

It was in 1873, just two years before Mazuchelli penned her book on the
mountains of India, that Isabella Bird (1832–1904) (see figure 41) had climbed
Long's Peak in the Rocky Mountains of Colorado. Bird was deeply stirred by a
kind of transcendental experience in the Rockies, but her written witness of
those mountains differs from Mazuchelli's of the Himalayas and offers another
version of the Victorian female sublime. Bird compared her newly discovered
mountains with the Alps, as had Mazuchelli, and Bird also drew careful pictures
of the dangers of mountain animals and situations. But in a cleaner, drier, more
matter-of-fact style, Bird far more often than Mazuchelli chose to objectify her
experience by depicting the mountains' unfamiliar vastness in scientific terms.
For example, of a hike through the winter mountains, she recounted: "We took
neither of the trails, but cut right through the forest to a place where, through an

Figure 40.   Marianne North, *Distant View of Kanchenjunga from Darjeeling*. Courtesy of the Royal Botanic Gardens at Kew.

opening in the foothills, the plains stretched to the horizon covered with snow, the surface of which, having melted and frozen, reflected as water would the pure blue of the sky, presenting a complete optical illusion. It required my knowledge of fact to assure me that I was not looking at the ocean" (171). Or again, describing the onset of a storm: "The purple sun rose in front. Had I known what

Figure 41. Isabella Bird.

made it purple I should certainly have gone no farther. Then clouds, the morning mist as I supposed, lifted themselves up rose-lighted, showing the sun's disc
as purple as one of the jars in a chemist's window" (163). In this second passage,
where Bird is not in possession of the scientific facts enabling her to read her
environment, color and danger are not domesticated through a household reference or an allusion to classical mythology but through an analogy to a chemical concoction.

What Bird would not do to a mountainscape like this—romanticize it
through the language of the picturesque—she was nevertheless quite willing to
do to a mountain man, the notorious "Rocky Mountain Jim," to whom she is
said to have been sexually attracted. In a reversal of the male view of woman as
nature, passive and appropriable—a sexual object to the male's subject—Bird
chooses here to make Jim the object, standing in for nature as fierce and dangerous, with Bird herself as the subject. Thus Jim serves a function in Bird's
book *A Lady's Life in the Rocky Mountains* (1879) rather like that of the native
bride in male narratives of travel and conquest. Hardly an optical illusion, Jim
personifies the nature of the new world and its rugged western mountains:

With a sort of breezy mountain recklessness in everything, he passes remarkably acute judgments on men and events; on women also. He has
pathos, poetry and humour, an intense love of nature, strong vanity in certain directions, an obvious desire to act and speak in character, and sustain
his reputation as a desperado. (86)

Bird's relationship with Jim Nugent began as mountain comradeship; he was
her guide to the unknown regions of the Rockies, her guardian on an ascent to
Long's Peak, the highlights of which she described in a sexualized version of the
Victorian female sublime. Like Mazuchelli, she stressed her physical contact
with the mountainside, but in her case this also included physical contact with
Rocky Mountain Jim:

> Never-to-be-forgotten glories they were, burnt in upon my memory by six
> succeeding hours of terror. You know I have no head and no ankles, and
> never ought to dream of mountaineering; and had I known that the ascent
> was a real mountaineering feat I should not have felt the slightest ambi-
> tion to perform it. As it is, I am only humiliated by my success, for 'Jim'
> dragged me up, like a bale of goods, by sheer force of muscle. At the Notch
> the real business of the ascent began. 2000 feet of solid rock towered above
> us, 4000 feet of broken rock shelved precipitously below; smooth granite
> ribs, with barely foothold, stood out here and there; melted snow, refrozen
> several times, presented a more serious obstacle; many of the rocks were
> loose, and tumbled down when touched. To me it was a time of extreme
> terror. (66)

Attached to Jim as through an umbilical cord, the forty-two-year-old, single Isabella Bird knows the sublimest fear of her life—a kind of primal sexuality linked
with horrible beauty, an out-of-body experience grounded deeply in the body.

This description is all the more interesting when we consider the audience
for which it was originally intended. *A Lady's Life* began as letters to Bird's sister, Henrietta, and was later polished and published with the encouragement of
Henrietta and the friends to whom she had read Isabella's letters. Given the personal involvement of the letters' audience with their author, we might venture
that this sexual variation on the female sublime presents another version of the
wedding of self and nature. On Long's Peak, Bird would also reveal, she and Jim
bonded in a way she had never bonded before. Jim later told her that he wanted
to marry her and that he had made up his mind on Long's Peak. Her reaction
was the same as to the sublime landscape: "I was terrified," she wrote to her sister Hennie, "it made me shake all over and cry" (qtd. in Barr 87).

In retrospect, Bird described her ascent as a sexual climax: "A more successful ascent of the Peak was never made, and I would not now exchange my memories of its perfect beauty and extraordinary sublimity for any other experience

of mountaineering in any part of the world" (*Lady's Life* 71). Here Bird transforms the gothic fear of male power and sexuality into a desire *not* to domesticate Jim, who had to remain wild. No conversions on the part of Jim would have suited Bird because, more than anything, she needed to keep her memory wild. Verbalizing what appears to have been the sublime climax of her life seems to have left Bird free in real life to say no to Jim. Yet she would need to console herself over his loss most of the rest of her life—much as Kingsley did for the peak experiences on the Ogowé. Even in this sexualized form of the Victorian female sublime, the loss of the thing felt in nature was what made the experience so memorable.

The Natural in the Aesthetic: Vernon Lee

Not one to physically ascend rugged mountain heights in the way that Bird described herself as doing, Vernon Lee (Violet Paget [1856–1935]) (see figure 42) nevertheless trained herself to plumb the depths of the human response to beauty, searching for connections between our human senses and our sense of the beautiful in nature. In describing the practitioners of the Victorian female sublime, I have used the word "aesthetics" loosely, to denote a literary response to nature in the form of the beauty and danger of unknown mountains. Lee's work was that of a more formal aesthetician who saw art and nature as akin. "By *aesthetic,*" she said, "I do not mean *artistic*. I mean . . . that which relates to the contemplation of such aspects as we call 'beautiful,' whether in art or in nature" (*The Handling of Words* 79). Lee was a prolific writer on European art and travel and, not incidentally, the redefiner and popularizer of the term "genius loci" at the turn of the century.

For Lee, the body was the primary source of our aesthetic pleasure. In the late 1880s, Lee and her friend Clementina (Kit) Anstruther-Thomson began a series of experiments in which they measured the human body's reaction to beauty. They would stand before art objects and record physiological effects that the objects might have on the body's temperature, equilibrium, respiration, and circulation. Then in "Beauty and Ugliness," an essay they wrote in 1897, Lee and Anstruther-Thomson proposed that "the aesthetic instinct, the imperious rejection of certain visual phenomena as ugly, and the passionate craving for certain others as beautiful" depended upon "one of the most constant and important intellectual activities, the perception of form" and that this, in turn, depended upon two bodily functions, respiration and equilibrium (225).

Lee and Anstruther-Thomson would be challenged on the originality of their theory by no less than Bernard Berenson (1865–1959), the eminent art critic and connoisseur, who believed that he initiated their ideas. He had been researching the nature of muscular sensations generated in the body when the

Figure 42.   John Singer Sargent, *Vernon Lee* (1881). Courtesy of the
Tate Picture Library, Tate Gallery, London.

Tuscan painters are viewed. But this kind of research was generally in the air
at that time. Karl Groos (1861–1946) and Theodor Lipps (1851–1914) were
working on similar theories in Germany, and Grant Allen, following Spencer,
had published his positivist *Physiological Aesthetics* in 1877. Like Lee in her early
work, Allen wanted to purge transcendental rhetoric from aesthetics; he would
show aesthetic feelings "as constant subjective counterparts of certain definite
nervous states" (viii). Lee herself would later modify her earlier position on
physiological aesthetics and bracket Anstruther-Thomson's contributions to
the 1897 essay in a reprint that was issued in 1912. This revisionism suggests,
as Lee herself put it, that she was increasingly "inclined to consider that mere
formal-dynamic empathy as such, that is to say considered as a mere mental
phenomenon (whatever its physiological origin or connexions), is the direct,
the primary explanation of the aesthetic phenomenon" ("*Beauty and Ugliness*"

153–54). Nevertheless, although Lee became successively more interested in empathy and morality and their connection to aesthetics, she would continue throughout her career to reflect on the human physical response to beauty.

For Lee, human beings fed both literally and emotionally on what she called "the Life of the World." In 1896, she pointed out that the great strength of the art of the Middle Ages was that it made the human self "cosubstantial" with this "Life" (*Renaissance Fancies* 8). Searching out, reviewing, and defining what might be "cosubstantial" between the human self and the life of the world became a focus of much of Lee's subsequent writing. For example, place or locality, Lee tells us in *Genius Loci* (1899), "can touch us like a living thing" (3), "immanent very often, and subduing our hearts most deeply" (6). That is because beneath place, as beneath art and the human reaction to art, lay nature—something very concrete and very substantial. Witnessing the quarries of Monte Altissimo in Italy and feeling the hardness underfoot, Lee realized that

> the works of modern sculpture, all this dead and dreary art, will have in future a living and wonderful side for me; in the fact of the marble in which they are carved, and the remembrance of the scent of sun-dried herbs, of the sound of the well-head at the base of the Altissimo, and the sight of the eagle circling above its spectral white crags. ("Among the Marble Mountains" in *Genius Loci* 70–71)

Like Gerard Manley Hopkins (1844–1889), her contemporary and fellow admirer of Walter Pater, Lee based much of her writing in her sensual response to the concrete "thinginess" of the universe. Substantial things inorganic—the white crags—as well as organic—sun-dried herbs—were for Lee the building blocks of the universe and of the world of art. Lee's description of asphodels, for example, charts what might be called, using Hopkins's parlance, the "inscapes," or inner scapes (*Journals* 200), of the flowers, first en masse and then individually:

> deep plantations, little fields, like those of cultivated narcissus, compact masses of their pale salmon and grey shot colours and greyish-green leaves, or fringes, each flower distinct against field or sky, on the ledges of rock and the high earth banks. . . . The beauty of the plant is in the candlestick thrust of the branches. The flower has a faint oniony smell, but fresh like box hedge. (*The Spirit of Rome* 70–71)

Human beings live with and respond to this landscape of flowers as they do with and to the rocks of Monte Altissimo. Then the genius loci, which is "of the substance of our heart and mind" as well as of the earth, returns to haunt them (*Genius Loci* 5). They become cosubstantial with substantial things. People embody place in memory, and place becomes so strong within them that it is what determines local and national characteristics of people (*The Sentimental Traveller* vii). It is our own physical "uprooting" from place that leads to our yearning for the genius loci. For Lee, as for the practitioners of the Victorian female sublime, this was the point of origin of travel books. Words fleshed out memories of things once sensed or perceived as substantial.

It was the "things" of places that captured Lee's imagination particularly strongly in her collection *Laurus Nobilis* (1909), where Lee once again shows the concreteness underpinning the beautiful. Here she also evinces the elusiveness in "things" and their beauty:

> Our language does not possess any single word wherewith to sum up the various categories of things (made by nature or made by man . . .) which minister to our organic and many-sided aesthetic instincts: the things affecting us in that absolutely special, unmistakable, and hitherto mysterious manner expressed in our finding them *beautiful.* (4)

Disciplining herself to focus her search upon one symbolic and natural thing, Lee alights upon the bay laurel (*Laurus nobilis*) to guide her through her reflections. The plant of poets, the plant into which Apollo metamorphosed, the cure for aches and pains, bay laurel can speak to the heart, the mind, and the body. Lee caresses the leaves, the twigs, and the bay trees themselves with words, searching for the links between plant and art. The mystery of the beautiful must come through some correspondence between the "primordial," "cosmic" power of the beautiful thing—the laurel, for instance—and the same sorts of qualities in the human being (12). "The power of Beauty, the essential power therefore of art, is due to the relations of certain visible and audible forms with the chief mental and vital functions of all human beings; relations established throughout the whole process of human and, perhaps even of animal evolution" (13).

In her search for the roots of cosubstantiality, Lee pioneered in something that Grant Allen seems to have missed: she associated contemporary aesthetics and psychology with Darwinian evolutionary theory. To her mind, human beings evolved in part in order to enjoy and appreciate. As early as the 1897 version of "Beauty and Ugliness" and here again in *Laurus* (4, 100), Lee used the phrase "aesthetic instinct." Even earlier, in "Vivisection: An Evolutionist to Evolutionists," a carefully argued essay that appeared in the *Contemporary Review* in 1882, Lee had defined herself as a Darwinian. In this essay, Lee had argued "as one who believes in scientific method, in human development, and in evolutional morality" (796). Vivisection is immoral because torture of other animals inevitably leads the torturers, the human species, into further moral backsliding. On these grounds alone, scientists ought to be persuaded to reconsider what they are doing and exercise willpower to rethink the implications of their work—not for human physical improvement but for human moral improvement. I have interrupted my discussion of *Laurus* to discuss this essay because

Lee's views on vivisection help to explain some of her ideas about nature and art in *Laurus*. Lee does not let "Christian" or "deist" arguments, as she calls them (796), sway her stance on antivivisection. Her own moralized, humanistic version of evolution—in which human beings individually and collectively must actively work toward the moral betterment of their kind—marked her work both early and late. From the beginning, then, Lee was interested in the nature of human nature as not only physical but moral as well.

Because Lee wanted a moral component to enter her theory, she always had difficulty in following her "aesthetic instinct" to its logical conclusion that humankind is nature beholding the natural:

> the aesthetic phenomenon *par excellence,* and such other heightening of vitality as we experience from going into fresh air and sunshine or taking fortifying food, the difference between the aesthetic and the mere physiological pleasurable excitement consists herein, that in the case of beauty, it is not merely our physical but our spiritual life which is suddenly rendered more vigorous. (*Laurus* 15)

On this particular issue, she refused to break with her teachers: "As every great writer on art has felt, from Plato to Ruskin, but none has expressed as clearly as Mr. Pater," she insisted, "in all true aesthetic training there must needs enter an ethical element" (17). Despite an earlier desire to purge transcendental rhetoric from aesthetics, Lee reinstated words like "spiritual" in her work and linked the spiritual to the ethical. She did not view the natural and the ethical as opposed; the idea of moral evolution was a reality to her.

Because she was so deeply attracted to Darwinian theory, Lee continued to find ways of incorporating it into her work. In *Genius Loci,* for example, places themselves evolve. "One wants," Lee says, "if one really cares for places . . . to feel what the life of that particular place has been striving after through the uneasy centuries—what has been, to put it pedantically, the formula of its evolutions" (109). And in *Renaissance Fancies and Studies,* where she discusses art as "Life," she also describes human artifacts in time in terms of evolutionary process:

> All the natural selection, all the outer pressure in the world, cannot make a stone become larger by cutting, cannot make colour less complex by mixing, cannot make the ear perceive a dissonance more easily than consonance, cannot make the human mind turn back from problems once opened up, or revert instantaneously to effects it is sick of; and a number of such immutable necessities constitute what we call the organism of an art, which can therefore respond only in one way and not another to the influences of surrounding civilisation. (38)

For Lee there was a natural determination in the history of art that paralleled the evolution of life-forms.

As in her earlier experiment with the body's reactions to beauty, Lee returned in *Laurus Nobilis* to her hopes that science might show the way not just to understanding the structure of our senses or organs but to understanding the mystery of beauty. "The habit of beauty," she says, "is the habit I believe scientific analysis of nature's ways and means will show us—of the growing of trees, the flowing of water, the perfect play of perfect muscles, all registered unconsciously in the very structure of our soul" (106). She knows that "the emotional communion of man with nature is through those various faculties which we call aesthetic" (110), but because of her commitment to an ethical aesthetics that may somehow lie beyond matter, she can refer to those faculties as "matter" only by way of queries. "If the soul be a function of matter, will not science recognise but the more, that the soul is an integral and vitally dependent portion of the material universe?" she asks (109). And then again she questions: "When, I wonder, will the forces *within* us be recognised as natural, in the same sense as those *without?*" (122). Lee's queries and ponderings in *Laurus* are logical concomitants of her quest for cosubstantiality and for the source of art. "The mountain forms, colour, water, etc., of a country are incorporated into its art less as that art's object of representation, than as the determinant of a given mode of vitality in the artist" (172). "The vitality of the artist"—here Lee reverts to the idea behind her experiments with Anstruther-Thomson—the bodily source of humankind's response to beauty. In *Laurus,* however, she is unwilling to return and refine her earlier physiological aesthetics.

Tentative about these materialist aesthetics, she moves more definitively in *Laurus* toward an altruistic aesthetic. Aesthetic pleasure, she points out, "is not in the least dependent upon the fact of personal ownership" (51). Arguing as she had in her essay on vivisection, she evokes a moral evolution which this time includes the arts:

> Many of the pleasures which we allow ourselves, and which all the world admits our right to, happen to be such as waste wealth and time, make light of the advantage of others, and of the good of our souls. This fact does not imply either original sinfulness or degeneracy—religious and scientific terms for the same thing—in poor mankind. It means merely that we are all of us as yet very undeveloped creatures. (45)

The raw "struggle for existence," Lee suggests, will not improve the species (46). Selfishness will persist unless human beings work to rid themselves of it, and one means of doing so is through "the enjoyment of beautiful things," which "is originally and intrinsically one of those which are heightened by sharing" (46). For her, "obsolescent instincts of rapacity and ruthlessness" can be made more genuinely obsolescent if "what the psychologists call the *contagion of emotion*" were redirected to encompass the beautiful rather than the greedy (46, 50). If human beings were to believe that to share ideas and beauties was as important as to share bread, this might alter "our views of loss and gain" and "lessen the destructive struggle of snatching and holding" (70). This altruistic aestheticism becomes Vernon Lee's answer to social Darwinism.

If in her altruistic, ethical aestheticism Lee is the child of her mid-Victorian heritage, she also offers something more naturalistic in other passages in her books. There, Lee becomes an impressionist, offering flashes of writing that capture quick insights into art and time, not just art and space. Particularly in her later work, she anticipates Virginia Woolf, simultaneously illuminating "things" and moments. In her "Lizard in the Abbey Church" in *"The Tower of Mirrors" and Other Essays on the Spirit of Place,* for example, Lee offers a meditation on lizards, time, and decay. Opening with a breathless staccato—"France once more, and at length the first autumn morning. The straggling village has that French air of little, close-fisted, *cossu* middle class" (7)—Lee next focuses our attention on the tree stump on which she sits, then on the "white hulk of the Abbey Church" on which she gazes (8). This building "is a phantom," unoccupied by its "village of unbelievers," and so Lee spends most of her time there, avoiding the unbelievers and "in dealings with a lizard" (10). As would Woolf in her prose piece about a mysterious "mark on the wall," Lee at first finds it difficult to determine just what she is seeing. The unexpected field lizard seems displaced, and Lee removes the creature to its natural habitat, alarmed that afterwards it "merely slipped behind some weeds and lay there like dead" (11). The next morning, when she returns to find it gone without a trace, Lee enters her meditation. She hopes that the morning dew has "washed the monastic foulness off" of the lizard and that it has returned to the nearby vineyard (11); or that "it was put to death mercifully by one of the swallows in their autumn hoverings" (12). But whatever has happened, in Lee's imaginings, nature in the form of the lizard has returned to nature to become part of the life cycle, whether its own or the swallow's. So too with the church:

> The vapours have drooped back on to the horizon faintly reddened by the invisible sunset. From the river meadows and the stubblefields rise white gauzes of mist, in which mingles the smoke of supper and of burning weeds. Above a red farm-roof, the moon, nearly full, floats white in the thin blue air. The great abbey church seems asleep, its high brown roof and turrets and buttresses unsubstantial among the poplars. An hour hence it will have vanished back into the distant ages. (12)

The day claims the church, but so does time. Having outlived its mission, it evaporates into memory, decay, and ultimately loss. Art and artifact and the institutions that make them, like things natural, live and die in a cycle of time. Lee's impressionism catches the drift of her "Life of the World" whereby art and the natural life cycle can be critiqued with one language. They have become cosubstantial.

Figure 43.   Gertrude Jekyll in her Spring Garden (1918).

The Aesthetic in the Natural: Gertrude Jekyll

Unlike Lee, who roamed Europe in search of genii loci, or the women practitioners of the female sublime, who confronted their sets of magnificent mountains as foreigners, gardener Gertrude Jekyll (1843–1932) was rarely distanced
from the nature about which she wrote (see figure 43). Never separated from
the practical effects of the gardens that she created for herself and for others,
Jekyll returned to her own garden over and over again not just to plan or plant
but to write on location—not through the scrim of memory. Two times a month
she would pick a spot and sit there for awhile, saturating herself in its sights and
scents. Then she would begin an article for the *Guardian*. What emerged from
these sittings were not just basic how-to essays but a unique kind of aestheticized nature writing that, like Jekyll's gardens, became her hallmark—an applied aesthetic based on Jekyll's successive careers as painter and gardener and

on her belief that garden writing is as important to our understanding of aesthetics as are meditations on art and art history.

During her lifetime, Jekyll wrote over fourteen books and two thousand notes and articles on gardening, all of which can offer insights into just how this kind of writing transforms the natural into the aesthetic. When Jekyll recast the site of the garden into the symbolic structure of garden writing, she was performing a double translation. The garden is itself a representation of nature revised by culture, a situation in which an aestheticized nature is already literally in place. Garden writing sets out to further reenvision this nature-as-garden linguistically, a daunting task for several reasons, especially for Jekyll. First of all, although the garden itself is a locus, the garden transformed into writing must become portable, representing a place but never literally tied to it. For a garden maker like Jekyll, this can be particularly stressful. Unlike the seventeenth-century poet Andrew Marvell, for example, who in his "Garden" was describing the garden work of someone else, Jekyll at Munstead was inscribing one of her own works of art. Artistic license was of little use to her; verbal accuracy was far more essential. Second, the garden itself is basically mute; it speaks primarily to the eye and the nose, not to the ear. When we add to this the fact that for all her verbal ability, Jekyll saw the garden as something yielding itself more readily to the sketch or photograph than to the word, we can appreciate how garden writing offered Jekyll challenges that in many ways exceeded those of laying out the garden itself. On the other hand, unlike the writers of the female sublime, who felt a sense of loss during the sublime encounter with nature and afterward, and unlike Vernon Lee, who struggled to aestheticize places lost, Jekyll always had as her primary achievement the garden itself, her self-created and already beautified natural space. Her writing did not have to compensate for a personal loss of nature in quite the same way as did theirs.

In her garden writing, Jekyll announced her own credo, something she often reiterated in her essays and books: "I hold the firm belief that the purpose of a garden is to give happiness and repose of mind, firstly and above all other considerations, and to give it through the representation of the best kind of pictorial beauty of flower and foliage that can be combined or invented" (*Wall and Water Gardens* 141). These two concepts underpinned all of Jekyll's work. What one reads first in this credo—the purpose of the garden—suggests Jekyll's understanding of a commonplace in garden theory. The garden is artifice, harking back to Eden. It is made to deliver us for a moment into a state of bliss that we can never really sustain. It is a place to which we can repair to restore ourselves. But what one reads second in the credo indicates the even greater allure of the garden for Jekyll. A painter before she was a professional gardener, Jekyll read color into the garden as had no one before her (or since). The garden for her was the site of artistic intentionality, a construction that above all else called for a painter's eye. A victim of failing eyesight, which of course made it difficult to paint or do other close work, Jekyll discovered in the garden a place where larger-scale vision could find one of its finest expressions. In Jekyll's gardens, nature is not simply imitated but reinterpreted in terms of what Jekyll called "garden pictures" (*Wood and Garden* 197). "Planting ground," Jekyll expounded, "is painting a landscape with living things; and as I hold that good gardening takes rank within the bounds of the fine arts, so I hold that to plant well needs an artist of no mean capacity. . . . his living picture must be right from all points, and in all lights" (*Wood and Garden* 156–57).

Because of her strong dedication to educating other people to see the garden fully, Jekyll freely used pictorial representations in her writing, regarding each book as a photo opportunity that was also part of a teaching assignment. In *Wall and Water Gardens* (1901), she realized that photos of gardens might in some ways be more instructive tools to use in teaching her readers about gardens than the gardens themselves. They could train the eye by setting a feature into bold relief or by providing a number of angles on one prospect or place. Through a photograph, Jekyll could, for example, illustrate just how improvements in landscape could be effected. Then she could revise the picture, sometimes with sketches and plans, sometimes with words, as here, where a photo reconstructs a scene that is then recaptured and refined verbally:

> Often one sees some piece of water that just misses being pictorial, and yet might easily be made so. Such a case is that of the sheet of water in the il-

Figure 44.   Gertrude Jekyll, *A Good Pond That Might Be Much Improved.*

Figure 45.   Gertrude Jekyll, *Tabby in the Cerastium.*

lustration [see figure 44]. A great improvement could be effected by a moderate amount of navvy's work, if it were directed to running a sharp-pointed bay into the rising ground on the right, and tipping the earth taken out into the square corner on the near right hand; saving the bed of rushy growth and planting it back on the new edge and into the bay. The exact position of the excavation would be chosen by following any indication to-wards a hollow form in the ground above, and by considering how its lines would harmonize with the lines already existing. The two sides of the bay would also be eased down after the manner of those hollow places one sometimes sees by pond or lake in rising ground where cattle or wild crea-tures come down to drink. (*Wall and Water Gardens* 159)

Jekyll was versatile with her use of photographs and at ease with a variety of audiences. In a later book, *Children and Gardens* (1908), Jekyll photographed and whimsically described a love second only to the garden itself—the cats which inhabited her garden:

One bank is covered with Cerastium; this he [Tabby] thinks is just suit-able for his bed [see figure 45]. I often find him there, and though it is not quite the best thing for the Cerastium I cannot help admiring his beauti-ful rich tabby coat, with its large black clouds, so well set off by the velvety grey of the little downy plant. (169)

As noteworthy here, artistic arrangement, color, and composition were ever Jekyll's primary concerns. Aesthetics were appropriate for children, as in this photographic and verbal reverie, just as they were for landscape gardeners in the detailed description of how to make a body of water more pictorial. Tabby in the garden, his cloudlike patches of black set off by the gray Cerastium, is an aesthetic portrait, a Whistlerian study in gray and black. Garden writing gave Jekyll an alternative canvas on which to spread her colors.

Carefully crafted narrative strategies enhanced Jekyll's painting in words. In her most mature and beautifully written garden book, *Colour Schemes for the Flower Garden* (1908), Jekyll continued to develop the art of word picturing along with the art of the imaginary walk. The former gives us a break to absorb the static pictures that Jekyll wants us to linger with for the moment, the latter kinesthetically moves her narrative forward. For example, Jekyll opens the first chapter with a delivery of the "year's first complete picture of flower-effect in the woodland landscape" (2),

> a place among silver-trunked Birches, with here and there the splendid richness of masses of dark Holly. The rest of the background above eye-level is of the warm bud-colour of the summer-leafing trees, and, below, the fading rust of the now nearly flattened fronds of last year's Bracken, and the still paler drifts of leaves from neighbouring Oaks and Chestnuts. The sunlight strikes brightly upon the silver stems of the Birches, and casts their shadows clear-cut across the grassy woodland ride. The grass is barely green as yet, but has the faint winter green of herbage not yet grown and still powdered with the short remnants of the fine-leaved, last-year-mown heath grasses. Brown leaves still hang on young Beech and Oak. The trunks of the Spanish Chestnuts are elephant-grey, a notable contrast to the sudden, vivid shafts of the Birches. Some groups of the pale early Pyrenean Daffodil gleam level on the ground a little way forward. (1–2)

With utter specificity, Jekyll's hyphenated adjectival phrases direct our eyes into the scene, and her colors, though subdued, are intricately hued. The effect is again Whistlerian, an arrangement in browns, silvers, and silvery greens. But once we have this picture etched in our minds, we are moved on through a kind of garden gallery to a wider field of observation, and Jekyll begins our walk through "dark masses of Rhododendron" onto a lawn, into a gray herb garden, on past some shrub clumps, and to a bulb garden. A garden plan of the bulb garden helps us on our way, as does a photo of a magnolia. Successively, the colors brighten in the text:

> The colour scheme begins with the pink of *Megasea ligulata,* and with the lower-toned pinks of *Fumaria bulbosa* and the Dog-tooth violets. At the back of these are Lent Hellebores of dull red colouring, agreeing charmingly with the colour of the bulbs. A few white Lent Hellebores are at the

end; they have turned to greenish white by the time the rather late *Scilla amoena* is in bloom. Then comes a brilliant patch of pure blue with white—*Scilla sibirica* and white Hyacinths . . . a long drift of white Crocus comes next, etc. (6)

I have lingered here in the garden that opens *Colour Schemes for the Flower Garden* to indicate how very carefully the reader's eye is controlled in a mature Jekyll text. But this is all a trompe l'oeil. Jekyll realizes that her reader will never see the garden as she has painted it. Her text offers a Marianne Moore garden, "an imaginary garden with real toads in it," and Gertrude Jekyll is a "literalist of the imagination."[1] Thus, what Jekyll establishes here is a sense of immediacy that represents *her* having been in this place at this time. The innocence, the directness of all of this vanishes when we begin to analyze exactly what is *not* going on here. Her readers are, in all probability, *not* in southern England in a bulb garden. Jekyll herself never lost sight of the illusions created by garden writing. This enabled her not only to describe the gardens she knew, but to describe the gardens she would never have or never make. In *Colour Schemes,* for example, she mentions that she does not have a rocky hillside in full sun and so cannot have something she can easily envision: "a rock garden on an immense scale, planted as Nature plants, with not many different things at a time" (40). The narrative of the bulb garden in *Colour Schemes* was successfully mediated through rhetoric in much the same way as is Jekyll's nonexistent rock garden. In both cases, we are in the presence of splashes of writing, not splashes of colorful flowers, but Jekyll nevertheless works hard to bond her reader to her illusory garden spaces.

For all of her skill in writing the garden, Jekyll sometimes became frustrated with verbal representation. Language's imprecision in representing color caused her particular distress. In *Wood and Garden* (1899), she tells us that she placed herself before a juniper, one whose stems were clothed in lichen, to practice the sorcery of wordcraft: "Standing before it [the juniper] and trying to put the colour into words, one repeats, again and again, pale-green silver—palest silvery green!" (31). Here she makes the reader work to conjure up the color of this

1.   These phrases are from the earlier, longer version of Marianne Moore's poem "Poetry," which appears in the notes to *The Complete Poems of Marianne Moore.*

>   when dragged into prominence by half poets, the
>   result is not poetry,
>   nor till the poets among us can be
>   "literalists of
>   the imagination"—above
>   insolence and triviality and can present
>
>   for inspection, "imaginary gardens with real toads in them,"
>   shall we have
>   it.

color. Then we authorize her because of her struggles with words, and, as a result, her verbal picture insinuates itself into the reader's vision. Take her thoughts on the color gold as another example of how this works. Again in *Wood and Garden*, Jekyll emphasizes that no flower "matches or even approaches the true colour of gold" and derides the use of the word "gold" to describe what she calls "bright yellow" (222). Pollen-covered anthers or dying beech leaves may approximate gold, but even they are not gold. But, she goes on, "in literature it is quite another matter; when the poet or imaginative writer says, 'a field of golden buttercups,' or 'a golden sunset,' he is quite right, because he appeals to our artistic perception, and in such case only uses the word as an image of something that is rich and sumptuous and glowing" (222). An image, not reality. All this time, Jekyll is, of course, educating other eyes to work like hers in ways of perceiving both gardens and garden texts, for she believed that her work might train other human minds "to perception of beauty," so that they might "find more opportunity of exercising this precious gift" (10).

In her later books, Jekyll was determined to educate her readers' eyes still further—to the *tricks* of perception. In *Colour Schemes*, she shows how easily a gardener can manipulate color to fool the eye. After describing how an eye can become filled with gray and blue, she shows what happens when, in turn, it avidly seeks the brilliance of yellows, then "scarlets, blood-reds, clarets," and then yellows again. "Now the eye," she says, "has again become saturated, this time with the rich colouring, and has therefore, by the law of complementary colour, acquired a strong appetite for the greys and purples. These therefore assume an appearance of brilliancy that they would not have had without the preparation provided by their recently received complementary colour" (55). In such passages, the readers are not just witnesses to her gardening, as they are in the word pictures and walks; they are instead potential painters of gardens. If, following in the tradition of women educators, Jekyll attempts to activate the artistic potential of the reader, then, following in the footsteps of women popularizers of science, Jekyll also reminds us how the same trompe l'oeil can be demonstrated empirically, through colored words. If we look for a long time at a word written in red and then shut our eyes, we see this same word written in green by our mind's eye. When Jekyll herself paints with highly colored words, something of the same effect takes place: we are being impressed by the power of her expert gaze. Jekyll's words gain color through her knowledge of how the reader's mind works, and we in turn respond to passages like this one about the leaves of tree peonies:

> Their colour is peculiar, being bluish, but pervaded with a suspicion of pink
> or pinkish-bronze, sometimes of a metallic quality that faintly recalls some
> of the variously-coloured alloys of metal that the Japanese bronze-workers
> make and use with such consummate skill. (*Wood and Garden* 73)

Just in case we have come too completely to trust Jekyll's own consummate skill in representing color through colorful words, in *Colour Schemes* she again disillusions us. "It is a curious thing," Jekyll muses, "that people will sometimes spoil some garden project for the sake of a word. For instance, a blue garden, for beauty's sake, may be hungering for a group of white Lilies, or for something of palest lemon-yellow, but it is not allowed to have it because it is called a blue garden, and there must be no flowers in it but blue flowers. . . . Surely the business of the blue garden is to be beautiful first, and then just as blue as may be consistent with its best possible beauty" (98–99). The word is not the thing, naming is not being, nor does it bring anything other than words into being—and this includes colorful words. In the misunderstood blue garden, word-deluded planners have mistaken the sign of the thing for the thing itself. Naming has distanced them from gardening. In this same chapter, Jekyll returns to the word "gold," which had troubled her in her first book, *Wood and Garden.* Now more of an expert with words as well as with gardens, she relishes the metaphoricity of the word and feels free to use it as poets might:

> The word "gold" in itself is, of course, an absurdity; no growing leaf or flower has the least resemblance to the colour of gold. But the word may be used because it has passed into the language with a commonly accepted meaning. (*Colour Schemes* 108)

Even we, the uninitiated in color and gardens, may use it. Words like "botany," as she tells children in *Children and Gardens* (again in the tradition of women popularizers of science), are nothing to fear (86). For Jekyll, naming becomes a tool; she wants to keep it clean and sharp like a garden spade, but in order best to use it, not to be intimidated by it.

If Jekyll uncovers the power of language in order to present garden pictures—the second of the two parts of the credo with which I began the discussion of garden pictures—she also unmasks the power of the garden to impart the paradisal rest which she describes in the first part of that credo. For if a feeling of paradise resides in the garden, it is a feeling brought about not just by the work of words but by hard physical labor. When it comes to gardening, the aesthetic end-product is a result both of mental ingenuity and of human sweat. By way of contrast, in Oscar Wilde's brand of aestheticism, the effete and languorous Cyril and Vivian in the critical dialogue "The Decay of Lying" shun the garden, for them a dwelling place of raw nature—like bugs—and not of the kind of refined beauty they seek.

Throughout her texts, Jekyll directly addresses the physical aspects of gardening. With an air of Victorian classism, she assumes the role of overseer of workmen who need to be monitored at every turn by the educated eye and mind of a Gertrude Jekyll—or her intended, late-Victorian reader. Gardens do not simply just happen. They are planned, and then they are achieved, and then maintained. Nor are they free from wild nature's encroachments. Sometimes wonderful effects appear that the gardener would never imagine, as plants creep out of cracks or wander off into a different garden.

As words give only the illusion of gardens, gardens give only the illusion of paradise:

> The early summer air is of the perfect temperature, the soft coo of the wood-dove comes down from the near wood, the nightingale sings almost overhead, but—either human happiness may never be quite complete, or else one is not philosophic enough to contemn life's lesser evils, for—oh, the midges! (*Wood and Garden* 220)

Here Jekyll discerningly resists her own constructions, and here she deflates both of the premises of her credo. She eschews garden pictures, substituting evocations of sound and feeling, and she then sets out to undermine the illusion of paradise that she has created. Wilde's bugs did indeed reside in Jekyll's fictional gardens. Jekyll and Wilde both understood clearly that the dazzling effects of the art they so loved and dedicated themselves to depended on the deliberate, painstaking contrivings of the artificer, the puppeteer who pulls the strings. As Jekyll reminds us in *Wood and Garden*, "It is not the paint that makes the picture, but the brain and heart and hand of the man who uses it" (157). This multitalented woman, who was never above filling in her gardens' bare spaces with potted plants and who counseled careful concealment of all garden props and stakes, was an aesthete in three media. All art must be illusion, said this discerning fin-de-siècle painter-turned-gardener-turned-writer. In her garden writing as in her gardening, Jekyll never lost sight of the fact that although the garden was art made from living things, it was unredemptive and reconstructible—nature understood and nature controlled. For her, land did not resist being aestheticized. In helping determine a new British landscape by bringing the "gardenesque" style to its apex of color and by grouping plants in informal masses and drifts, she had put the genius in the locus.

Naturalizing Space and Time

We have always assumed that something odd happens at the ends of centuries—a sense of dis-ease, of loss, of disempowerment—emotions Elaine Scarry insightfully reviews in her essay "Counting at Dusk" (*Fins de Siècle*). Scarry ponders the ways in which final decades tend to "disempower and reinvigorate the human will," particularly in men's poetry (10). In *Victorian Suicide*, I saw this time frame as symptomatic of what Thomas Hardy called "the coming universal wish not to live" (the title I gave to chapter 8 of my book). In my study as well, men in particular looked at the end of the century as lifeless. But century's ends also mix and muddle categories; they confuse people. Thus Elaine Showalter envisions the fin de siècle in the nineteenth century as a time of "sexual anarchy," when gender roles and sexual identities were questioned and reconstituted and when, in literature, women were disengaged from their stronghold in the novel (*Sexual Anarchy*).

At the end of our own century, it may be time to turn back and think about just why none of this cultural confusion or doom and gloom pervades the work of Gertrude Jekyll or Vernon Lee. To the contrary, the end of their century marked, for them, the beginning of thriving careers. As the work of both of these women confirms, there was a turn-of-the-century women's aesthetic based in perceptions of nature. It stemmed from British romanticism and entered Victorian culture not through the cities or through Oxford (Dowling)—as did the decadent fin-de-siècle aestheticism most often associated with Oscar Wilde—but through female literary and domestic spaces such as travel writing and horticulture. In this sense, it was akin to the travel and rustic writing of W. H. Hudson, Richard Jefferies, and Frances Kilvert, but it was not nostalgic for the British rural worlds that either these men or Thomas Hardy celebrated.[2] Women like Lee and Jekyll were far more involved in the business of describing, discussing, and theorizing beauty per se than in representing a disappearing British way of life.

Our failure to acknowledge garden and travel writing such as theirs as promoting a natural aesthetic is one of the factors that has disabled us from more boldly writing women into late-century aesthetics. This failure has instead encouraged frequent reappraisals of the longer-established, male, often homoerotic aestheticism, which is far more precious and world-weary. If, again, we take Wilde to represent this decadent aesthetic—with his pronouncements that one "should either be a work of art or wear a work of art" ("Phrases and Philosophies for the Use of the Young," *Collected Works* 14: 177) and that "all art is quite useless" (preface to *The Picture of Dorian Gray, Collected Works* 6: xi)—it becomes clear that, for the Wildean, art has become allure, its object artificial or "unnatural" rather than natural. Nature, correspondingly, is devalued. As Wilde's Vivian says in "The Decay of Lying," "Enjoy Nature! I am glad to say that I have entirely lost that faculty. People tell us that Art makes us love Nature more than we loved her before; . . . My own experience is that the more we study Art, the less we care for Nature. What Art really reveals to us is Nature's lack of design" (*Collected Works* 8: 3). "All bad art comes from returning to Life and Nature," he concludes (8: 55).

---

2. For an excellent study of this nostalgia, see Glen Cavaliero, *The Rural Tradition in the English Novel, 1900–1939,* particularly the first chapter, "The Land and the City."

In striking contrast, the women at the end of the nineteenth century were eager to aestheticize the natural and to promote their aestheticism socially and, often, commercially. In this sense, there was little that was precious about them. Gertrude Jekyll both wrote about plants and started a flourishing business by selling surplus plants from her home, Munstead Wood. In her later years, she spent much of her time developing this sales nursery and responding to correspondence about plants. Like Jekyll, Vernon Lee, was vigorous and prodigious, a writer who every few years set a new volume before the public. Thus if it was difficult for women to gain recognition for their efforts to promote the new in science at the end of the century or to sustain their position in the lucrative business of what Gaye Tuchman calls the "high-culture novel" (*Edging Women Out* 5), they were nevertheless successful—both critically and financially—in adding to the store of knowledge via the business of natural aesthetics. They revised the paradigm of woman as nature that had obsessed the Pre-Raphaelite and classical Victorian painters in England and haunted the Viennese: the paradigm of woman IN nature—both domesticated and wild. These two women—Lee in all probability a lesbian, Jekyll a spinster—were not obsessed with aestheticizing woman's nature, either in the form of demon or of Mother Nature. Instead, they aestheticized nature as nature, an accessible realm that could be domesticated by art.

This use of nature as the stuff of art led both of them to develop a different sense not only of space but of time. As Scarry has shown, at century's end there is always a need to deal with the problem of calendar time. Time as human construct gets in the way of natural time, and the cycles of the moon and the seasons give way to a preoccupation with regulated, human time. Reenvisioning space rather than time and addressing natural cycles of the vegetable year rather than apocalyptic endings, Jekyll's writing serves as a contrast to decadent fin-de-siècle writing, preoccupied as it often was with more linear time. And for Lee, whose peak years of writing overlapped Jekyll's, the nature that engulfed the place of travel offered both a site parallel to the garden and a similar conception of time. Sunsets and sunrises over Italy and France continually recur in her writing; lizards come and lizards go. Even Lee's art history becomes more cyclical than linear as she returns to sites like Rome and relates time to life cycles—including her own—rather than to the linear calendar. As Scarry says, "The evening voluntary and the garden voluntary, though never confined to the ends of centuries, continually recur there" (23). In the nineteenth century, they recur most often in women's writing—because at the end of Darwin's century, women like Jekyll and Lee utilized, reconstituted, and embraced rather than feared nature. They naturalized both space and time.

7

Hunting and Gathering Writing

Not all of women's writing about nature was appreciative, benign, or protective. If Vernon Lee and Gertrude Jekyll aesthetically reconstituted nature, and if Frances Power Cobbe and others penned bold essays to encourage animal protection, by the end of the nineteenth century other women felt free to write with equal gusto about their exploits destroying wild animals. By the last decades of the century, women broke into new realms of activity like big-game hunting and came to pride themselves on their prowess in the hunt. Hunting for new audiences as well, in the 1890s they ventured onto the gendered turf of men's writing, where they learned to wield new forms like the hunting narrative and the fishing logbook. Still, they also wished to court an audience of women readers accustomed to popular subgenres—domestic romances, travel adventures, educational tracts, how-to guides, and the like. As a result, a number of late-century women evolved some surprising and ingeniously hybridized literary forms that helped them to tell distinctive tales of their appropriative embrace of nature.

Game Writing: Capturing the Wild

Take, for example, the work of Mrs. R. H. Tyacke, a late-Victorian writer-hunter who was especially proud of her game list:

> Our bag for one year was as follows: pheasants, 137; chikor, 321; cock, 49; snipe, 9; duck, 3; barking deer, 7; goral, 3; black bears, 6; red bears, 8; and musk-deer, 3; and this might have been considerably increased, had we cared to go in for slaughter. (*How I Shot My Bears* 16)

This tally of a slaughter that was no slaughter belongs to a woman who actually styled herself a lover of animals and yet who herself shot many of the wild animals she cataloged. The title of her book on the hunt is particularly telling: *How I Shot My Bears; or, Two Years' Tent Life in Kullu and Lahoul* (1893). The bears Tyacke describes are *her* bears; shooting game is *her* right—she appropriates their lives for her own "tent life." But there is a second sense of appropriation here as well: the words "my bears" can also be read as terms of endearment.

In *How I Shot My Bears,* Tyacke employs both senses of the word "my" by wedding the male hunting narrative, with its tallies of dead game and its literary formulas for heightening the moment of the kill, to female domestic narratives about nurturing young orphans. Tyacke thereby authorizes herself as a professional in two popular, very marketable kinds of writing—one traditionally associated with men, the other with women. In her book, Tyacke's persona appreciates, shoots, and mothers with no sense of the disparity inherent in her responses to wildlife. She would observe the beauty and familial charm of a mother bear cavorting with her cub and then report to her readers just how inconveniently the two bears fell when her husband shot them dead. But if she showed little sympathy for the dead mother bear and her cub, she could patiently nurture a snow leopard cub whose mother had likewise been shot. After trying to help the leopard cub nurse from a glove with a hole cut in it, and then feeding it via a sponge and a piece of India-rubber tubing, she offered the baby to her pet goat, which agreed to suckle it. Tyacke emphasizes this cub's survival as a deeply gratifying success story (268–72).

The apparent absurdities and moral inconsistencies of shooting baby bears and suckling baby leopards and then tying their two narratives together did not trouble Tyacke, in part because it would not have worried many of her contemporaries. Despite the growth of animal protection movements, shooting was a favored pastime among the late-Victorian and Edwardian well-to-do, just as was domesticating wild animals.[1] Sport for the late Victorians was seen as a contest between a human's canniness, intelligence, and prowess, on the one hand, and an animal's instincts and strength, on the other. It was also a means of upward social mobility (Lowerson). Well-to-do middle-class people gained prestige by participating and excelling in upper-class blood sports. The bag was sheerly a reward for one's skill; one simply appropriated what one deserved. Of course, domestication, particularly of wildlings, could also be appropriative. Thus if the bears Tyacke shot were her bears, the snow leopard cub she gentled also became her leopard because her sentimental attitudes toward the animals were similarly possessive. In each case, the animal wholly lost its independent identity, but Tyacke suggests that as a socially superior member of a superior species she had a right to this kind of approach.[2] In this respect, Tyacke's work is consistent with male hunting narratives like Frederick Courteney Selous's famous *Travel and Adventure in South-East Africa* (1893), which recounts a decade of hunting wild animals and sometimes trapping them for European zoos and museums. Selous (1851–1917), who is reputed to have shot thirty-one lions and two hundred buffalo (viii), became a prototypical "great white hunter."

1. For a fuller discussion of the role of these pursuits under the British Empire, see part 3 of Harriet Ritvo's book *The Animal Estate: The English and Other Creatures in the Victorian Age.*

2. Tyacke's attitudes parallel those represented in the 1984 antihunting film *The Shooting Party,* an indictment of callousness and bloodlust in Edwardian upper-class hunters.

He was also a voracious collector: once, but typically, when he only partially in-
jured an eland he had shot, he took a second look at her, decided that "besides
being fat, she was a beautiful specimen of a striped eland, one that would do
very well for the British Museum," and "resolved to despatch her at once" (75).

Throughout her own narrative, Tyacke captures not just animals but aspects
of the landscape she traverses. Whereas other women travelers romanticized
the aesthetic pleasures of the sublime alpine landscape, she rhapsodized over
the environs of the hunt:

> Consider the joy of shooting in these lovely mountains, in a perfect cli-
> mate, where, of sporting purposed, the whole place belongs to you; where
> you take out no licence, pay no keepers; where the birds are *bona fide* wild
> ones, and take a lot of shooting; where you generally carry a rifle in addi-
> tion to a gun, and run the chance of knocking over a bear or a panther, as
> well as a pheasant. (17)

The mountainous country where Tyacke "knocked over" animal after animal
was again colonial India, this time viewed neither as picturesque nor sublime
but simply as fair game. In this special preserve of the privileged English hunter,
Tyacke represents herself as completely at home—as at home as she is in a
book that freely crosses the travel and domestic narratives with the true-life adventure tale. As we have seen in Mary Kingsley's work, authorizing one's experience with nature by writing one's story for commercial consumption was a
source of self-pride as well as money for traveling women. Travel books were,
as Maria Frawley has shown, lucrative "bread and butter" books for some publishers (28). And hunting books about exotic species in the far reaches of the
empire were also very popular.[3] So was any writing that might take advantage
of the nineteenth-century passion for animal trophies. Sarah Bowdich Lee was
proud to have issued the first British handbook of taxidermy in 1843. She had
hoped to anticipate the market for trophy preservation, but at the same time
she was also "finding it absolutely necessary to understand the Art [taxidermy]"
herself, faced with the necessity of preserving specimens in her own work in
natural history (*Taxidermy* iii). Tyacke may not have been adept at the art of
taxidermy, but she was a trophy hunter par excellence, motivated by the pursuit
of excitement and the excitement of the pursuit.

Tyacke seems never to have lost her zeal for the hunt. Nor did many of her
contemporaries, especially the foxhunters among them. Like Tyacke, Victorian
foxhunters were often inconsistent in their attitudes toward animals—deeply,
sentimentally fond of domestic dogs, for example, while at the same time ruthlessly indifferent to the wild fox. Foxhunting was a more acceptable form of
hunting for women than was big-game hunting, which until the 1920s carried

3. See Ritvo, chapter 6, "The Thrill of the Chase."

with it a taint of impropriety, even raffishness (Aitken ch. 4). As early as the 1850s, women were known to excel in foxhunting,[4] but by the 1890s, in the wake of the protests we have seen on behalf of nonhuman species, at least one of those women was moved to turn her back on the sport. A onetime "female Nimrod" (49), as she would call herself in her essay "The Horrors of Sport," Lady Florence Dixie recounted how she became filled with revulsion over her own involvement with hunting both at home and abroad.[5] Acknowledging the excitement of stalking prey, this famous convert from hunting to species preservation wrote to advocate interrupting the hunt at the stage of the stalk, recommending that a "drag" of an animal's scent might serve for as sporting a hunt as a kill of the fox. Like Vernon Lee and Frances Power Cobbe, Dixie came to see the destruction of other species as a mark of human regression. For her, humanity created a "holocaust of animal suffering" through hunting for sport, a "remnant of barbarism in our natures" (53, 50).

What had converted Dixie was what seems to have left Tyacke and others unmoved—the pain and silent reproaches of dying animals:

> I have seen the beautiful eye of deer and its different kind, glaze and grow dim as the bright life, my shot had arrested in its happy course, sped onward into the unknown; I have ended with the sharp yet merciful knife the dying sufferings of poor beasts who had never harmed me, yet whom I had laid low under the veil of sport; I have seen the terror-stricken orb of the red deer, dark, full of tears, glaring at me with mute reproach as it sobbed its life away, and that same look I have seen in the eyes of the glorious-orbed guanaco of Patagonia, the timid, gentle gazelle, the graceful and beautiful kooddoo, springbok, &c., of South Africa, seemingly as it were, reproaching me for thus lightly taking the life I could never bring back. ("The Horrors of Sport" 49)

Although it offers a stark contrast to Tyacke's game list, this sentimental litany of anguished sights presents another catalog of animals considered to be fair game in the British Isles and throughout the empire, this time couched as polemic. "I will never in life again," Dixie emphatically avows, "raise gun or rifle to destroy the glorious Animal Life of Creation" (52).

All the same, other Englishwomen would continue to hunt down a multiplicity of "glorious-orbed" animals the world over. One even devised a hunting narrative meant to serve as a recruiting and advice manual for prospective female big-game hunters. Isabel Savory's book *A Sportswoman in India* (1900), set out to capture women as potential hunters by capturing the thrill of the

4. See John M. MacKenzie, *The Empire of Nature: Hunting, Conservation, and British Imperialism*, 21–22.

5. On the prevalence of foxhunting in Britain at the time Dixie wrote, Erich Hobusch tells us in *Fair Game: A History of Hunting, Shooting, and Animal Conservation*, that "in 1895 there existed altogether three hundred and twenty-three packs in Britain, and some five million pounds were needed to keep the horses and the 20,835 hounds" (205).

hunt. In an attempt to suggest the uniqueness of her own hunting book in its address to women, she pointed out that "it is these highlands of India which are specially connected in the mind with tigers and tiger-shooting—a theme which, I venture to hope, is not, from a woman's point of view, yet worn threadbare" (255). Set in some of the same alien territory as were numerous travel narratives by purveyors of the Victorian female sublime, her book is filled with both caveats and promotions: "Unless a woman is physically strong, it would be foolhardiness to spend eight weeks under such conditions," she warns (283). "But, after all, it is worth it, and a high price has to be paid *because* it is worth it" (283).

Savory fanned her readers' interest in the hunt both by describing the excitement of the stalk and by verbally masculinizing her game, to increase the sense of power of her female audience: "The sight of such consummate power [as a tiger's], as he swung along, licking his lips and his moustache after his feed, was one of those things not soon to be forgotten" (266). Here begins a hunting narrative's version of the Victorian female sublime. The quarry—in this case a mustachioed male animal, more frightening and more other than any female and therefore more capable of stimulating a sublime response—presents danger and arouses fear, hallmarks of the sublime. But as Nina Mazuchelli did in her night walk, Savory will do more than just brave danger. A stalker of beast as Mazuchelli was a stalker of beauty, Savory will emerge as an appropriator of nature. Hunters like Savory incorporate themselves into the very mind of the beast; for a time, they become the other, much as Mazuchelli became the eagle. But after that, they kill, and the beasts live on only in their imaginations. To rekindle the experience, the heightened moment must be recaptured in another kill or in writing.

Throughout her book, Savory's reader is firmly situated in the hunting memsahib's territory, and *A Sportswoman in India* accordingly sets multiple snares for its real quarry, the reader. Although purportedly instructing women in the art of the hunt, Savory also capitalizes on the popularity of hunting books by men—Selous's books, and Victorian adventure stories like Rider Haggard's *King Solomon's Mines* (1886) and *Allan Quartermain* (1887), for example. Adventure stories, according to Martin Green in *Dreams of Adventure, Deeds of Empire*, offer "a series of events, partly but not wholly accidental, in settings remote from the domestic and probably from the civilized (at least in the psychological sense of remote), which constitute a challenge to the central character. In meeting this challenge, he/she performs a series of exploits which make him/her a hero, eminent in virtues such as courage, fortitude, cunning, strength, leadership, and persistence" (23). The reader will notice the psychological similarities between this kind of experience and those of the women experiencing the female sublime.

Highly charged with anticipation and following a pattern similar to that described by Green, Savory's tale of a bear shoot unfolds, revealing the remoteness, the challenge, the courage, and the skill of the hunters. First, an old native beater falls to the bear's claws—"With furious growls the bear sprang towards the half-naked coolie" (224). The bear, erect on his hind feet, hits "the man on the top of the skull a buffet with one great forepaw" and simultaneously bites the man in the chest (224). Enter the great white hunters, female (Savory) and male (her husband). Their foe is monstrous: "an old male, measuring six feet three inches, with worn-down teeth," rearing to seven feet when alarmed and on the attack (226). But age does not slow this creature, for "on the old bear came, in far less time than it takes to read this" (225). Readers beware: we are mentally engaged here, but this is not our story. It is the hunter's, and in this case Savory's husband ends the charge by firing a well-aimed bullet, hitting the bear's head behind its ear. All are once again safe.

In most of her miniadventure narratives in *A Sportswoman in India,* Savory herself, not her husband, emerges as savior. In these cases, Savory's stories offer women readers the kind of personal satisfaction that pervades the bravado episodes in travel narratives by women like Mary Kingsley. For instance, in Savory's book a woman is always close to the kill. If Savory herself did not have time to grab her gun in the written version of the bear hunt, the picture that accompanies this vignette nevertheless shows her pointing directly at the bear, standing alongside her husband, her own trigger finger as near to the quarry as his gun. In *A Sportswoman in India,* there are no cowering Victorian females needing human male protection from large King Kong–like animals, nor are there fallen superwomen like She to be reckoned with. The drama here lies neither in saving women from dangerous animals, nor in diminishing their prowess through human sacrifices made for "love" (as Haggard did with Ayesha's), but in empowering women to kill. In another hunting vignette, Savory's own dead eye enables her to fell a charging tiger that two men have missed (see figure 46), an animal that can spring "upon a man, seizing the shoulder in his mouth, while his teeth penetrate right through chest and back to the lungs" but yields itself to a woman (275). Savory describes herself as "a well-known Mem-sahib who has taken part in almost every variation of sport in India," one who wants Indian wildlife preserved not for its own sake but to enable other women to test their mettle (255). Women of the British Empire, she suggests, can wield technology such as guns and compasses with as much prowess as men can. Regardless of gender, only the brave deserve the spoil.

The kind of hunt that Tyacke and Savory described and Dixie came to deprecate was certainly different from the kind of specimen hunting that Mary Kingsley and Margaret Fountaine pursued in the name of science. But the implications were similar: creatures died as these women did what they did. Kingsley distanced herself from women like Tyacke when she declared, "I never hurt a leopard intentionally; I am habitually kind to animals, and besides I do not think it is ladylike to go shooting things with a gun" (*Travels in West Africa* 545). All the same, Kingsley would risk life and limb to kill a fish, and Fountaine loved the excitement of the chase when she began hunting for butterflies.

WITH MY LAST BARREL I FIRED.

Figure 46.   *With My Last Barrel I Fired,* illustration from
*A Sportswoman in India: Personal Adventures and Experiences
of Travel in Known and Unknown India* (1900), by Isabel
Savory.

In the 1890s, after a decade of indulging in butterfly hunting, Fountaine began to question the pain caused to lepidoptera by her passion for collecting. Of
a butterfly-hunting excursion near Florence, she confessed: "I caught a splen-
did specimen of male Brimstone, thinking that though it was common enough
in England I should always love to think that it was caught in Italy." But this
conspicuous consumption also pricked her conscience: "It gave me a pang of re-
morse to take this beautiful creature away from her flowers and her sunshine,
which I too knew so well how to enjoy; the death of the butterfly is the one
drawback of an entymological [*sic*] career" (*Love among the Butterflies* 59). Despite this identification with the pleasures of her prey, Fountaine continued to
collect. In 1894, two years after the diary entry quoted above, she reinscribed

her thoughts on the pains of collecting as she once again pursued butterflies in the Italian hills: "The entire female population of *P. Napi* was represented by var. *Vryonia*. Directly I saw the males on the wind I conjectured that at this elevation the females would most probably be of this variety and I was glad to find that I had conjectured rightly; it seemed so brutal to rob them of all their little, dusky wives and the mothers of the next brood, but there was no choice but to take a good thing when I saw it or give up collecting altogether" (79–81).

Fountaine's anthropomorphizing, like Tyacke's, seems neither to have deterred nor deferred the decision to kill. Each for her own reasons, these two women needed to validate their prowess in the hunt more than they needed to spare the creatures that populate their narratives. In their writing, too, they domesticated nature not to spare it but to bring it under the power of their pens as well as their guns or nets. Ironically, it seemed easier to destroy for the sake of showing or telling if, in the accounts of destruction, these writers noted the closeness to humanity of the species they were destroying. Hence, their writing does not truly domesticate its subjects; it only adds a contrasting element of domesticity that actually heightens the adventure of their narratives.

The kind of perverse sanitizing-by-humanizing of the animal world found in Tyacke and Fountaine is an exact reversal of what Charlotte Brontë had done in *Jane Eyre* with Bertha Mason: Brontë bestialized her in order to kill her off with authorial impunity. But it corroborates James Turner's observation that latter-day Victorians "reclaimed the beast," by giving it "a mind and, more important, a heart. They ended with a new picture: no longer the beast but the animal, an image so appealing that it not only quelled the fears of man's bestial past but served as an emblem of the heart and an example to the human race" (78). In the cases just described, however, the heart was insufficient to stop the hunt. The domestication of the butterflies as wives and husbands or bears as mother and child can hardly seem to make their deaths more palatable. It could nevertheless increase a reader's horror or *Schadenfreude*—to use the term for taking pleasure in another's pain favored in an essay bearing that title by Frances Power Cobbe—and in so doing create a perverse kind of pleasure for the reader-spectator.

Fishing Sites

No Victorian or Edwardian species was entirely free from the hunt, and women's desire to take part in outdoor sports had stimulated an increased interest in fishing as well as hunting. In the late 1820s, Sarah Bowdich Lee needed to find fishermen to gather specimens for her to illustrate, but by the 1890s, the fisherwoman that George Egerton (pseudonym for fiction writer Mary Chavelita Dunne [1859–1945]) depicted in "A Cross Line" was such a familiar figure that she was unremarkable not only in the pages of a short story but on the banks of a real river. In Egerton's story, a sporting man, searching for something, runs into a woman, and the following dialogue ensues:

"I am looking for a trout stream, but the directions I got were rather vague; might I—"
"It's straight ahead; but you won't catch anything now, at least not here,—sun's too
    glaring and water too low; a mile up you may in an hour's time."
"Oh, thanks awfully for the tip. You fish then?"
"Yes, sometimes."
"Trout run big here? (What odd eyes the woman has! Kind of magnetic.)
"No, seldom over a pound; but they are very game."
"Rare good sport, isn't it, whipping a stream? There is so much besides the mere
    catching of fish; the river and the trees and the quiet set a fellow thinking; kind
    of sermon; makes a chap feel good, don't it?" (13)

Here in *Keynotes*, George Egerton herself sports with a cliché—that of "old boy" meeting New Woman. The man, temporarily lost in his quest for a fishing spot and taken aback by the woman's knowledge of fish and fishing, begins to hunt, viewing her as prey and first sizing up the power in her eyes. Puzzled by her in-scrutability, in both self-justification and self-defense he breaks into a hail-fisher-well-met parlance, trying to communicate and at the same time impress the woman with both his prowess and his sensitivity. But the woman is the one who knows the fish and their favored spots, and in this dialogue she openly claims her knowledge of fishing and of herself. She outfoxes him both as a hunter of women and a hunter of fish. Gendered angling and an angling woman step to the fore as George Egerton offers her readers a New Woman fiction anchored in fishing.

    Egerton's nameless heroine eventually walks away from the fishing stream and glides into more conventional domestic settings, like parlors and gardens. While at home, however, she certainly could have perused one of the many pop-ular manly accounts of the art of fishing published during the 1880s and 1890s. Frank Buckland (1826–1880), for example, depicted his love of the sport with great gusto. Buckland's *Natural History of British Fishes; Their Structure, Economic Uses, and Capture by Net and Rod* (1881) seems to have had the subject of fishing just about covered, as its comprehensive title might suggest. For Buck-land, the art of sport fishing was itself serious business; his entry in the presti-gious *Dictionary of National Biography* actually mentions that he was "a good salmon fisher, but, probably from want of leisure, was not equally skilled in fly-fishing for trout" (204). Quite aside from his prowess in salmon fishing as touted in the *DNB*, Buckland's expertise on fish of all sorts was witnessed by a variety of late-Victorian interest groups. As inspector of salmon fisheries, he helped to help enact the Norfolk and Suffolk Fisheries Act and was networked (so to speak) with fishermen all over the country; as the son of William Buck-land, the famous geologist and canon of Westminster, he had his own private line to God and could interpret the wonders of fish as his father had interpreted the wonders of fossils; as curator of his own museum of fishing apparatus in South Kensington, he could speak with the authority of an expert on tackle. The product of a man with all of these connections, his *Natural History of British Fishes* tosses off allusions to everything from lengthy stays in country houses to collecting expeditions to forage for "sea serpents" with his father and Sir Robert Peel. Moreover, it had the godly imprimatur of the Society for Promoting Christian Knowledge. Self-validated, Buckland was also revalidated wherever he turned.

If the old *Dictionary of National Biography* could also say of Frank Buckland that "genial, sagacious, enthusiastic, always prone to look at the humorous side of a subject, Buckland aimed . . . at enlisting the sympathies of others in his favourite studies" (204), it was unlikely ever to so characterize a woman. Women who fished often fished privately, as did Muriel Foster (b. 1884), whose work offers an interesting contrast to Buckland's. Foster not only fished but used her professional training in drawing to record the aesthetics of her sport and document the nature of her catch. Not long after the remarkable financial success of the publication in 1977 of *Country Diary of an Edwardian Lady*, by Edith Holden (1871–1920), Viking issued *Muriel Foster's Fishing Diary* (1980). Foster's was an equivalently beautiful book and another work that had originally been produced privately and was therefore little known for decades. The diary is prefaced with an illuminated medieval border, illustrated with watercolors of fish, their habitats, and fishing lures, and chronicling Foster's fishing years from 1913 to 1947. The *Fishing Diary* is unquestionably the work of an expert—a practiced fisherwoman who knew her species and their environments and kept a careful log, as did more widely acknowledged experts like Buckland. But Foster's book differs considerably from Buckland's *Logbook of a Fisherman and Zoologist*, whose very title (flaunting the word "zoologist") authorizes it as the record of a professional scientist. Foster was a talented artist whose illustrated diary focuses not just on prose entries about fish species and sizes but on delicate watercolor representations of animals and the passing seasons. As did several other women in this chapter, Foster wedded gendered arts formerly kept separate—in her case, the fishing log and the illustrated diary of natural history. One side of her diary takes the form of a traditional list of fishes, which includes records of the geographic places where the fish were caught, the precise body of water, the number of rods, the flies (often illustrated), and the captured fish with their weights. The opposite leaf has a place for remarks, a space which Foster used far more for watercolor drawing than for written comment. In Foster's work, male and female skills and pastimes confront each other across the adeptly illustrated pages.

As a natural history collector and gardener as well as fisher, Foster developed a remarkable eye for the web of nature in a given environment. Like Mary Kingsley, who believed that without a knowledge of its environment "you cannot know a thing" (*West African Studies* x), Foster defined not just her fish and tackle but whatever she saw around her as she fished. Primary among those sights were other fishers, less often the persons who showed up in her chosen spots than the terns, kingfishers, and otters that fished alongside her. Nearly as important as these predators were the prey of the fish themselves—mayflies, dragonflies, moths, butterflies, and other insects that front the cunningly tied flies on the pages opposite them. To gaze at Foster's diary is thus to enter the entire ecosystem of a given lake or stream or pool or seashore, the sort of thing that Elizabeth Gould was beginning to work toward in her illustrations of birds in the 1830s. To compare Foster's work with Gould's shows an increasing movement toward environmental sensitivity, even among certain hunters. Both of these women have an "ecological vision," a way of seeing that complements what James Krasner calls "evolutionary vision" (55). If "evolutionary vision" stems from Darwinian roots but addresses not a "single organic form" (Krasner 55), ecological vision addresses a multiplicity of allied organic forms. It offers a distinct contrast to Tyacke's appropriative hunting and boastful storytelling. In her self-representation, Foster paints herself small, an unassuming figure setting out in a raincoat with her fishing tackle in hand—just another part of the environment.

Farming Narratives

Thirty years in time and an entirely different philosophy of the hunt separated Tyacke from Foster. During those years, women not only hunted and fished but domesticated nature by raising farm animals and working the land. Before turning to several privileged Victorian female agriculturists who had the time to write of life on the farm, I would like to acknowledge the hard, often backbreaking farmwork of women who did not write their stories and therefore have little part in this book. In her *Victorian Countrywomen*, Pamela Horn documents the lives of British women who were farm laborers and more prosperous farmers, noting that "most accounts of nineteenth-century agriculture pay little attention to the contributions made by wives and daughters to the prosperity of farming" (103). As Horn also shows, it was not just prosperity that was at stake for women on farms. Subsistence for farmworkers often meant that daughters either worked on the land with the men, or in gangs, or that they went out into service to help support themselves and families. Moreover, as the middle-class Victorian ideal that a "lady" did not work was still upheld throughout most of the nineteenth century, women who did work—as managers, dairywomen, supplementary gardeners, and laborers—tended to be overlooked by their written culture, as they have been by ours. Rarely did such women have the time or the ability or the inclination to produce written narratives about their own lives; consequently, their advice or reminiscences about their experiences do not survive.

Not until the 1880s and 1890s were there training opportunities that enabled women to become professional horticulturalists, for example. Mrs. Tubbs, who attended the International Congress of Women in 1899 (the congress that Margaretta Lemon addressed so passionately on bird protection), pointed out that women still badly needed to professionalize their gardening skills. "Let it not be supposed," she urged, "that the woman who intends to take up gardening as a profession can dispense with thorough training" (*Women in Professions* 153). A few distinctive and mainly self-taught individuals like Gertrude Jekyll did not make up a body of professionals. Hence, Tubbs counseled that women needed to take advantage of new educational opportunities and attend schools like the women's branch of the Horticultural College at Swanley, Kent (154).

By the late nineteenth century, however, advice manuals for gentlewomen farmers had, it must be pointed out, existed for some time. Until late in the century, they tended to be written by women who were professional writers rather than professional farmers. One of the most famous of these was Jane Loudon, whose story is woven throughout this book because Loudon survived by knowing her audiences and writing exactly what they bought—which meant everything from gothic potboilers to botany books to scientific popularization. Loudon also produced one of the nineteenth-century's most popular agricultural advice books, *The Lady's Country Companion* (1845). Founder and editor of the *Ladies' Companion at Home and Abroad,* a large-format Saturday weekly that put her in direct touch with hundreds of women readers, Loudon perceived the need for a companion book for countrywomen and first imagined her *Lady's Country Companion* as a series of letters to a young wife. But in her eventual compendium of explanations and hints for better country living, Loudon would come to address not just young wives but all "ladies who from circumstances have been induced to reside in the country" (iii). A latter-day Martha Stewart, she offered her readers information on everything from making fires to cooking to animal husbandry. Her knowledge on each of these topics was both practical and up-to-date, arranged by topic and made easily accessible by its encyclopedic format, which would set the pattern for books like *Mrs. Beeton's Book of Household Management* (1859–1861).

Loudon also established a precedent for later writers who would embellish or refocus the agricultural self-help book, as did the political economist and novelist Harriet Martineau (1802–1876) in her instructive narrative, *Our Farm of Two Acres* (1865), a pamphlet based on a series of essays for *Once A Week* (1859). Its advice was aimed toward small landowners, "ladies, who happen to have a little ground attached to their dwellings, from which it is just as well to derive comfort and luxury, or pecuniary profit, as not" (*Our Farm* 4). Martineau suggested that even a household of middle-class women can keep a small farm going and offer work to local laborers as well. Her model had come from her own experience with a "small patch of land for the production of comforts for my own household" (7), a plot which for eleven years gave her fresh fruits and vegetables, eggs and ham, and dairy products. Martineau became so good at this that she began to turn a small profit by selling her surplus. Carefully reckoned ledgers of profit and loss, a plea for better veterinary services in the countryside, and useful suggestions for innovations like stall feeding for cows help make this pamphlet a miniature Victorian "economy."

Throughout, it is clear that the pamphlet is the product of the social class and learning of its author. Very much the gentlewomanly part-time farmer, Martineau insists that she and her companions at the two-acre farm still "have an abundance of social duties and literary pleasures, in parlor and kitchen; but these are promoted, and not hindered, by our out-door interests" (*Our Farm* 45). Yet Martineau's belief in the land deepened with her knowledge of agriculture. She actually came to feel differently about life because of the small tragedies and miracles she witnessed on the farm. "Whoever grows any thing feels a new interest in every thing that grows," she observed with sensitivity (46). If Octavia Hill advocated the necessity of green spaces for the working class, here Harriet Martineau did something similar for middle-class women. "To women who do not know a cock from a hen, or green crops from white, or fruit-trees from forest-trees, or how to produce herb, flower, or root, from the soil, it would be new life to turn up the ground which lies about them," she passionately advocates (48).

Martineau's household economy strove toward a balanced form of agriculture and a generally benevolent farm ecology. When her cats ate her birds, she would tie the dead bird around the neck of the cat and leave it there for a few days, thus deterring the cat from further stalking. When sparrows would attack her seeds, she would assume that they needed the food. Other Victorian women were less patient with similar agricultural annoyances, both at home and abroad. Recall that Eleanor Ormerod had recommended the destruction of house sparrows to preserve agriculturally beneficial insects. To her way of thinking, sparrows had "enormous powers of increase," which were fostered by protection and "absolute fostering" to the extent that their numbers were raised "so disproportionately as to destroy the natural balance" (*Eleanor Ormerod* 161). And, far from taking time to train farm cats, Annie Martin, in her *Home Life on an Ostrich Farm* (1890), discusses the feeding of kittens to a pet secretary bird to stop cat attacks on domestic fowl in South Africa. Kittens, Martin tells us, were Jacob the secretary bird's favorite "delicacy, and he was fortunate enough while at Walmer [her farm] to get plenty of them." "His enormous appetite, and our difficulty in satisfying it," she continues, "were well known in the neighbourhood, and the owners of several prolific cats, instead of drowning the superfluous progeny, bestowed them on us as offerings to Jacob. They were killed and given to him at the rate of one a day" (29).

In contrast to Martineau, Martin's total insensitivity to the young cats is characteristic of her insensitivity to many of the animals that were neither her particular pets nor the money-yielding produce of her ostrich farm—the exotic subject of her book. If Tyacke's narrative offered an imperialist hunting mentality, Martin's volunteers an imperialistic brand of husbandry. Her narrative encapsulates the attitudes of a colonialist who is both curious about native fauna and wholly unsympathetic toward them.[6] When animals could be domesticated, either as pets or as contributors to the farm's profitability, Martin tells us she favored them; when they were not, they were dispensable, as we have seen with the overly abundant kittens. Honey birds were therefore praised because they helped her in gathering honey, but bee-eaters were abominated for their feasting on the bees (232–34). Even the ostriches, whose feathers were the main crop on Martin's farm, captured little of her respect. Martin considered them stupid because they ran into fences; it never occurred to her that they were programmed for wide-open spaces and therefore unable to adapt to artificial barriers. When frightened, they kept on the run at all costs. Similarly, Martin betrays her imperialist attitude in her belief that ostriches are full of conceit because they failed to recognize their keepers when a keeper changed clothing or hats. Martin finds this characteristic a sign of ingratitude; ostriches "resent the idea of being looked after by [their] human friends" (147).

Because she holds these birds accountable for everything that happens to them, few of their natural propensities are revealed as such to readers of her narrative, nor does Martin take responsibility for what occurs when one of the ostriches becomes tamer than the rest. "Jackie," an incubator bird that imprinted on people, learned to take food from the hand. But Jackie became a nuisance when he then started to steal food from kitchen pots and from young children on the farm. Martin virtually gloats when Jackie gets his comeuppance after attempting to grab an edible from a young African child, a "little animated nude bronze" lunching on a river bank—another colonized feature of the farm as seen by Martin and one seemingly of less interest to her than the ostrich. During this last and failed snatch, Jackie tumbled down the bank and broke his leg and, consequently, "had to be killed"—silly bird (122).

Only once in her book does Martin show any sympathy toward an ostrich, for "the bare idea of there being anything pathetic about an ostrich seems absurd" (118). This occurs when one of the birds loses his mate and wanders "up and down, up and down, the length of his camp, in the hard, beaten track worn by his restless feet along the side of the fence" in the disconsolate, repetitive motion of a mourner (118). In her book about "home life," Martin domesticates this incident by calling this ostrich a "widower" and his dead mate a "wife" (117–18). Only the dance of anthropomorphism—the same dance that called

6. In her attitude toward native animals, Martin of course parallels British colonial attitudes toward indigenous colonial peoples, so well described in books like Douglas Lorimer's *Colour, Class, and the Victorians: English Attitudes to the Negro in the Mid-Nineteenth Century,* and Vron Ware's *Beyond the Pale: White Women, Racism, and History.*

out so strongly to both Fountaine and Tyacke—enables Martin to move toward compassion for her ostriches.

Martin's book is certainly a potpourri: some facts and a few gratuitous "how-tos" about beginning and enduring in ostrich farming; some tidbits about odd native species; some science popularization about ostriches, which are "nine cases out of ten" made into "ludicrously incorrect" drawings by Europeans (102); and all offered up with a dash of humor here or a pinch of anthropomorphism there. In terms of its temporal literary positioning, *Home Life on an Ostrich Farm* is an imperialist work that looks backward to earlier books on husbandry and encounters with exotic species and forward to the animal stories that were soon to become so popular. A far cry from avant-garde romances like Olive Schreiner's *Story of an African Farm* (1883), written and set in the same country, Annie Martin's book courted readers not with promises of love stories similar to those long known at home but with descriptions of strangeness and difference not just in landscape but in life-forms. Martin wrote because she was surprised "to find out how little is known in England about ostrich farming," so little, she decided that "any information on the subject" must seem "new to the hearers" (102). In the end, she herself returned to England—herself now a hybrid kind of life-form—"with dear, delightful, rough South African life . . . a thing of the past" (283).

8

Storied Animals

For all of her disdain for most of the birds that gave her her livelihood, when a homesick Annie Martin found herself back in London in the 1890s, she headed directly for the London Zoo in search of an ostrich. What she found was that there were no living specimens to view; in the zeal of their appreciation, the British public had poisoned them by tossing pennies their way. Martin's particular mix of contradictory attitudes—her contempt for the birds, coupled with her deep need to be near them—marked the blindnesses and the yearning of this British colonial. But many people at home had similar blindnesses; they were, after all, the ones who had tossed the coins that killed the ostriches. Nevertheless, like Martin, they too had a deep desire to be near the animals, somehow to offer them their obeisance.

The opening of the London Zoo in 1828 had long since stimulated a British craze for nonnative animals. With the expansion of the empire and the growth of interest in exotic animals in the nineteenth century, the British public grew more and more hungry to see little-known animals on display. Animals were gathered together like a mismatched bouquet; variety was what counted. In 1830, just a few years after the founding of the London Zoo, the *Zoological Keepsake* featured the following poem:

> In short, whatever folks might trace
> In Noah's famous ark
> (If ever there was such a place,)
> Are in the Regent's Park.
> (Qtd. in Blunt, *The Ark in the Park,* opposite the foreword)

Not just the London Zoo but private menageries burgeoned. The Pre-Raphaelite poet Dante Gabriel Rossetti (1828–1882) kept many animal curiosities in his house in Chelsea, among them a wombat that slept in a lamp. Rossetti would sketch himself desperately mourning the animal only two months after its arrival, when it died and left him with nothing to do but to have it stuffed and placed in his vestibule. All of this interest in exotics led to artistic expressions of all sorts, and writing about domesticated animals became an especially popular pursuit. Because of their established audiences among women and children, their part in the preservation of species, and their closeness to domestic animals in menageries in the home, women writers would come to dominate new kinds of nonfiction and fiction that featured animals.

Gathering Animals/Gathering Stories

To provide a context for a set of women writers who drew both their pleasure and the subjects of their writing from menageries of domestic and exotic pets, I will isolate and review just a small part of the frequently told story of the London Zoo—the zoo as a source of animal stories (Altick; Blunt, *Ark;* Bostock; Ritvo). The London Zoo was meant to be the ultimate menagerie, a place for observation and a place for domestication. Even its well-respected founder, Sir Stanford Raffles, realized this. A firm believer in the scientific importance of the zoo in Regent's Park—what Wilfrid Blunt has called "the shop-window, as it were, of a scientific institution," the Zoological Society (*Ark* 23)—Raffles supervised an organization dedicated to

> the introduction of new varieties, breeds, and races of animals for the purpose of domestication or for stocking our farm-yards, woods, pleasure grounds, and wastes with the establishment of a general Zoological Collection, consisting of prepared specimens in the different classes and orders, so as to . . . point out the analogies between the animals already domesticated, and those which are similar in character upon which the first experiments may be made. (Qtd. in Matthews 281–82)

But although he was a scientist, Raffles was also another kind of domesticator of the animals behind the "shop window": he led them home, and then he told their stories. Take, for example, that of the Sun Bear from Malaysia. "He was brought up in the nursery with the children," said Raffles in a paper for the Linnean Society, "and when admitted to my table . . . gave a proof of his taste by refusing to eat any fruit but mangosteens, or to drink any wine but champagne. The only time I ever knew him out of humour was an occasion when no champagne was forthcoming" (qtd. in Blunt 24). This is what Victorian readers or listeners, apparently even the scientifically inclined, loved to hear: the story of an exotic animal who lives with people and acquires human taste, in this case the beast "reclaimed" as finicky boor (Turner 77–78). Like this anecdote, stories of odd animals that adapted to or bedeviled humans became commonplace by midcentury. In 1847, the popular nature writer W. J. Broderip (1789–1859) deliberately framed his *Zoological Recreations* to feature animals like a wanderloo monkey who would foil his viewers by feigning indifference and then dash up to them and steal their hats. These were the animals that spoke to people.

Because there was such widespread interest in exotic animals, writing about their own menageries also offered women another way of rhetorically undercutting the division between the private and public spheres. Menageries were themselves domestications—in the sense of things kept at home—and hence often came under the watchful eyes of women. All women needed to do to bring their own versions of this domestic world into a more public kind of prominence—as Anna Jameson (1794–1860) had suggested that Victorian women do for their own advantage (*Sisters of Charity*)—was to represent this world to others via writing. Annie Martin, of course, did exactly that in *Home Life on an Ostrich Farm*. With her characteristic lack of respect for the wildlife of her adopted country, Martin opened her second chapter by boldly announcing, "South Africa is the land of pet animals. The feathered and four-footed creatures are all delightful. They have the quaintest and most amusing ways, and they are very easily tamed" (25). Except for the ostriches, of course.

This tone of condescension greets all of the pet creatures of Martin's book—her "acquisitions," as she calls them (26). Secretary birds like Jacob and dikkops—birds that "possessed very foolish, vacant faces" and "large, round bright yellow eyes" that were "entirely void of expression, just as if a bird-stuffer had furnished them with two pairs of glass eyes many sizes too large" (31)—come in for particularly demeaning language. These animals are controlled on the farm and then again controlled with language, memorialized even before their time. But they also die off like flies. The death toll of the animals—one after another, they meet their end—is reminiscent of Tyacke's hunter's roll: Martin's animals pine away; they swallow the wrong substances; they hurt themselves; they are crushed under household trunks. Husbandry is no more the primary aim here than it had been in the larger public menageries established earlier in the century, when, as Altick recounts, "lions, tigers and pumas, on an average, lived no more than two years after arrival" in the London Zoo (*The Shows of London* 319). Just as the public zoo's dead animals went directly into the service of science as specimens for dissection, to be replaced by living counterparts as soon as was possible, so Martin's animals simply disappear from her text only to be replaced by a seemingly endless string of others. Her narrative moves from pet to pet, its primary intent being to amuse the reader with descriptions of otherness. Martin's secretary bird, for example, is an altogether "uncanny-looking creature, and one which, had he appeared in England some two or three centuries ago, would have stood a very fair chance of being burned alive in company with the old witches and their cats" (27). None of these animals is seen as more than a diversion for human beings. Martin's meerkats "were surely created for the express purpose of being made into pet animals. Certainly no prettier or funnier little live toys could possibly be imagined" (157), she tells her readers and then includes a photograph of one of them collared and on a lead (see figure 47).

As we have seen from the hunters and from popularizers like Louisa Meredith, Martin's were by no means the only attitudes toward exotic animals held by women who lived in the provinces of the British Empire during the Victorian and Edwardian periods. But they were typical of a certain kind of acquisitive colonial who captured and kept as pets living animals that entered her or

Figure 47.   A meerkat, photograph from *Home Life on an Ostrich Farm* (1890), by Annie Martin.

his sphere of influence. When Marianne North traveled the world, she visited home after home stocked with native animals serving as pets — macaws and parrots "with blue foreheads and yellow waistcoats" in Brazil, monkeys in Singapore, a mongoose in Ceylon (*Recollections* 1: 144). North herself found these animals exceptional not in their prevalence or their degree of domestication but in the opportunity they afforded her for a closer look at other species. Their omnipresence seems to have been more commonplace to her than the snake that Lucie Duff Gordon brought to table in the North's home when North was a young woman (1: 6). The British brought home exotic wild animals throughout the nineteenth century, sometimes to rule or treat as alien beings, but sometimes for different reasons — to tame, to study, to wonder at, or to nurture. They brought them home in the provinces and home to England. Recall Jane Loudon's railroad journey in the 1840s (see chapter 2 above), when a gentle and curious mother and daughter, returning to their house in Bayswater from a trip around the British countryside visiting various menageries, brought home a monkey to foster.

The taming of the wild became an oft-told tale in Victorian and Edwardian Britain, one that eventually became a special province of women. When, late in this time frame, Olivia Fanny Tonge (1858–1949) journeyed through India (from 1908 to 1913), her aims were both to validate herself in late middle age and to study and draw the exotic animals of the subcontinent. Her beautifully illustrated notebooks survive in the library of the British Museum of Natural History and are prefaced with this curious statement:

> And it came to pass, that a certain Grandmother, when that she had come to nigh on two score years and ten; and had gotten long in the tooth, spake to herself thus.—Lo, will I now paint. And she took much gold, yea much fine gold, and got her a book, and in the book, so that all men might see, painted she all the things that crawled upon the face of the earth, and all things seemly, lo, that flew in the air, and all the things that swam in the waters that are under the earth . . . and verily no man mote stop her. (Preface to *The Sketchbooks of Mrs. O. F. Tonge*)

Tonge endowed herself and her text with biblical authority—the authority to look and to name and to do. In her Indian notebooks, she kept a detailed written record of animals and birdlife she encountered, with observations and lore and facts about their behavior (see figure 48). But she enters the present chapter because she also tamed and then briefly wrote about these creatures. There was "Cupid, my pet mugger [crocodile] who hisses and growls and snaps like any Wild Cat, except when he is full of Beef, when he unbends somewhat, and is comparatively affable" and there was "a little jungle Hedge Hog, tamed and unafraid. It differs from the British Species in having fur of a cool brown grey colour, instead of foxy red, and in the longer light coloured Ears." Even without a public audience, Tonge the journal writer recounted her experiences divertingly, like a published writer of animal curiosities.

In some ways, the keeping of exotic pets was an outgrowth of the keeping of wild British species, just as interest in alien flora was an outgrowth of "pteridomania" and other British botanical fads. All of these pursuits were related to the keenness for observation I discussed in chapter 3. Emily Shore (1819–1839), who watched British wild birds carefully enough to write essays on bird behavior for the *Penny Magazine* in the 1830s, also kept native species as pets, partly in order to study their behavior more closely. Her journal, like Tonge's more than half a century later, records these observations in some detail. The Shores had a scientific interest in birdlife. Each member of the family seems deliberately to have taken on a different species as his or her special preserve for study and enjoyment. When Emily returned home from a trip, the first thing she did was to check on this avian menagerie:

> I am very glad to return at last to the quiet of Woodbury, much as I have liked this little excursion. We find everybody well, and the number of our

The Chambered, or Pearly Nautilus,
Nautilus Pompilius, unfortunately for the Poets, only Pearly
when the outer Porcelain like Covering
has been broken off.

A Curlew
much esteemed for
Food in
India.

An
Eyshter
"Bed,"
otherwise Oyster Catcher.

Figure 48.   Olivia Fanny Tonge, *Curlew, Oyster Catcher, and Nautilus Shell,* illustration from *The Sketchbooks of Mrs. O. F. Tonge* (c. 1908–13), sketchbook 9, leaf 3. With the permission of the Trustees of The Natural History Museum, London.

> bird pets somewhat increased. A cock bullfinch, shy as the species is, two days ago flew into the schoolroom; its head was bare of feathers, probably with fighting. Richard introduced him to his hen bullfinch; they live very amicably together. Mackworth is rearing a young blackbird, and Arabella and Louisa have two young chaffinches, which the mother feeds. A few days after we went to town, M. found a coal-tit's nest with six or seven young ones. He brought it to the house, and the mother came every day to feed them. (104)

Ten days later, Shore's own mother "bought a young jay, not quite fledged, which is to be her pet" (105). The house and its grounds must have been swarming with semidomesticated birds, for Shore kept larks and a cuckoo and a jackdaw as well. A self-styled birdwoman, she even requested that her death portrait represent her holding a stuffed bee-eater (see figure 49). Shore believed that she was engaged in natural history, a study in which she thought "it is particularly important not to come too hastily to conclusions, but to study facts from observation frequently and most carefully before any inference is drawn from them" (119). Her semidomesticated menagerie of British birds, like her bedroom with its "deal box filled with birds eggs" and "System of Birds" and "registering book of birds' songs" (218), enabled her information-gathering version of ornithology.

Figure 49.   Emily Shore.

Animal Biographies

Emily Shore's was a personal story personally told via her journals, but the animal descriptions in these volumes and in her bird essays of the 1830s were, like Jane Loudon's railway journey, important precursors of a kind of popular writing that reached its zenith in the 1890s: the animal biography, a form in which women unquestionably excelled. Animal biographies would encompass two shorter kinds of animal stories, the brief animal anecdote and the animal chronicle, which details a pet animal's life from birth to death or from acquisition to loss. Annie Martin's book featured elements of the animal chronicle; it told the story of numerous pets from their acquisition to their demise. Her narrative is nevertheless dominated by ostrich farming, not pet stories, and so is not an animal biography in the stricter sense in which I am defining the term. Louisa Meredith's books like *My Home in Tasmania* (1852) also interspersed descriptions of wild animals and plants with anecdotal interludes about domesticated wild animals. In *My Home,* Meredith was still writing for the British reader, tailoring her stories to their supposed ignorance of Australian species, with digressions into anecdotes about pets; all of these animals, wild and tamed, were meant to give her readers a closer look at the behavior of native species via vignettes. For example, a longish anecdote about a tame possum, Willy, the "spirit of fidget" (9), features the animal's nocturnal antics around her home. These included keeping people awake most of the night until a night of storms, when it tucked itself into a hat for protection—much as it would have into a tree hole had it been free to do so. In *My Home,* Meredith clearly did not intend to write a book about tamed animals but simply utilized the animal anecdote to help her tell the story of science. Meredith carefully apologizes to the reader who might have expected purer science, not a possum story: "If any of my readers find this memoir of a pet "Phalanger," somewhat prolix, they must attribute my tediousness to my zeal for science, and my desire to make known whatever knowledge I may possess on this interesting subject[;] . . . these creatures are not very well known" (13).

As we have seen in chapter 2, other women who wrote popular science used similar strategies to build interest in the facts of natural history that they wanted to relay. In preparing to write her *Parables from Nature,* for example, Margaret Gatty was eager to find the old and new literary forms that were best suited to her scientific purposes—and to her moral purposes as well. Her daughter, Juliana Horatia Ewing, tells us that Gatty had an interest in Adams's "Allegories" in the later 1840s, when she was thinking about producing her *Parables from Nature* (1855–1871). But Gatty was appalled by things like "'dear green lizards' being made emblems of sin" (xix). Her own parables would draw on Adams and on Francis Quarles's seventeenth-century *Book of Emblems,* but they would also bear animal anecdotes and animal information that would be truer to the various species she represented. Gatty could tailor her tales to offer the morals expected by readers of parables but at the same time tailor her facts to science. Acutely aware of the limitations of children's understanding of the natural world, she believed that her parables could bridge the gulf between animal life and the human species.

In "Inferior Animals," Gatty illustrates this intent by describing a child who is nipped by a cat. The child does not know why the intriguing, attractive animal has treated her so; she sees it as a "soft plaything" (214). But Gatty diagnoses the problem:

> . . . while mama tells her little one that poor pussy does not know what she means, cannot hear what she says, cannot talk as she can, has no sense to know how much she loves her, and therefore is not to blame for biting, although she must be slapped when she does it, to make her remember not to do it again;—behold! how the wistful eyes of the listening child haze

over with a dull dreaminess as she becomes more and more perplexed. It is all far too puzzling for her to understand, and when she turns again to puss—as if by looking at her to make it out—lo! the veil between the two natures remains as thick as before; neither the bite, nor anything else, has been explained. (215)

Attempting to lift that veil, Gatty allowed cats and rooks and spiders and birds to speak their special knowledge of the world.

By the later part of the nineteenth century, animal anecdotes became an important tool not just in science popularization but in species preservation. Even the eloquent and persuasive animal rights essayist Frances Power Cobbe stopped to write true-life animal vignettes in "Dogs Whom I Have Met" for the *Cornhill Magazine.* Cobbe's essay is polemical, of course, but it also offers a series of animal anecdotes, as when Cobbe recounts the story of her own dog as a tiny puppy that kissed and bit her ear. The pup then disappeared for nine weeks, presumed gone forever. But it was eventually returned, and all but Cobbe were doubtful that the now larger, different-looking pup was really hers. The returned dog passed the grade, however, when she gave Cobbe "the identical little gentle bite she had been wont to do two months before, and which she never gave to anybody else" (665).

This story of Yama the dog's return home was a forerunner of many that would be told by professional practitioners of the animal biography in the 1890s, a decade that saw the flowering of this kind of literature. Two women especially, Eliza Brightwen and Alice Dew-Smith, became well known for their animal biographies and offer an interesting contrast in their individual use of this popular subgenre of true-life animal stories. A preserver of wild things, Brightwen was also their intimate observer, particularly in and around her estate and retreat in Stanmore, which offered her lakes, woods, and a large garden. There she kept copious notes on local birds, plants, and animals and developed a menagerie of exotics as well. And there, in her sixtieth year, she began assembling her work for publication. Her hope, according to Edmund Gosse, who introduced her autobiography, was to produce a body of "purely original work, carried out within limits so strictly defined and owing nothing to previous literature, [that] might, simply recorded not fail of some welcome from the public" (*Eliza Brightwen* xiii–xiv). The first literary result of this intent was *Wild Nature Won by Kindness* (1890), an unqualified success, which made Brightwen one of the most popular natural history writers of her day. *Wild Nature* was followed by *More about Wild Nature* (1892) (see figure 50), *Inmates of My House and Garden* (1895), *Glimpses into Plant Life* (1897), *Rambles with Nature Students* (1899), and *Quiet Hours with Nature* (1903). During this entire period, Brightwen remained sequestered at Stanmore and carried on a wide correspondence about natural history, most of which came about through inquiries from her readers.

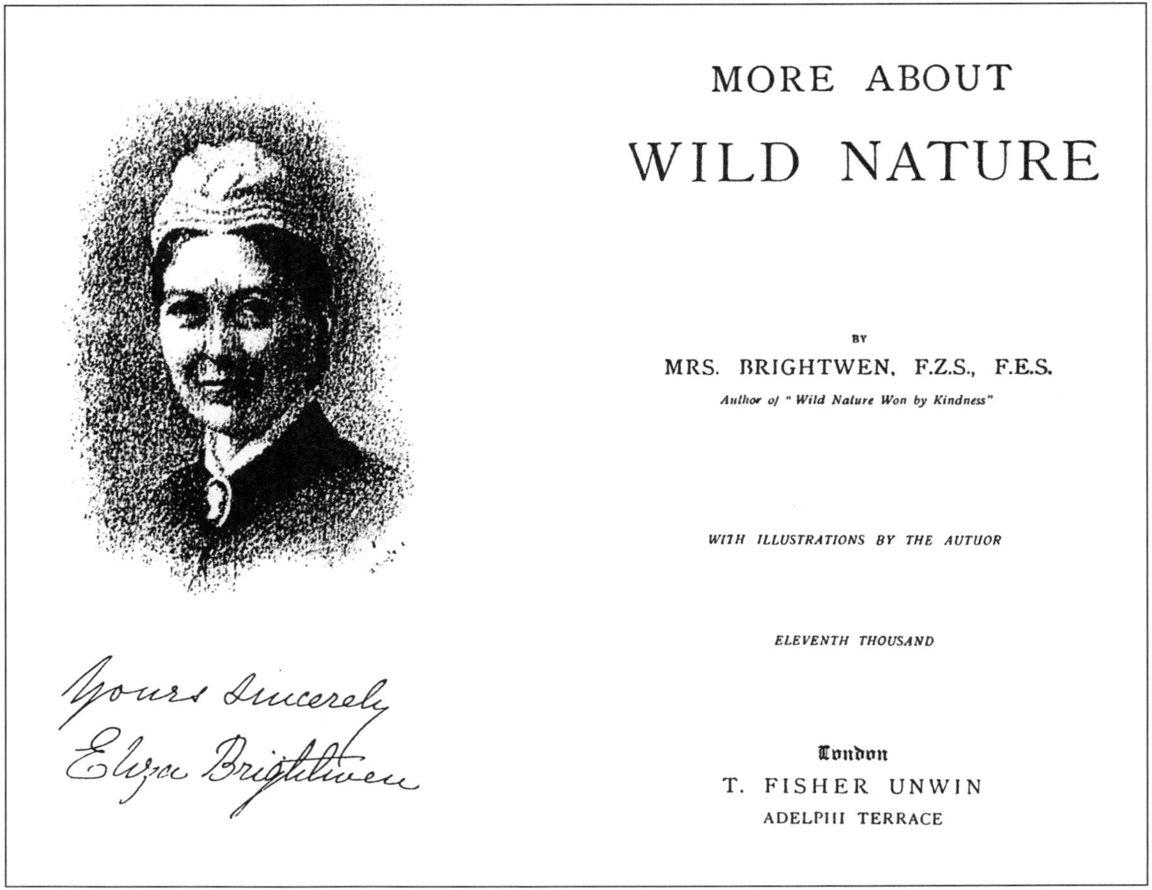

MORE ABOUT
WILD NATURE

BY

MRS. BRIGHTWEN. F.Z.S, F.E.S.

Author of "Wild Nature Won by Kindness"

WITH ILLUSTRATIONS BY THE AUTUOR

ELEVENTH THOUSAND

London

T. FISHER UNWIN

ADELPHI TERRACE

Figure 50. Title page (with portrait of Eliza Brightwen), *More about Wild Nature* (1892), by Eliza Brightwen.

Brightwen also believed in educating the public about animal preservation. She rescued animals, opposed falconry, wrote the pamphlets and essays deploring the use of feathers for the trimming of human clothing described in chapter 4, and lectured in local schools about bird trapping and the destruction of nestlings. Her concern for other species stemmed in part from her close observation of nature and in part from her evangelical religion. To her mind, creation was "all out of order for a time" (*Eliza Brightwen* 131) because of humanity's fall and, as a result, humans had inappropriate responses to animals.

Despite her popularity, Brightwen continued to keep herself to herself. Like Shore's, her essays were outgrowths of private journal entries and natural history observation. Since she rarely left her estate, her fame and success as a professional writer so late in life took her by surprise:

> When I put forth, with much diffidence and many apprehensions, the simple account of my adventures with my favourite animals and birds, I little dreamed of the kind reception which it was destined to meet with from the critics and from the general public. That several thousand copies of "Wild Nature Won By Kindness" would be sold within the first twelve months of publication was not within my most sanguine anticipations. (*More about Wild Nature* x)

Here, perhaps in an effort either to be modest or to single out her own success, Brightwen ignores or seems unaware of the immense interest in storied animals prepared for by the combined influences of natural history, high incidence of household pets, and travel narratives that engulfed her culture.

Alice Dew-Smith's personal story is very different from Brightwen's. Dew-Smith was a New Woman, a feminist and professional journalist. She contributed regularly to the column "The Wares of Autolycus" in the *Pall Mall Gazette*, where her animal stories were published before they were gathered together in popular books like *Confidences of an Amateur Gardener* (1897) and *Tom Tug and Others: Sketches in a Domestic Menagerie* (1898) (see figure 51). In Dew-Smith's highly polished stories, traditional views about the godhead are absent, not reinscribed for a later generation of post-Paleyites as they were by Gatty and Brightwen, and children are not the intended audience. Ignoring or defying the conventions set down by women naturalists earlier in the century, Dew-Smith talks to adult men and women, frequently about their differing perceptions of animal life and of each other. Nor does she look upon animal protection with conventional eyes. In this area more than any other, there are interesting contrasts between Dew-Smith and Brightwen. If Brightwen strongly supported the Royal Society for the Protection of Birds in its efforts to ban bird plumes in hats, she extended this support in her "wild animals" books. In *Inmates of My House and Garden*, she tells the story of a tiny willow-wren whose wings have been glued together by birdlime. She manages to unstick the wings

TOM TUG AND OTHERS

SKETCHES
IN A DOMESTIC MENAGERIE

A. M.,
BY
MRS. DEW-SMITH

AUTHOR OF 'CONFIDENCES OF AN AMATEUR GARDENER,'
'THE WHITE UMBRELLA,' ETC.

WITH ILLUSTRATIONS BY
ELINOR M. MONSELL

LONDON
SEELEY AND CO. LIMITED
38 GREAT RUSSELL STREET
1898

Figure 51. Title page, *Tom Tug and Others: Sketches in a Domestic Menagerie* (1898),
by Mrs. A. W. Dew-Smith.

and takes the bird home to recover. Realizing that this is a mother bird, she also brings along its nestlings, and she and the mother bird together nurture the young. When the mother does recover, Brightwen sets the whole family free and later remarks in *Inmates*, "Can any one conceive my having had her killed and stuffed, and then placed as a trimming on my bonnet! The thought of the willow-wren's mother-love ought to make such an idea abhorrent to any gentle-minded woman" (87).

Dew-Smith finds cruelty elsewhere—in the keeping of caged birds and in the confinement of any wild creature, as Brightwen was certainly likely to do in the process of taming them. Dew-Smith went so far as to suggest that caging was far worse than killing, and that included fox killing by hounds:

> A natural fear of death causes many people to regard the mere killing of an animal with undue horror. People who shudder at the thought of the fox's run for life and rapid death, torn to pieces by the hounds, will gaze unmoved at the same creature condemned to the horrors of perpetual confinement in a small cage in a menagerie. Apart from the naturalists, with whose distress at the destruction of small birds every one sympathizes, there are hundreds of people whose feelings are outraged by the sight of a hat shop decorated with trophies of slaughtered wild birds, and who will experience no distress of mind on seeing a bird shop full of living wild birds beating their wings against the bars of cages so small that they can barely turn round. The point of view of such people seems unreasonable. The fox in being killed, the birds in being shot do but anticipate a little their inevitable fate. (*Tom Tug and Others* 64–65)

In Dew-Smith's writing, this issue resurfaces again and again: there is more cruelty in disabling or attempting to "tame" animal lives than in ending them altogether.

Dew-Smith was also radical among late-Victorian animal writers in her belief that there was no hierarchy of animal species. Dogs were not better than spiders or flies, nor plants lesser living things than animals. When Dew-Smith watched a pitcher plant and wondered whether it was getting enough insect life to sustain its need for protein, she found it difficult to decide whether she was on the side of the plant or the insects it needed to digest. Musing on this dilemma, she observed that "in Nature one's sympathies are continually being divided. One is sorry for the hungry spider, who must go without his dinner for want of a fly, and extremely sorry for the fly whose lot it is to provide the much-wished-for-meal" (*Confidences of an Amateur Gardener* 59). In this unconventional attitude, Dew-Smith also differed considerably from Brightwen. Like Gatty, Brightwen wanted to "lift the veil which divides us from the kingdom of fur and feathers, and so increase the circle of students and lovers of pet creatures" (*More about Wild Nature* xi). All of her "little series of narratives" was geared toward this (x). But Brightwen nevertheless kept part of the veil in place as she judged animals according to their usefulness or tamability. Brightwen believed that the animal world existed partly to provide pleasure to people, and her stewardship reflected this attitude. Until human beings "try to write down what we have been taking in with our senses," she suggested, "we shall not be aware of how much we have missed of the real beauty of the delicate things that are given for our enjoyment" (131). Brightwen never doubted that aesthetic enjoyment of animals was a human prerogative.

Such enjoyment was Brightwen's right because her pets—the wildlings that she tamed, in particular—belonged to her. Of two wild bats she would say, "a pair of noctules were seen flying in the park, so I live in hopes that some day a young one will come into my possession"; of wild butterflies, "my tame butterflies were delightful pets, coming on my finger for their daily drop of honey, and when I took them into the garden they would enjoy short flights to and fro, and yet they were quite willing to come on my hand and return to their cage" (*More about Wild Nature* 44, 239). Brightwen was yet another gatherer, a collector. She not only kept a varied menagerie of wild things from a mongoose to lemurs to the butterflies but also told people how to build menageries for themselves and how to appreciate museums and zoos. She had no compunction about giving her lemurs to the London Zoo when she discovered that they were ultimately untamable and then recommending that her readers go to the zoo to see the very pets she had described in what she called "word pictures" (133). "Visitors to the monkey-house can identify them from the description I have here given" (*Inmates* 25), she suggested.

These opposed attitudes of Dew-Smith and Brightwen fostered divergent emphases in their respective styles of animal biography. Dew-Smith seems not to have kept exotics. The menagerie she writes of in *Tom Tug and Others* consists of cats and dogs, like Tom Tug, and observable household insects, like spiders and flies. When she does venture into the world of exotics, as when describing Whishton, a Mexican marmot, she writes of someone else's pet, not her own.

Comparing Dew-Smith's chronicle of Whishton the marmot with Brightwen's Mungo the mongoose points up these differences in their writing. Both women use anecdotes within the biographies: Mungo gets lost, is found in a spring trap, loses a leg, and eventually learns to get by with three; Whishton attempts to hibernate in a stored rug in his mistress's garret and is repeatedly removed to a straw box downstairs. But each essay offers something more than anecdote; we get a stronger sense of the animals' lives—from the writer's discovery of them up through the writer's conclusions about them. These are not just stories offering animal curiosities or subjects for sentimentality. The essays are crafted to show something about the animal's raison d'être, its needs, and its personality.

Mungo, Brightwen tells us, fascinated her because "a wild creature rendered perfectly tame by unvarying kind treatment gives one an excellent opportunity of observing the real nature of the animal" (*Inmates* 47). We see Mungo in a number of instances—recovering from his injury, hobbling around ignoring it, and baying at the lemurs Brightwen kept in her conservatory. But according to Brightwen, Mungo's real nature was "selfish, his one idea is to enjoy perfect liberty and have his own way in everything" (47). Brightwen goes on to point out that after four years of petting and cuddling, Mungo remained indifferent to her except as a source of warmth and food. Still, she would forgive Mungo for being intractable and not judge all of his kind by his behavior:

> Possibly Mungo may be a selfish specimen of his race, and there may exist brilliant exceptions abounding in affection and other noble qualities. I can only describe him as he is, and, judging by his small cranium and its pecu-liarly flattened formation, I should imagine he is formed to be, not a pat-tern of all the virtues, but a creature of one idea, and that—snake-killing! To be proficient in that art all the characteristics I have noted in this animal are specially needed, such as lynx-like watchfulness, undaunted courage in fight, persistent curiosity and determination to care for himself under all circumstances. (49)

So Mungo passes the test in terms of adaptation, and his natural history is com-plete. This leaves only Brightwen's Christian and moral conclusion to be dealt with: "We must therefore wink at his failure in moral goodness, and admire the way in which he carries out the purpose for which he was made. He worthily adorns his own special niche in Creation" (49). Mungo has been chronicled ac-cording to the omniscient Eliza Brightwen's values. He is not much of a pet, but his kind has its place in the web of nature, according to God's intent. If Mun-go's is a Christian biography, Mungo certainly fails as a subject for hagiography.

Alice Dew-Smith approaches the story of Whishton from a radically differ-ent point of view, one which enables her animal biography to verge on autobi-ography. Attempting to find her way into animal intelligence, she imagines what it must feel like to be a Mexican marmot kept in chilly England. Whish-ton seeks warmth whenever possible—on the hearth, from which he is inces-santly removed until he gives up, and in the rolled-up carpet in the garret. He is, Dew-Smith reveals, forced "like other victims of domesticity . . . to adapt himself to circumstances—not of his own choosing" (*Tom Tug and Others* 156). Via ventriloquist Dew-Smith, Whishton then turns the tables on human be-ings, wondering, "'Why can't people live happily in the woods, where they can do as they like, go to bed when they like, get up when they like, and eat what and when they like; instead of in a stupid, stuffy house, where you can't go any-where without waiting to have a door opened, and where you can't even dig a hole without having your ears boxed?'" (154–55). The worst ignominy that Whishton has to endure in Dew-Smith's account is to be transported to a cat-and-rabbit show full of other caged animals, where he tears madly at his own cage. Having already transcribed part of Whishton's self-told story, Dew-

Smith thinks about this part of his life as well: "If Whishton could write his autobiography, what he endured at that show would, I am sure, fill many pages" (159). But, of course, it does not fill those pages because he cannot write them, a fact implied throughout Dew-Smith's fictionalized essay. We can speak for animals, but there is no guarantee that we can ever get their story right. The reader's last view of Whishton is Dew-Smith's, as she watches him silently look longingly out of the window at the garden and trees. His storyteller says sadly: "I could not help feeling that he was feverishly making plans to escape from domesticity and be a little wild marmot once again" (160).

Dew-Smith and Brightwen typify two poles in the range of fin-de-siècle women writers: the new-style feminist and the woman who, representing "timeless" Christian values, writes what amounts to a turn-of-the-century variation on the narrative of natural theology. But in writing their animal biographies, Dew-Smith and Brightwen were both working in a genre of familiar, life-at-home pieces that lay somewhere between the polemical essays of Lemon, Phillips, and Cobbe and the polemical fictions of Julia Horatia Ewing and E. Nesbit. When her sympathetic, anecdotal style led Dew-Smith momentarily into a kind of ventriloquism, however, it took her into the province of yet another kind of writing—close to the borderlands of the fable of talking plants and animals. Dew-Smith put a different spin on this kind of writing; her animals do not speak to say pleasant and humanlike things. In fact, they talk back. With notable exceptions—think of the beasts in Lewis Carroll's *Alice* books— most Victorian talking animals served quite different functions, giving free reign either to the sentimental and nostalgic or to the moral.

As Harriet Ritvo has shown, sentimental attachment to pets and to animals in general became increasingly strong in the first half of the nineteenth century, when "nature ceased to be a constant antagonist" (3). A genre as old as Aesop, the beast fable therefore took on new and growing interest in Victorian Britain, allied to the debate on animal intelligence. From midcentury on, Victorians involved themselves in defining whether or not animals reasoned and, if so, just how. Was there a hierarchy of animal intelligence? Did plants as well as animals know or feel? Such questions occupied scientists as well as the general public. As people realized that they, too, were animals, they wanted to know exactly how they differed from the other kinds (Ritvo introduction; Turner ch. 4). The debate relating to these issues was waged in the pages of journals such as the *Zoologist* and the *Westminster Review* and extended to full-length studies like George Romanes's *Animal Intelligence* (1884). In this exhaustive book, Romanes moves up the scale of being from protozoa to the apes and evaluates each species by gathering and assessing observations and anecdotes from multiple observers.

To look at Romanes's disclaimers in view of work like Brightwen's or Dew-Smith's reveals something of the deep and long-standing kinship between Victorian science and Victorian storytelling (Beer, *Darwin's Plots;* Ritvo;

Levine, *Darwin and the Novelists*). Romanes struggles hard to divorce these two enterprises. In *Animal Intelligence*, he elects not to be seen as a popularizer of any sort and protests rather too strongly that his work is of another order:

> Were the purpose of this work that of accumulating anecdotes of animal intelligence, this would be the place to let loose a flood of facts, which might all be well attested, relating to the high intelligence of dogs. But as my aim is rather that of suppressing anecdotes, except in so far as facts are required to prove the presence in animals of the sundry psychological difficulties which I believe the different classes to present, I shall here, as elsewhere, follow the method of not multiplying anecdotes further than seems necessary fully to demonstrate the highest level of intelligence to which the animal under consideration can certainly be said to attain. (447–48)

This is a roundabout way of saying: there is a flood of animal anecdotes in my book; however, they are there not to entertain you but for the sake of science. All the same, whatever his intents and disclaimers, in Romanes's book anecdotes abound.

Not just Victorian animals but Victorian plants too had their intelligence measured. If Romanes attempted to segregate his work from that of people like Brightwen, J. E. Taylor (1837–1895) instead chose an opposite course and alluded to writers like Gatty when he wrote his preface to *The Sagacity and Morality of Plants*. Stressing similarities, not differences, between science and literature, Taylor's book is full of parables because, he points out, botany "is now a science of *Living Things*, and not of mechanical automata" (v). For Taylor, intuition had begun to count in reading otherness. "Sagacity" such as Taylor's plants were demonstrating was, as Ritvo has shown, a term often applied to lower animals, one which "indicated not the ability to manipulate mechanical contraptions or solve logical problems, but a more diffuse kind of mental power" (37). In Taylor's book, it would be demonstrated through a catalog of wonders like the cooperation of plants in perfume production, the dangers of parasitism from fungi, and the adaptations of the pitcher plant and other insect-"eaters."

In Victorian England, the idea of sagacity sometimes led to absurdities when it was applied to plants. It was easily spoofed, as when Lewis Carroll took on Tennyson for his conversational flowers in *Maud* (*Poems of Tennyson* 1076) with his own talking flowers in *Through the Looking Glass and What Alice Found There* (138–43). But plants had been talking in texts before either *Maud* or the Alice books were conceived, and by the late nineteenth century, the sacredness of trees and their closeness to vegetation rites and numinous human beliefs were being explored both by anthropologists like Sir James Frazer (1854–1941) in his *Golden Bough* and by women like Mrs. J. H. Philpot in her *Sacred Tree*, a compendium of information on tree worship. Late-Victorian people were not just crazed by plants; they felt a real kinship with them. What was said of Frances Hope (d.1880), author of *Notes and Thoughts on Gardens and Woodlands* (1881), was true of many: "Her plants were her pets" (from a "Memorial Extract" in the *Gardener's Chronicle* 8 May 1880, qtd. in *Notes and Thoughts* xi). Why, then, might plants not speak to people in their own special plant language? Certainly, an entire second language for human beings had been devised around them: a well-known language of flowers, which enabled people to send coded messages of love, or hate, or sorrow via floral gifts and allusions.[1]

And so it came about that in Victorian books, plants were permitted to deliver the spoken word just as animals were. Victorian science and Victorian anthropology would enhance this ventriloquism, and women would become as proficient at speaking for plants as they were in crusading for their preservation. Ancient literary conventions dating back to Aesop were thus given new life in the nineteenth century, and women of a later day, like Alice Dew-Smith, did not need to justify giving voice to other species.

Reenter Beatrix Potter, Victrix

Beatrix Potter, who had failed to win scientific recognition for her groundbreaking study of fungi, would find she had plenty of room to succeed brilliantly when it came to talking animals. Her work is, of course, the apotheosis of the animal story, partly because she was especially well equipped for this enterprise. As a gatherer of specimens and an amateur naturalist, she kept and observed a menagerie of animals that included dormice, a hedgehog, and Benjamin Bouncer, the model for her rabbits in her now renowned little books. From an early age, she knew her animals as she would come to know her fungi—from a scientific perspective. As a youngster, she wrote to her brother suggesting that since the long-eared bats they kept as pets were not eating, they might be set free. With apparently few compunctions—since it could no longer survive in the wild—she also seems to have acceded to his return request that the weakest among them be killed and stuffed by Beatrix;[2] it would then serve for their scientific study and illustration. Later, before tackling her own stories, Potter also illustrated other people's work and produced greeting cards full of animals. Like Lewis Carroll, she wrote entertaining letters to children in which she made up animal stories. And then she put it all together. In her work, scientific knowledge and fablelike stories converge, and animal biographies and talking animals emerge in one seamless art form.

1. For an excellent recent study of this fascinating and complex subject, see Beverly Seaton's *The Language of Flowers: A History.*

2. This anecdote is discussed in *Beatrix Potter, 1866–1943: The Artist and Her World,* ed. Judy Taylor, Joyce Irene Whalley, Anne Stevenson Hobbs, and Elizabeth M. Battrick, 42.

Having studied animals at close quarters, Potter tried never to moralize or misrepresent animal behavior. Nor did she fully humanize the animals in her tales. They live in a never-never land somewhere between people and real-life animals, crisscrossing a set of fluid borders with ease. If they talk, they also act out their animal natures. For a rabbit like Peter or Benjamin Bunny, to steal a carrot is to need a carrot to live. But when a rabbit is wearing a waistcoat and acting like a boy, it can be condemned for stealing what belongs to another's sweated labor. Animals are like people because people are animals, but animals are never fully people in Potter's books. When they are the most dangerous or saddest is not when they are most fully represented in their animal nature but when they are the most uncomfortably anthropomorphized. Like Potter's long-eared bats, they need to return to their animal natures. Looking carefully at one of the most enigmatic of the Potter characters—Mrs. Tiggy-Winkle, the hedgehog-washerwoman, in whose character the scientific and the literary, the animal and the human converge, will illustrate this point further.

Potter kept pet hedgehogs for a number of years and, true to her own nature, studied them sedulously. In an unpublished essay on the hedgehog,[3] Potter suggests both the inattention usually given to hedgehogs and the care with which she observed her pet animal:

> Although sufficiently common animals, hedgehogs appear to have been very little studied by naturalists, judging from the letters that occasionally appear in the *Field*. The animal moults about $\frac{1}{3}$ of its spines every spring, the spines being moulted after the rest of the fur. It will be noticed that the fur and spines pass from one form to the other—stiff bristly hairs gradating into thin spines at the borders of the prickly jacket. The spines are attached to the skin by a slight knob. I believe that they fall out, I do not think that they are pushed out by a new spine growing in the old socket. This is a point of interest because new spines grown at odd times to replace broken ones, are I think grown from the old root; and they are white and soft like those of a young hedgehog. ("Hedgehogs")

In this essay, Potter goes on carefully to describe, in even more minute detail, the spines, which obviously fascinated her, pointing out where they erupt on the "prickle jacket." She then concludes her brief essay with a second set of observations, this time about the painstaking way the animal goes into and out of its cataleptic states, observing that, contrary to common belief, this action is not entirely determined by temperature.

Potter seems to have needed to convey what she had learned about hedgehogs to a wider audience. In 1896, she began to think about writing a hedgehog story

---

3. For my information about this essay (Ms. BP 1306 Victoria and Albert Museum Library, London), I am deeply indebted to Anne Stevenson Hobbs, who led me to the right archive and allowed me to read it in the Victoria and Albert Museum Library.

and, in 1901, began to draft *The Tale of Mrs. Tiggy-Winkle,* continuing to use her pet hedgehog, Mrs. Tiggy, as a model. A number of letters follow, as she reflects on turning knowledge into story, animal into person. To Norman Warne, her dear friend and publisher, she wrote that "Mrs. Tiggy as a model is comical; so long as she can go to sleep on my knee she is delighted, but if she is propped up on end for half an hour, she first begins to yawn pathetically, and then she *does* bite! Never the less she is a dear person" (12 November 1904, *Letters* 107). Although the biting hedgehog was discarded as a live model in favor of a stuffed effigy, Potter's interest in the story seems to have fueled more interest in the pet and more letters as well. In 1905, Potter wrote to young Winifred Warne about one of Mrs. Tiggy's periods of hibernation, showing the snoring animal in a bed asleep, with a nightcap over her head (Taylor et al. 135–37). Writing to children seems to have helped clarify portions of her stories for Potter. Her Peter Rabbit was, of course, conceived in a letter to a child.

The Tale of Mrs. Tiggy-Winkle was published in 1905, a compendium of knowledge about hedgehogs; love of the scenery around Newlands near Derwentwater, which provided the site for the tale; and respect for a real-life washerwoman, Kitty McDonald. After a visit to Tayside in the 1890s, Potter described Kitty as "a comical, round little woman, as brown as a berry and wear[ing] a multitude of petticoats and a white mutch" (Taylor et al. 121). If it is a story more about a child's losing her handkerchiefs than about a hedgehog, it is the hedgehog that most of us will remember. Mrs. Tiggy-Winkle does not appear until midway through the story and remains something of a mystery until its end. Lucie, the little girl, is looking for her handkerchiefs and discovers Mrs. Tiggy-Winkle hard at work laundering animal waistcoats and lost handkerchiefs alike. The hedgehog says little and speaks only when spoken to, industriously ironing away as Lucie chats to her. Instead of garrulity in her companion, Lucie finds a "little black nose" that goes "sniffle, sniffle, snuffle" and eyes that "twinkle, twinkle" (*Complete Tales* 92). Mrs. Tiggy-Winkle signals animalness but is carefully dressed in the kind of clothes Kitty McDonald must have worn. Still, she is strange, for "underneath her cap—where Lucie had yellow curls—that person had PRICKLES!" (see figure 52). Potter lets Mrs. Tiggy-Winkle's animal nature shine through in characteristic behaviors and adaptations that cannot be altered by dressing her up. The nose, the eyes, the spines will out, regardless. In the end, the fully garbed Mrs. Tiggy-Winkle vanishes from Lucie's eyes, and a real hedgehog, all spines exposed, appears and is seen running up the hill. Potter leaves us guessing—Was this all a dream? Did Lucie imagine the encounter? Her narrator cautions us—maybe not; she herself is "very well acquainted with dear Mrs. Tiggy-Winkle" (100).

Just what is Potter doing here? Is Lucie projecting the weight of civilization—dressing up to cover one's self, talking, ironing—onto the little creature? Or why is Potter doing so, if her Lucie is not? Part of the answer seems to lie in

Figure 52.   Beatrix Potter, *My Name Is Mrs. Tiggy-Winkle,* from *The Tale of Mrs. Tiggy-Winkle,* by Beatrix Potter. © Frederick Warne & Co., 1905, 1987. Reproduced by kind permission of Frederick Warne & Co.

clothes. As Carole Scott has argued, writers like Potter used clothing to convey different messages about the worlds of animals and people. Potter's animals like to doff their clothes—Benjamin Bunny his clogs, Tom Kitten his jacket—and become real animals in the course of her stories. Scott sees this as a message to children about themselves: "Clothes and the social self they represent, are imprisoning; they mar and hide the real, natural self, rather than provide a means to express it" (79). But it sends another message as well: our imaginations may dress animals up to suit our needs—as in finding one's lost handkerchiefs—but animals will continue to dress us down for these dreams.

The final image of the hedgehog is not one of a stuffed animal set up before Potter's drawing board, nor of a washerwoman-hedgehog, but of a hedge-

Figure 53.   Beatrix Potter, *Mrs. Tiggy-Winkle without Her Clothes,* from *The Tale of Mrs. Tiggy-Winkle,* by Beatrix Potter. © Frederick Warne & Co., 1905, 1987. Reproduced by kind permisson of Frederick Warne & Co.

hog running wild and free, unencumbered by domestication of any sort. Here, Potter stresses not the similarity between animals and humans but their difference. The prickles can be covered up for only so long before a real hedgehog will emerge to bite—as did Potter's modeling pet—or run away, as in this story. If in *The Tale of Mrs. Tiggy-Winkle,* Potter gives human voice to animals, in the end, her images tell a different story from her words. If the narrator claims to know Mrs. Tiggy-Winkle, the illustrator offers the last image—a brown, fully spined hedgehog running fast, through fields of green. Potter's hedgehog seems to escape the page to live out its own story (see figure 53).

9

Kindred Natures: The Earthlings

Edwardians, writing in the afterglow of the nineteenth century, realized interconnections between women and nature different from those represented by John Ruskin's Sphinx or Holman Hunt's *Awakening Conscience*. Both womanhood and nature had been reappraised. Born of a cultural need to essentialize women, revised in the light of Darwin's theory of natural selection, and realigned both by radical women like Frances Swiney and eugenicists like Frances Galton and Mary Scharlieb, Victorian myths of women and nature had undergone a thorough remodeling by the early twentieth century. To more modern eyes, the Victorian woman was not really wild, nor was nature simply something "out there," to be run toward to escape the possessive sexuality of the Victorian parlor. By the time of the Edwardians, women and men alike needed not to further mythologize but, rather, to *de*mystify their sexual lives, as Marie Stopes and Havelock Ellis kept repeating in their passionately committed, radically different books. Indeed, the earth itself had been rethought and rewritten. To many, it seemed more fragile, less overwhelming, more in need of appreciation and stewardship than mastery and control. If anything, this new view made the lure of nature and the earth as literary subjects more appealing than ever. I would like to probe more deeply into just a few of the changes in the apprehension of womanhood and nature that took place between the beginning of the nineteenth century and the Great War by reading these changes through the scrim of three Edwardian fictions—*Green Mansions*, by W. H. Hudson (1841–1922); *The Secret Garden*, by Frances Hodgson Burnett (1849–1924); and *Gone to Earth*, by Mary Webb (1881–1927).

In all three fictional works, myths of woman and nature that I discussed in chapter 1 were discarded or radically reenvisioned. By the late nineteenth century, the cultural flexibility of myths had, of course, been fully acknowledged. Mythographers such as E. B. Tylor, James Frazer, and Jane Harrison (1850–1928) had studied myth sufficiently to theorize that myths were mutable, inflected by particularities of time and locale. It was in line with this kind of thinking that Oxonian A. H. Sayce (1845–1933) supposed that "myth takes its coloring from each generation that repeats it, and clothes it with the passions and the interests and the knowledge of the men in whose mouths it lives and grows" (*Principles of Comparative Philology* 320n.). Sayce's suppositions are especially true of nature myths, which, as Northrop Frye has shown (*A Study of English Romanticism* ch. 1), have had an especially high rate of mortality in the West. Throughout time, such myths have nevertheless been central to civilizations of all sorts; they enable the people of a certain culture or time frame to apprehend the external world as animated by a unifying power and to explain the nonhuman world in accordance both with this power and with human nature. Hence the potent mythic qualities of the book of Genesis and of Gerard Manley Hopkins's latter-day world "charged" with "the grandeur of God" ("God's Grandeur" 1); hence Wordsworth's desire to be a "Pagan suckled in a creed outworn," seeing Proteus rising from the ocean ("The World Is Too Much with Us" 3: 18); or the Navajos' creation myth, where humans emerge from underground darkness in consort with the animals which will live near them in the light world of the present day.

Reenter the Wild Woman, Spiritualized and Cremated

Abel, W. H. Hudson's hero in *Green Mansions* (1904), tries to envision something equally satisfying by investing Rima, a South American jungle girl, with supernatural powers that extend to her communion with the animals around her. In recounting his story, Hudson's narrator therefore spins a tale of enchantment. Desiring more knowledge of "the world of nature and the spirit" (4), he has asked Abel to recall his time in the rain forests of South America, where Abel went to collect information about the natives and "the vegetable products" of the continent (10). Abel reveals that he fell in with a tribe of natives who told him of the strange Daughter of the Didi, who inhabited the forest near their village. The natives were fearful of her, believing her to be the supernatural protectress of the forest. Since to destroy her animals could be a source of danger to them if she became angered, they outlawed hunting in her territory. Himself undaunted, Abel enters this forest preserve and listens to a strange, unearthly warbling, not quite human, not quite birdlike. It is the voice of the Daughter of the Didi—Rima, as she is called by her grandfather. In the thick jungle, Abel slowly begins to discern her concealed form, dressed in a fabric woven from spiderwebs. He learns, too, to know her grandfather, who is not a Didi at all but a hermitic old man, and slowly Abel begins to communicate with Rima, never himself learning to warble but capable of teaching her more Spanish than she already knows, trying to tame his wild woman. *Green Mansions: A Romance of the Tropical Forest* is not just another romance with nature; it also holds out the promise of Abel's romance and possible sexual union with Rima. Eventually, Abel makes a pilgrimage with the grandfather and Rima to find her place of origin. Disappointed in what she finds, Rima flees back to her forest preserve, tripping quickly through wild areas that Abel and the grandfather find more difficult to traverse. Meanwhile, believing that she has left for good, the native tribe begins to hunt in Rima's forest; when they discover that she has returned, they are loathe to give up their reclaimed hunting rights. Instead, they trap her in the top of a huge tree and burn it until Rima plunges to her death. Abel returns to discover this tragedy and mourns her for the rest of his life.

The story of Abel's inner life is more complicated than this summary of the story's action might suggest. For Abel has invested Rima not just with his human hopes for companionship but with his larger spiritual hopes, his "strange sense and apprehension of a secret innocence and spirituality in nature—a prescience of some bourn, incalculably distant perhaps, to which we are all moving; of a time when the heavenly rain shall have washed us clean from all spot and blemish" (21). Through Abel, then, Hudson has invested Rima with both romantic and Victorian stereotypes about nature and woman. Grafting his romantic millennialist hopes onto the stories of the natives, Abel transforms this nature woman into something supernatural. However, having invested Rima with powers that exceed her own knowledge of the jungle, Abel ultimately is forced after Rima's demise to discover in himself a world-weary, disbelieving son of the turn of the century, no longer willing to thank "the Author of my being for the gift of that wild forest, those green mansions where I had found so great a happiness!" (61).

Certainly, if there is fault behind all of this loss, it lies with Abel himself. From the beginning, Abel does not just observe Rima, as he does the other creatures of the forest, but in his mind forces her to conform to a preordained image which she defies in her day-to-day being. For Abel, Rima becomes the perfect woman, a projected figure, natural yet intelligent—a union of the Victorian wild woman and the gentler Victorian image of woman as protectress of nature and man. But, alas for Abel, Hudson has devised a Rima who is also an independent being totally suited to her environment and requiring no Abel for her survival.

An ornithologist and arch-observer of South American nature, Hudson rendered Rima's jungle world, replete with spiders and snakes and monkeys, with utter vividness. Guided by her own deep knowledge of this diverse world and by her own mental construction of her dead mother—whom she invests with the powers of a Mother Nature—Rima lives self-sufficiently in her forest. Misunderstanding this self-sufficiency, Abel works to make Rima conform with his pre-Darwinian apprehension of nature and womanhood. "Listen, Rima," he whispers, "you are like all beautiful things in the wood—flower, and bird, and butterfly, and green leaf, and frond, and little silky-haired monkey up high in the trees. When I look at you I see them all—all and more, a thousand times, for I see Rima herself" (120–21). There is none of Haggard's female atavism here; Abel imagines sensitive, vegetarian, animal-loving Rima as would a man determined to find both his god and his ideal woman in the world of nature.

"Listening to her I was no longer the enlightened, the creedless man. She herself was so near to the supernatural that it seemed brought near me" (178). Self-converted, Abel is lost in desire for this creature of his own mind—deeply attracted to his woman for all seasons.

Rima's death therefore leaves Abel both sexually and spiritually bankrupt, a sterile colonial marooned in his own antiquated romantic mythmaking, an adventurer who could not, in this turn on the adventure-story plot, rescue his beloved. Having believed in a spirit inherent in nature, Abel lives for a time within the shell of his beliefs, not killing a large hermit spider for the sake of the memory of Rima but wanting badly "to strike off one of his legs, which would not be missed much, as they were many" (288). Like Emily Brontë's Heathcliff in *Wuthering Heights*, he feels like a cruel "I, no longer I, in a universe where *she* was not, and God was not" (297). But, eventually, with the idea of Rima's natural supernaturalism gone, Abel's earthly paradise becomes "an earthly inferno" (309). When he leaves the site of her fiery death, Abel claims to have escaped this mental prison; he gathers Rima's ashes and is followed by a large snake. Is it a minion of Rima's? Or is it Rima's incarnation? Her spirit? Neither Abel nor Hudson tells us, but Hudson never shows us a healed hero, only a man broken by loss. With his spirit guide missing, Abel lives on only in the hope that Rima has forgiven him for her death, a death he believes he has caused through his curiosity and intervention in her life. For him, Rima has now become a new, more typically Victorian symbol, another route to salvation, preaching a gospel not of kindness to the earth's creatures but of self-forgiveness:

> In those darkest days in the forest I had her as a visitor—a Rima of the mind, whose words when she spoke reflected my despair. Yet even then I was not entirely without hope. . . . she also said that if I forgive myself Heaven would say no word, nor would she. (314)

Here, as in most of this novel, Hudson is not representing Abel's as a course to emulate. Hudson's protagonist embraces myths and stereotypes about woman and nature, and then Hudson uncovers him, to reveal Abel as an unenviable last romantic. Abel remains unredeemable except by Rima, his forever absent spiritual deliverer. In *Green Mansions*, mythologies of womanhood and nature both become dead ends. Rima is killed by them and—except in some small courtesies extended toward spiders—so is Abel, at least as a moral being. By the end of W. H. Hudson's "romance," any preconceptions Hudson's reader might have had about female nature as dangerous wild-woman nature are incinerated along with Rima, but so too are ideas of woman as redemptive or of nature as a female principle that can serve as spirit guide for the male soul. Hudson's Abel has been wholly disabled by this latter philosophy. The heart of darkness in Hudson's novel stems neither from the jungle, nor from Rima, but from the unrealistic expectations of a wild woman that Hudson's hero has set for himself. In the end, Abel's own heart encases an untenanted hollow at its very core.

Down-to-Earth Mary

Frances Hodgson Burnett's *Secret Garden* (1911) offers its readers something quite different from Abel's male-driven tale of loss and disillusionment. *The Secret Garden* is a conversion story for children, a kind of feminized *Christmas Carol.* Sour Mary, "quite contrary," according to her own cousins and just about everyone else who meets her in the early pages of her story, has been left alone in the world after the deaths of her parents in a typhoid epidemic in India. Transported to England, she is wasting away from lack of contact with human love and, it turns out, with nature as well. But she is lucky in the housemaid who looks after her, who in turn is lucky in her mother—another kind of Mother Nature figure—and her brother—a nature boy who talks to the animals. In this familiar story, Mary discovers an overgrown garden on her uncle's property, and with the nature boy, Dickon, helps it again come alive with flowers. In the bargain, she saves her bedridden cousin Colin, who is also converted to the garden and what he calls its "magic." These two ignored and petulant children ultimately turn into hopeful and caring people. Like Scrooge, Mary becomes good by helping others—and finds a kind of religion in the bargain.

But unlike the Dickens story, the story of Dickon and Mary and Colin is mediated through kindred nature, not through the ghosts of former selves, and through a very young woman, not a man's aging conscience. Once she gets digging in the ground and finds that she likes "to smell the earth when it's turned up" (106), Mary becomes more and more down-to-earth in every sense of the word. Bursting with desire for a garden of her own, she musters the courage to issue to her physically and emotionally remote uncle the one and only request she will make of him: "Might I have a bit of earth?" (118). Request granted, her conversion begins. Mary's will not be a "'gardener's garden,'" as the narrator is quick to say, but a "wilderness of growing things" (165). As in the borderlands of a Gertrude Jekyll garden, where the cultivated grew out into the wild with a natural ease, this garden is ready to go wild at any moment. It is the barely tamable power of nature that rules here at all times, and the young gardener needs fully to respect and work with this energy, to chart its magic. This, of course, is one of the lessons of Dickon, who speaks to foxes and crows and can coax wild things from the ground as well as from the moors.

If Dickon is the nature boy in this story, Mary is the nature girl, learning and revealing the language of living things, both literally and symbolically. She begins her English life out-of-doors by listening to a robin; after this initial contact, Mary takes time to observe how just how Dickon speaks with the birds:

Dickon has become like them—round-eyed, and blue-eyed from looking sky-ward—and Mary too learns their language. She soon comes to kiss the flowers, she loves them so much, but it takes her awhile to believe that human beings are equally worthy of love (157). Imperious and standoffish in the beginning, Mary nevertheless comes to mellow even toward people. No longer does she order them around as does Colin. Instead, she learns the Yorkshire dialect and uses it freely when talking with others who use it, like Dickon and gardener, Ben Weatherstaff. Unlike Abel, Mary listens to earthlings rather than asking them to speak her language. In short, Mary goes native, feeling in touch with roots of the earth and the roots of the people of the place she has come to inhabit. Her racism and classism, evident in the early parts of the book where she treats servants with hauteur and remarks that the dark-skinned Indian people waited on her hand and foot, vanish as she becomes preoccupied with a world outside the self—the transforming world of the garden. Mary is the instrument of healing—of the earth and of the domestic world of Misselthwaite Manor. Her female agency allows for an appropriate taming of the wildness that the garden has become. She achieves the difficult compromise between post-Darwinian fear of the wild and social Darwinist domination of the earth.

Mary differs from Dickon in the uses to which she puts her new knowledge. Like so many of the women in this book, Mary becomes a storytelling educator, reviewing the story of nature for others. She does not remain out-of-doors as Dickon does but returns inside to convert Colin after she has learned to speak nature's language. If Colin's father has wished that his son were not on earth at all (161), down-to-earth Mary wishes him closer to earth. Mary has grown like the garden; by the last third of the book, where the conversion of Colin becomes prominent, Mary has become "un-hysterical and natural" (190). She has matured before Colin begins to grow and is ready to reveal the healing-garden story to him, whetting his appetite for life as she whets his appetite for the garden. In control of a difficult situation, like Scheherazade she withholds her story. When Colin becomes petulant, she gives him an incentive to alter his behavior by refusing to tell him anything more about the garden, its inhabitants, and Dickon until he becomes more civil—as though she were controlling a child much younger than herself. The withheld storytelling does the trick; Colin improves his disposition and then improves physically when finally exposed to the real, not just the fictional, garden.

Mary is a fine teacher. Once converted, Mary's pupil Colin is enabled to take nature's story in an entirely different direction from hers. I do not agree with Heather Murray's assessment that Mary's presence "shrinks" in the last part of the story as Colin's "grows" (39). On the contrary, Mary's role waxes in the natural course of her own development from spoiled child to sensible, sensitive young woman. Through understanding the garden, she has gained enough selfhood to allow another to grow freely. Burnett seems to be saying that working-class Dickon can live the garden's influence one way, literate female Mary another, and educated, upper-class male Colin a third way.

Colin, like so many of the Victorian males we saw in chapter 1 of this study, and like Abel, too, needs to read science and religion into the natural. First of all, Colin is quick to realize his kinship with nature because he already knows that he too is animal. He expects to like Dickon because "he's a sort of animal-charmer and I am a boy animal" (154). Colin thus begins as a post-Darwinian and develops a natural historian's powers of close observation. Watching and waiting, Colin learns the "ants' ways, beetles' ways, bees' ways, frogs' ways, birds' ways, plants' ways," and so on (237). In a phraseology reminiscent of Arabella Buckley's *Fairy-land of Science,* Colin also looks for the principles underlying these "ways." "I am sure," he says, "that there is Magic in everything, only we have not sense enough to get hold of it and make it do things for us—like electricity and horses and steam" (239). But Colin vows to get this "sense" through science, for "scientific people are always curious, and I am going to be scientific," says Colin. "I keep saying to myself, 'What is it? What is it?' It's something. It can't be nothing! I don't know its name, so I call it Magic" (239). Colin wills to know the secrets of nature.

But this kind of magic is Life—to use Arabella Buckley's term. It is in Colin, in the flowers, in the sun, in everything in *The Secret Garden,* including the narrator, who says:

> One knows it sometimes when one gets up at the tender, solemn dawntime and goes out and stands alone and throws one's head far back and looks up and up and watches the pale sky slowly changing and flushing and marvellous unknown things happening until the East almost makes one cry out and one's heart stands still at the strange, unchanging majesty of the rising of the sun. (215)

Colin and the youngsters in this novel find out that "in the garden there was nothing which was not quite like themselves" (261). And so it proves to be. Mrs. Sowerby, Dickon's wonderful, understanding mother is "Magic," and so is the influence of Colin's dead mother "Magic." In "Gardens, Houses, and Nurturant Power," Phyllis Bixler reads all of *The Secret Garden* as a book whose heroes are "its community of mothers centered in the secret garden" and makes this point very effectively (213). But "Magic" extends even further than this. It is in all the characters, including the garden itself and the robin and the gardener and even Colin's cold father, who comes back into the warmth of the growing garden and the world of living things. Nature is everywhere; it is every living thing. Mary is not the inheritor of the mantle of natural woman in this story; she is no more natural than are the male characters. Instead, she is the inheritor of a kind of female teaching and storytelling about nature that has been the subject of much of *Kindred Nature*. She is a verbal being whose embrace of nature translates into caring words about it.

Burnett thus spins a benign romantic tale from threads of stories we have heard before, and not just the famous Christmas story by Dickens or Brontë's *Jane Eyre*, often mentioned as an inspiration for Burnett (Bixler 217–19). Burnett seems more informed by the story of boys and girls and science as told by the Mother Natures of my chapter 2; and by the story of the importance of altruism and species preservation as told by Julia Horatia Ewing and other women predecessors in children's literature; and by the story of the beautiful garden as told by Gertrude Jekyll and countless other Victorian and Edwardian women; and by the story of talking animals so well devised by Margaret Gatty and Beatrix Potter; and, finally, by the story of the ecological web of life and the magic it entails as told by Florence Dixie. In this light, it does not do us any great service to reduce the stature of Burnett's story merely because some of its plot's devices may seem familiar; rather, we do better to recall the strength of the many female traditions that have nourished it and the warmth it has retained in the memories of so many generations of people since it was published in 1911. To my mind, Burnett did not end up giving away the power of her heroine to Colin or even to Dickon. She put her Mary in a down-to-earth context that placed her squarely in a female tradition of literature about nature. Mary learns and Mary teaches and Mary heals. Without her, Colin's science would not have been possible; without her storytelling, Dickon's mute but beautiful male sensitivity would have gone unknown beyond the garden wall.

Gone-to-Earth Hazel

Burnett inscribes a bright halo around the world of kindred natures and offers a happy ending for those who heed nature's magic. Escaped from hothouses and stuffed pillows, Mary and Colin are saved by their contact with the earth, freed to live adult lives in a world made better by Mary's experiences with the garden. But we never see those adult lives. Sexuality enters this book only as it does in Elizabeth Wolstenholme Elmy's sexual primers for children: through animal analogies, like the nest building and the changed demeanor of the male robin during mating season. The triangle of Dickon-Mary-Colin does not become problematic, because it does not reach beyond puberty. But in Mary Webb's *Gone to Earth* (1917), eighteen-year-old Hazel Woodus is undone by the forcefulness of a similar triangle. For her, awakening to sexuality leads not to fulfillment but to death—as it did for Rima. A nature girl from name to temperament, Hazel is a kind of female Dickon, protectress of wildlings like a pet fox, Foxy, and menagerie of hurt and abandoned animals. However, Hazel's closeness to nonhuman nature in no way prepares her to chart her path through the world of men. Like Rima, she stands outside of culture—again, a very untenable position in the mind of her Edwardian author.

Mary Webb wrote *Gone to Earth* not just during the foment of the Great War but in the wake of a sexual revolution as well. A less well known writer than her contemporaries D. H. Lawrence (1885–1930) and James Joyce (1882–1941), she was as concerned as they were about the effects this revolution would have on definitions of woman's nature. For them, as Robert Adams has suggested, "the religion of woman [as ideal, as spiritual guide], with relatively few tonal changes transformed itself during the early twentieth century into something very like the religion of sex. . . . a very masculine phenomenon, based on various mystiques about women" (187). For Webb, women needed to take care to stay out of the center of both the religion of woman and the religion of sex. A fictional representation of the women for whom Lady Florence Dixie feared and for whom Marie Stopes wrote, Webb's Hazel is caught up in both religions and understands neither. For Hazel, wholly ignorant of her own sexual powers, marriage means neither sexuality nor lifelong human commitment but simply the chance to leave an uncomfortable home with a crotchety father and make a safer place for her menagerie in the home of a young preacher. Hazel is a complete naïf, a kind of nature-loving, creature-rescuing primitive on whom all of Webb's sympathy is showered but through whom endless warnings are issued.

Webb's sympathies with Hazel clearly derived from her own deep love of the natural world, but Webb herself was always unsentimental about nature. A student of Darwin, Huxley, and Haeckel, Webb schooled herself in evolutionary science. In "Sense and Sensibility Out of Doors," one of a number of familiar essays she wrote for the *Spectator,* she reminded her readers that "it is as unwise to be sentimental towards Nature as it would be to sonnetize in her presence the rosy lips of a cannibal queen" (qtd. in Coles 195). This knowledge did not, however, prevent Webb from rhapsodizing over natural beauty or from immersing herself in mythologies based in nature. Webb read and was intrigued by William Sharp as Fiona Macleod—quite taken with her/his Celtic lore and sense of wild beauty and the rhythms of his/her prose. Webb also read folklore, including Charlotte S. Brune's *Shropshire Folk Lore* (1883), an early and massive compendium of county life and lore. All of this reading was fueled by her own deep passion for the earth. "Everybody," she would say, "talks of 'love of nature', everybody writes 'nature books', everybody is 'fond of the country'. If you are a child of the earth you are not 'fond' but impassioned, devastated, recreated by these things" (qtd. in Coles 195). Webb had herself been so "recreated." In her essay *"Vis Medicatrix Naturae,"* she counseled, "Ceasing for a time to question and strive, let us dare to be merely receptive" (*Mary Webb: The*

Spring of Joy 135). Being "merely receptive" of the nonhuman natural world had helped Webb through severe bouts of illness with Graves' disease.

In Hazel, most of Webb's attitudes toward nature converged. Hazel has "so deep a kinship with the trees, so intuitive a sympathy with leaf and flower, that it seemed as if the blood in her was not slow-moving human blood, but volatile sap. She was of a race that will come in the far future, when we shall have out-grown our egoism—the brainless egoism of a boy pulling off flies wings" (*Gone to Earth* 163). Potentially, like Rima, the herald of a coming race, Hazel has trouble living with the current human race and instead identifies herself "with Foxy, and so with all things hunted and snared and destroyed" (17). Childlike, she talks through the fox and to the fox, and Mary Webb's fox in turn enters this Hazel-driven text like a human character: "In the middle of the night Foxy woke. The moon filled her kennel-mouth like a door, and the light shone in her eyes" (16). The bond between these two persists until their simultaneous end. It is meant to remind the reader of his or her animal origins—that "echoes are in us of great voices long gone hence, the unknown cries of huge beasts on the mountains; the sullen aims of creatures in the slime; the love call of the bittern" (62). If the story of Hazel takes us forward toward a coming race of more nature-sensitive human beings, it takes us back, too, to our evolutionary beginnings.

Hazel, "though sexless as a leaf" (16), will not be left untouched by the de-sires of men. Edward, the preacher whom she marries to find a better home for her wildlings, can neither grasp her primitive nature nor see "that Hazel was enchained by the earth, prisoner to it only a little less than the beech and the hyacinth—bond serf of the sod" (71). He marries her hoping somehow to civ-ilize her without destroying her innocence. When she explains her superstitions about the Black Huntsman—a folkloric master hunter who traverses the earth by night with a wild dog pack—Edward observes to her that "myths are inter-esting . . . especially nature myths" (72). Innocent Hazel responds: "What's a myth, Mr. Marston?" (73). Just as innocently, she does not understand mar-riage and never sleeps with Marston. "It was not a question of marrying or not marrying in Hazel's eyes. It was a matter of primitive instinct," Webb tells us (40). Hazel always assumes that she belongs to no one but herself.

This innocent independence and her husband's ignoring of her latent sexual-ity set the stage for the entry of Webb's Lawrencian character, Reddin, hunter of foxes and women. Reddin seduces Hazel and impregnates her, stealing her away from the repressed Edward Marston. But he robs her of more than maiden-hood, for he begins to erode her "sacramental love of Nature" (255). Imprisoned by his lust, Hazel will eventually make her way back to the broken Marston—but too late for any of the three of them to recover themselves. When Foxy es-capes from Marston's place and Hazel pursues her to save her from the hunt, she in turn is chased by foxhunters. In a final desire to save both herself and

Foxy from further captivity and harm, Hazel, holding Foxy in her arms, jumps over a precipice as the hunt closes in on them. Both go back to earth.

In *Gone to Earth*, Mary Webb gives the lie not just to the myths of woman as angel and woman as nature-embodying demon but to the myth of a natural sexuality innately known to womankind. Until her rude sexual awakening, Hazel lives in innocent harmony with herself. Self-contained, she wants neither Marston nor Reddin. Webb condones Hazel's ways with animals and flowers but not her naïveté with men. Throughout her novel, she seems to be reinforcing Havelock Ellis's popular contentions that the female sex life is extremely central to women's well-being but that it must be properly awakened and conditioned by men. Her Marston is incapable of this because he is daunted by Hazel's naïveté; her Reddin incapable because he would dispense with courtship and responsibility in his desire to swiftly initiate and complete the sex act. Hazel fulfills the stereotype of the uninitiated Victorian woman in all of this; she cannot imagine motherhood, and she likes but does not understand sexuality. She is like a Marie Stopes on her wedding night, dangerously caught up in something she fails to fathom.

Of course, Mary Webb was not replaying *Married Love* in *Gone to Earth*. Hazel's story is situated more deeply and comprehensively in nature than it would be were it only a story of a tragic sexual awakening. If Hazel is brought from the out-of-doors into the drawing room in an action directly opposite to that of Holman Hunt's awakened woman, her life continues to center around her sense of the earth even at Marston's vicarage. Her tragedy is not that of Thomas Hardy's *Tess of the D'Urbervilles* (1891), a fallen woman with nowhere to go but toward death. Hazel's distinctive tragedy lies in her hypersensitivity toward the suffering beauty of animal life. Hazel feels her kinship with the earth too passionately. Like the crusading women who chose to nurture wounded nature by engaging in political action, fictional Hazel knows the painful reality other beings experience. But through this kinship with animal otherness, she reaches too far toward the unnameable, where, as her narrator tells us

> all the outcries of all creatures, living and dying, sink in its depth as in an unbounded ocean. Whether this listening silence, incurious, yet hearing all, is benignant or malevolent, who can say? The willful dreams of man haunt this theme forever; the creeds of men are so many keys that do not fit the lock. We ponder it in our hearts, and some find peace, and some find terror. The silence presses upon us ever more heavily until Death comes with his cajoling voice and promises us the key. Then we run after him into the stillness, and are heard no more. (53)

This wartime novel, fraught with its author's hopes for the earth and fears for earthlings, thus takes us to the dark edge of naturalism. If Webb advocated nature as "re-creation" for herself and others of the breed "impassioned" by nature, through Hazel she also revealed the "devastation" that can befall the impassioned. Hazel moves closer and closer to and finally over the verge into silence. Her human nature is, Webb seems to be telling us, too sensitive for its time and place. In 1871, George Eliot had told an earlier generation that "*if* we had a keen vision and feeling of all ordinary human life, it would be like hearing the grass grow and the squirrel's heart beat, and we should die of that roar which lies on the other side of silence" (*Middlemarch* 189; my emphasis). In 1917, Mary Webb goes a step further: *when* we do hear the squirrel's heart beat and the grass grow, she seems to be saying, we can die from our sensitivity to their calls, because we ourselves are then too close to the "unnameable" mystery that in the end contains death as well as life.

In *Gone to Earth*, Webb reinscribes, in order to give the lie to, most of the Victorian myths about womanhood: Hazel is no do-gooder Saint Teresa, no wild woman, no young person eagerly awaiting heterosexual love, no demon or mythical beast. She is only a sensitive, nature-loving person in need of a culture that is itself badly in need of her kind of sensitivity but unable properly to cultivate it. Here is the source of her tragedy: ordinary human life does not feel her enduring need to be kindred with growing grass and with animal hearts and dreams. She is a woman both behind and ahead of her time.

Despite very real limitations imposed by their culture, the women in this book entered the fields of science, environmental protection, illustration (both commercial and scientific), and nature writing and, in doing so, helped to shape modern ideas about the natural world. Because so many of those women were forward-looking, I end this study of Victorians and Edwardians by regrouping some of these women and briefly writing them into the future, reinforcing their significance and expanding upon some of the arguments and issues raised in *Kindred Nature*. Forgotten though many of them have been, the women of these pages have prepared ground for us here and now at the end of the twentieth century in what is a very different space and, for some of us, a very different place from theirs. I thought of the crusaders on behalf of animals recently, when international television featured groups of British women holding up large placards saying, "Ban Blood Sports." This was early during the day (28 November 1997) that British members of Parliament voted overwhelmingly, 411 to 151, to ban the hunting of wild animals with horses and hounds. It was the same day that people in San Francisco unfurled a huge banner reading "Ban Furs" from a towering building and were joined across the country by women in New York City marching through the streets under a similar banner. Frances Power Cobbe and Lady Florence Dixie would have been proud of all of these people, if disappointed that such protesting was still necessary.

The diversity of the women in this book—some feminists, some clearly not; some religionists, some clearly not; some essentialists, some clearly not; some allied with others, some clearly not—complicates and challenges contemporary assumptions about women in earlier historical periods. Like ourselves, these earlier women were a mixed lot with different aims and talents, and certainly with different agendas. Grouping them, except as they grouped themselves—as did, for instance, the women of the Royal Society for the Protection of Birds— is a treacherous business. But what they do tell us, when we listen to them collectively, is that they were very active agents, not just passive recipients, in their culture, active, too, in directions in which we still move. I will briefly reintroduce just three, of many, areas in which their achievements have been more extensive and far-reaching than we have usually assumed: first, in the reinterpretation of Darwin that has continued from his time to ours; second, in the development of an ecological consciousness; and, finally, in the pioneering of nature writing.

Victorian women's reactions to Darwin have recently found considerable favor with women scholars. For example, in a fascinating essay, Rosemary Jann has written of Eliza Burt Gamble (1841–1920), an American Victorian suffragette who responded to Darwin with "a counternarrative that rewrote female power over sexuality as the missing link between biology and culture" ("Revising the Descent of Woman" 149). And on the British side, Evelleen Richards, an Australian critic, has deployed the divergent viewpoints of Frances Power Cobbe and Eliza Lynn Linton to reexamine the implications of Darwin's theories for women ("Redrawing the Boundaries"). *Kindred Nature*, too, has contributed to the reappraisal of Cobbe as an anti-Darwinian and also looked at other women, like Frances Swiney, in that light. But Darwinism, I would like to emphasize, put women into a double bind. If they accepted Darwin's theories in the *Descent of Man* as inaugurating a new, liberating era of science and allied themselves with the Darwinians, they were also accepting theories that helped make women reproductively potent and culturally potentially impotent. If they did not accept Darwin, as Cobbe did not in her linking of women's plight to that of animals, or as Swiney did not in her arguing for women's superiority, they often allied women with causes that might serve to essentialize them anyway—in these two cases, by emphasizing women's closeness to animals and by announcing a human need for sexual purity, respectively. Continuing to explore this double bind today by measuring women's reactions to the biological determinism that would culturally limit them is important. This is why such analysis has become a significant part of the feminist study of gender and the history of science. Nevertheless, this kind of analysis has itself put contemporary feminist critics into a double bind: as we continue to reframe the stories of the women trapped by ideas of biological determinism, we continue to reiterate stories of female impotence. This is something I did not wish to highlight in a book devoted to women's varied accomplishments in the cultural construction of nature.

If *Kindred Nature* engages in this kind of gender analysis, it also points elsewhere, showing that not all intelligent women in my time frame had an interest in critiquing Darwin on women. The cultural work that comes with redefinitions of nature is only partly the work of science, or even of what we have come to call social science. Much of it comes through education and through aesthetics. Within science study itself, women used their supple minds to reappraise Darwin's thinking about nonhuman nature as well as his thoughts about women in the *Descent*. In evaluating Darwin's views on other species for new audiences, these women's thoughts were as important, and in many cases as forward-looking, as were their challenges to Darwin's or Spencer's science of women.

Take, for just one example, Arabella Buckley's writing. As we saw in chapter 2, Buckley's interest in the importance of altruism and mutualism to species

theory anticipated the significance of these ideas, which still haunt evolutionary biology. Her most avid interests lay in morality—in the stories about cooperation that she wanted to pass on to children—and in the biological sciences
she so loved. But Buckley was even more in advance of her time in her discussions on the life force than she was in her advocacy of mutuality as an evolutionary principle. Buckley's "Life," the term she used for the life force, has much
in common with the Gaia of the Gaia hypothesis only recently set forth by Lynn
Margulis and James Lovelock. For them, Gaia, like Buckley's "Life," becomes
a precise and appropriate metaphor for describing that collectively evolving organism—the life-form of Earth herself—in whose own evolution cooperation
and mutualism have been even stronger forces than has competition.

Buckley's altruism can be connected not just with Gaia theory but also with
the ecological consciousness common to numerous women in *Kindred Nature.*
Buckley was not a "Green," like the crusaders for the protection of plants and
animals, but she had no doubts about the interrelatedness of all life and the in-
terdependence of organisms and their environments in what we now call our
ecosystem. The word "ecology" dates back to 1866, to Ernst Haeckel, who
wanted to introduce Darwin to the German scientific community and who, accordingly, defined his own new science as "the study of all those complex in-
terrelationships referred to by Darwin as the conditions of the struggle for existence" (qtd. in Kroeber 23). Yet, as we have seen, even before there was a word
for it, pre-Dawinian women understood the interrelatedness of things organic.
Among Elizabeth Gould's contributions to science illustration were her insights
into the plant communities that supported her birds. Later, something similar
would be true of Marianne North, who watched the insects that pollinated her
plants. Later still, among Muriel Foster's drawings of fish are drawings of the
waters in which they swim, the birds that fish those waters, and the dragonflies
that fly just above them. Beatrix Potter knew where hedgehogs lived and how
they survived in the British climate and how squirrels and owls were dependent
upon the same trees.

All these Victorian women helped pave the way for one of the most influential women of our century, Rachel Carson. "I have tried," said Carson, "to say
that all the life of the planet is interrelated, that each species has its own ties to
others, and that all are related to the earth. This is the theme of *The Sea Around
Us* [1951] and the other sea books, and it is also the message of *Silent Spring*
[1962]" (qtd. in Graham 53). Because of the importance of her work and the
enormous amount of publicity that surrounded it, Carson is often considered
the mother of ecology. Certainly she is the woman who, in *Silent Spring*, brought
home to the twentieth century the dire necessity of an ecological point of view.
But Carson's daring and influential work can also be seen as the culmination of
a long line of literary texts. It encapsulates and crowns three traditions in wom-
en's writing featured in *Kindred Nature*—popularization of science, crusading

on behalf of endangered species, and writing from an ecological perspective. All of these arts were practiced by concerned and observant women from at least the time of the Victorians.

If Potter and Gould observed animals and thought about their connectedness to their natural environment, Alice Dew-Smith and Mary Webb, following Frances Power Cobbe, watched how the animals in their world were subject to male dominance just as were women. These three women developed not just an ecological consciousness but an ecofeminist consciousness, a worldview that remained untheorized until the 1970s. Of course, all of the women I have mentioned found the world interesting not only because it contained the things people did but also because it contained things nonhuman. They did not think of the natural world "as man's oyster, or even as his garden," to quote Joseph Meeker (xix), but as a place belonging to many species. I am not here suggesting that men did not notice similar things but simply that the women of my time frame, the Victorian and Edwardian periods, had begun to think in ways that many people believe date only from an ecological revolution that began in the 1960s and 1970s.

Ecological consciousness did not arrive then but, like feminism, came in waves. So did what we have come to call "ecofeminism." When I taught a course on this subject five years ago, a student who was helping me to research the writing of Anna Kingsford and Frances Power Cobbe said to the others in the class, "But ecofeminism isn't new. I've just been reading women who said the same things a hundred years ago!" She was right, of course. When concerned that the mistreatment of animals can parallel the mistreatment of people, Kingsford and Cobbe are akin to contemporary Americans like Carol Adams in her book *The Sexual Politics of Meat* (1990) and Susan Griffin in *Woman and Nature: The Roaring inside Her* (1978). Similarly, ecofeminist theologians, such as Rosemary Radford Ruether, recall the earnest attempts of Anna Kingsford and Arabella Buckley to wed God and Gaia.

Certainly, not just polemic but natural beauty has for centuries also drawn women to write about nature. The wonders of nature as viewed and recorded by women like Anne Pratt and dozens of others established yet another tradition in women's writing, one that continues to this day. When I asked her about such a tradition involving women, nature writing, and science popularization, Diane Ackerman answered, "people . . . want a sense of the beauty of the world, a way to understand the mysteries they move among" (qtd. in Gates and Shteir 263). Ackerman believes that her "natural history" books and her books about vanishing species provide a sense of beauty by probing mystery with scientific understanding and encompassing it with language.

If popular science like hers is a subgenre in which women have long been comfortable, garden writing and flower books offer another example of long-term female commitment to yet another form of nature writing. From long before the time of Jane Loudon, both garden writing and the garden itself were female preserves. For women residing at home, the garden was and is a place close-by, a form of nature domesticated, a place often to be described for others. As Loudon led to Jekyll, Jekyll in turn led to Virginia Woolf's friend Vita Sackville-West. Sackville-West paid tribute to earlier garden writers when she bemoaned that "it is very difficult to write about flowers. Think—if we are to come down to details—how difficult it is even to express in ordinary language so simple a fact as that a flower smells good" (Sackville-West 12). Writing earlier in this century about her renowned garden at Sissinghurst—a place now frequented by the public—Sackville-West in turn influenced a multitude of garden writers today. Some write about their own gardens, some about the gardens of others, including the gardens of Jekyll and Sackville-West. Shelves and shelves at places like the Royal Botanic Garden at Kew and Longwood Gardens in Pennsylvania are devoted to garden books by women. Gardens and the books and magazines that describe them proliferate and thrive, as do their writers—many of them women.

In fact, dozens of kinds of writing practiced by women discussing nature in the nineteenth and early twentieth centuries have paved the way for similar writing today, in the late twentieth century. We still tell science stories to youngsters in simple, more appealing ways. We still buy short, well-illustrated children's books about little mice and cats and frogs. New renditions appear every year and are often packaged like the storied animals of Beatrix Potter and her contemporaries; meanwhile, Potter's books themselves remain best-sellers. Longer children's books, like Marguerite Henry's Misty stories, recall Anna Sewell's tributes to Black Beauty. Handbooks of birds and wildflowers and travel narratives by women still pack the shelves of contemporary book supermarkets. When Arlene Blum wrote of the exciting and tragic ascent of Annapurna by herself and eight other women in 1978, she paid tribute to foremothers like Isabella Bird and Fanny Bullock Workman (introduction to *Annapurna*). Annie Dillard's and Gretel Erlich's poetic prose describing self and natural place echo aesthetic musings like Vernon Lee's and again link to women's abiding interest in ecology (Dillard, *Pilgrim at Tinker Creek;* Erlich, *The Solace of Open Spaces*). More radical books about ecofeminist nature religions written by women like Starhawk and science fictions about superwomen with powers to better the future of the planet both have threads in common with utopias by Florence Dixie. As any reader of nature writing knows, this catalog of similarities could wind on. Whole anthologies—for instance, Lorraine Anderson's collection, *Sisters of the Earth*—help characterize and capitalize on current interest in women's nature writing.

But the point must already be clear. More than we tend to admit, we today are heirs to a rich legacy from earlier women who wrote and rethought nature. We ourselves are kindred to those Victorian and Edwardian women who made nature kindred in so many, different ways.

BIBLIOGRAPHY: WORKS

CONSULTED

Abir-Am, Pnina, and Dorinda Outram, eds. *Uneasy Careers and Intimate Lives: Women in Science, 1789–1979.* New Brunswick: Rutgers UP, 1987.

Adams, Carol J. *The Sexual Politics of Meat: A Feminist-Vegetarian Critical Theory.* New York: Continuum, 1990.

Adams, James Eli. "Woman Red in Tooth and Claw: Nature and the Feminine in Tennyson and Darwin." *Victorian Studies* 33 (1989): 7–28.

Adams, J. F. A. "Is Botany a Suitable Study for Young Men?" *Science* 9 (1887): 116–17.

Adams, Robert M. "Religion of Man, Religion of Woman." *Art, Politics, and Will: Essays in Honor of Lionel Trilling.* Ed. Quentin Anderson, Stephen Donadio, and Stephen Marcus. New York: Basic Books, 1977. 173–90.

Ahearn, Edward J. *Visionary Fictions: Apocalyptic Writing from Blake to the Modern Age.* New Haven: Yale UP, 1996.

Ainley, Marianne Gosztonyi. "Science in Canada's Backwoods: Catharine Parr Traill." *Natural Eloquence: Women Reinscribe Science.* Ed. Barbara T. Gates and Ann B. Shteir. Madison: U of Wisconsin Press, 1997. 79–97.

Aitken, Maria. *A Girdle Round the Earth.* London: Constable, 1987.

Alaya, Flavia. "Victorian Science and the 'Genius' of Woman." *Journal of the History of Ideas* 38 (1977): 261–80.

———. *William Sharp—"Fiona Macleod," 1855–1905.* Cambridge: Harvard UP, 1970.

Albinski, Nan Bowman. *Women's Utopias in British and American Fiction.* London: Routledge, 1988.

Alic, Margaret. *Hypatia's Heritage: A History of Women in Science from Antiquity through the Nineteenth Century.* Boston: Beacon, 1986.

Allen, Charles. *A Glimpse of the Burning Plain: Leaves from the Indian Journals of Charlotte Canning.* London: Michael Joseph, 1986.

Allen, David Elliston. "Natural History and Visual Taste: Some Parallel Tendencies." *The Natural Sciences and the Arts: Aspects of Interaction from the Renaissance to the Twentieth Century: An International Symposium.* Stockholm: Almquist and Wiksell, 1985. 32–45.

———. "The Women Members of the Botanical Society of London." *British Journal for the History of Science* 13 (1980): 240–54.

Allen, Grant. *Physiological Aesthetics.* London: Henry S. King and Co., 1877.

———. *The Woman Who Did.* London: John Lane, 1895.

Altick, Richard. *The Shows of London.* Cambridge: Belknap, 1978.

Anderson, Elizabeth Garrett. "Sex in Mind and Education: A Reply." *Fortnightly Review* 38 (1874): 582–94.

Anderson, Lorraine, ed. *Sisters of the Earth: Women's Prose and Poetry about Nature.* New York: Random House, 1991.

Anderson, Olive. "Women Preachers in Mid-Victorian Britain: Some Reflexions on Feminism, Popular Religion, and Social Change." *Historical Journal.* 12.3 (1969): 467–84.

Ardis, Ann. "'The Journey from Fantasy to Politics': Representations of Socialism and Feminism in *Gloriana* and *The Image-Breakers.*" *Rediscovering Forgotten Radicals: British Women Writers, 1889–1939.* Ed. Angela Ingram and Daphne Patai. Chapel Hill: U of North Carolina P, 1993. 43–56.

———. *New Women, New Novels: Feminism and Early Modernism.* New Brunswick: Rutgers UP, 1990.

Armstrong, Nancy. *Desire and Domestic Fiction: A Political History of the Novel.* Oxford: Oxford UP, 1987.

Atkins, Anna. *British Algae: Cyanotype Impressions.* 3 vols. Halstead: Sevenoaks (privately published), 1843–53.

Atwood, Margaret. *Surfacing.* New York: Popular Library, 1972.

Auerbach, Nina. *Woman and the Demon: The Life of a Victorian Myth.* Cambridge: Harvard UP, 1982.

Auerbach, Nina, and U. C. Knoepflmacher. *Forbidden Journeys: Fairy Tales and Fantasies by Victorian Women Writers.* Chicago: U of Chicago P, 1992.

Barber, Lynn. *The Heyday of Natural History, 1820–1870.* London: J. Cape, 1980.

Barr, Pat. *A Curious Life for a Lady: The Story of Isabella Bird.* London: Macmillan, 1970.

Barthes, Roland. "Myth Today." *Mythologies.* Trans. Annette Lavers. New York: Noonday Press, 1972. 109–59.

Barton, Ruth. "The Purposes of Science and the Purposes of Popularization." Paper presented to the Australasian Victorian Studies Association. Adelaide, Australia, Feb. 1996.

Basalla, George, William Coleman, and Robert H. Kargon, eds. *Victorian Science: A Self-Portrait from the Presidential Addresses of the British Association for the Advancement of Science.* Garden City: Doubleday-Anchor, 1970.

Becker, Lydia. "Is There Any Specific Distinction between Male and Female Intellect?" *Englishwoman's Review* 8 (1868): 483–91.

———. "On the Study of Science by Women." *Contemporary Review* 10 (1869): 386–404.

Beer, Gillian. *Darwin's Plots.* London: Routledge and Kegan Paul, 1983.

———. "'The Face of Nature': Anthropomorphic Elements in the Language of *The Origin of Species.*" *Languages of Nature: Critical Essays in Science and Literature.* Ed. L. J. Jordanova. London: Free Association, 1986. 207–43.

———. *Open Fields: Science in Cultural Encounter.* Oxford: Oxford UP, 1996.

Beeton, Isabella Mary. *The Book of Household Management.* London: Ward, Lock and Tyler, 1869.

Bell, E. Moberly. *Josephine Butler.* London: Constable, 1962.

———. *Octavia Hill: A Biography.* London: Constable, 1942.

Benjamin, Marina, ed. *A Question of Identity: Women, Science, and Literature.* New Brunswick: Rutgers UP, 1993.

———, ed. *Science and Sensibility: Gender and Scientific Enquiry, 1780–1945.* Oxford: Basil Blackwell, 1991.

Bennett, Jennifer. *Lilies of the Hearth: The Historical Relationship between Women and Plants.* Camden, Ontario: Camden House, 1991.

Bernard, H. M., and M. Bernard. *Woman and Evolution.* London: Frank Palmer, 1909.

Bird, Isabella. *A Lady's Life in the Rocky Mountains.* London: Folio Society, 1988.

Rev. of *The Birds of Australia,* by John Gould (2 vols. London, 1837). *Naturalist* 2 (1837): 47.

Birke, Lynda. *Women, Feminism, and Biology.* New York: Methuen, 1986.

Bixler, Phyllis. "Gardens, Houses, and Nurturant Power." *Romanticism and Children's Literature in Nineteenth-Century England.* Ed. James Holt McGavran, Jr. Athens: UP of Georgia, 1991. 208–24.

Blackburn, Jane (Jemima). *Birds Drawn from Nature.* Edinburgh: Edmonston & Douglas, 1862.

————. *Birds from Moidart and Elsewhere.* Edinburgh: David Douglas, 1895.

————. *Caw! Caw! or, The Chronicle of Crows: A Tale of the Spring-Time.* Glasgow: James Maclehose, 1870.

————. *The Pipits.* Glasgow: James Maclehose, 1872.

Bland, Lucy. *Banishing the Beast: English Feminism and Sexual Morality, 1885–1914.* Harmondsworth: Penguin Books, 1995.

Bleier, Ruth. *Science and Gender: A Critique of Biology and Its Theories on Women.* New York: Pergamon, 1984.

Blum, Ann Shelby. *Picturing Nature: American Nineteenth-Century Zoological Illustration.* Princeton: Princeton UP, 1993.

Blum, Arlene. *Annapurna: A Woman's Place.* San Francisco: Sierra Club Books, 1980.

Blunt, Wilfrid. *The Ark in the Park: The Zoo in the Nineteenth-Century.* London: Hamish Hamilton, 1976.

————. *The Art of Botanical Illustration.* London: Collins, 1950.

Bodington, Alice. *Studies in Evolution and Biology.* London: Elliot Stock, 1890.

Bohls, Elizabeth A. *Women Travel Writers and the Language of Aesthetics, 1716–1818.* Cambridge: Cambridge UP, 1995.

Bonavia, E. M. "Women's Frontal Lobes. A Biological and Social Question." *Provincial Medical Journal* 1 July 1892: 358–62.

Bordo, Susan. *The Flight to Objectivity: Essays on Cartesianism and Culture.* Albany: State U of New York P, 1987.

Bostock, Stephen St. C. *Zoos and Animal Rights: The Ethics of Keeping Animals.* London: Routledge, 1993.

"A Botanical Picture Gallery." Rev. of Marianne North's gallery. *Daily News* [London] 8 June 1882.

Boyd, Nancy. *Josephine Butler, Octavia Hill, Florence Nightingale: Three Victorian Women Who Changed the World.* London: Macmillan, 1982.

Brantlinger, Patrick. *The Rule of Darkness: British Literature and Imperialism, 1830–1914.* Ithaca: Cornell UP, 1988.

Bridson, Gavin D. R. *Plant, Animal, and Anatomical Illustration in Art and Science: A Bibliographical Guide from the Sixteenth Century to the Present Day.* Detroit: Omnigraphics, 1990.

Briggs, Asa. *Victorian Things.* London: B. T. Batsford, 1988.

Briggs, Julia. *A Woman of Passion: The Life of E. Nesbit, 1858–1924.* London: Hutchinson, 1987.

Brightwen, Eliza. *Eliza Brightwen: The Life and Thoughts of a Naturalist.* Ed. W. H. Chesson. Intro. Edmund Gosse. London: T. Fisher Unwin, 1909.

———. *Glimpses of Plant Life: An Easy Guide.* London: T. Fisher Unwin, 1897.

———. *Inmates of My House and Garden.* New York: Macmillan, 1895.

———. *More about Wild Nature.* London: T. Fisher Unwin, 1892.

———. *A Talk about Birds.* Leaflet no. 9. London: Society for the Protection of Birds, n.d. [after 1892].

———. *Wild Nature Won by Kindness.* London: T. Fisher Unwin, 1890.

Brock, W. H. "*Glaucus:* Kingsley and the Seaside Naturalists." *Cahiers Victoriens et Edouardiens* 3 (1976): 25–36.

Broderip, W. J. *Zoological Recreations.* London: Henry Colburn, 1847.

Brody, Judit. "The Pen Is Mightier than the Test Tube." *New Scientist* 105 (1985): 56–58.

Brontë, Anne. *The Tenant of Wildfell Hall.* 1848. London: Penguin Books, 1979.

Brookshaw, George. *A New Treatise on Flower Painting; or, Every Lady Her Own Drawing Master.* London: Longman, Hurst, Rees, Orme and Brown, 1816.

Brown, Penelope and L. J. Jordanova. "Oppressive Dichotomies: The Nature/Culture Debate." *Women in Society: Interdisciplinary Essays Compiled and Edited by the Cambridge Women's Studies Group.* London: Virago, 1981. 224–41.

Brück, M. T. "Alice Everett and Annie Russell Maunder: Torch-Bearing Women Astronomers." *Irish Astronomical Journal* 21 (1994): 281–90.

———. "Lady Computers at Greenwich in the Early 1890s." *Quarterly Journal of the Royal Astronomical Society.* 36 (1995): 83–95.

Bryan, Margaret. *Lectures of Natural Philosophy, the Result of Many Years' Practical Experience of the Facts Elucidated.* London: J. Murray, 1806.

Buckland, Frank. *Logbook of a Fisherman and Zoologist.* London: Chapman and Hall, 1875.

———. *Natural History of British Fishes: Their Structure, Economic Uses, and Capture by Net and Rod.* London: Society for Promoting Christian Knowledge, 1881.

Buckley, Arabella. "Darwinism and Religion." *Macmillan's* 24 (1871): 45–51.

———. *The Fairy-land of Science.* London: Edward Stanford, 1879.

———. *Life and Her Children: Glimpses of Animal Life from the Amoeba to the Insects.* London: Edward Stanford, 1881.

———. "Lyell, Charles." *Encyclopaedia Britannica.* 9th ed. 1878.

———. *Moral Teachings of Science.* London: Edward Stanford, 1891.

———. *A Short History of Natural Science.* London: John Murray, 1876.

———. "The Soul and the Theory of Evolution." *University Magazine* 93 (1879): 1–10.

———. *Through Magic Glasses.* London: Edward Stanford, 1890.

———. *Winners in Life's Race; or, The Great Backboned Family.* London: Edward Stanford, 1883.

Burfield, Diana. "Theosophy and Feminism: Some Explorations in Nineteenth-Century Biography." *Women's Religious Experience.* Ed. Pat Holden. London: Croom Helm, 1983. 27–55.

Burke, Edmund. *A Philosophical Enquiry into the Origin of Our Ideas of the Sublime and the Beautiful.* 2nd ed., 1759. Menston: Scolar Books, 1970.

Burnett, Frances Hodgson. *The Secret Garden.* 1911. London: Puffin Books, 1994.

Burstyn, Joan. "Education and Sex: The Medical Case against Higher Education for

Women in England, 1870–1900." *Proceedings of the American Philosophical Society* 117 (1973): 79–89.

Butler, Josephine. *Personal Reminiscences of a Great Crusade.* London: Horace Marshall and Son, 1898.

———. "Woman's Place in Church Work." *Review of the Churches* Feb. 1892: 30–32.

Caird, Mona. "A Defence of the So-Called 'Wild Women.'" *Nineteenth Century* 31 (1892): 811–29.

Carlyle, Thomas. *Past and Present.* 1843. New York: Scribner's, 1899.

Carpenter, Edward. *Love's Coming of Age: A Series of Papers on the Relations of the Sexes.* Manchester: Labour Press, 1896.

Carroll, Lewis. *"Alice's Adventures in Wonderland" and "Through the Looking Glass."* Ed. Roger Lancelyn Green. London: Oxford UP, 1971.

Cavaliero, Glen. *The Rural Tradition in the English Novel, 1900–1939.* Totowa, NJ: Rowman and Littlefield, 1977.

Chant, Laura Ormiston. "Woman as an Athlete: A Reply to Dr. Arabella Kenealy." *Nineteenth Century* 45 (May 1899): 745–54.

Chesser, Elizabeth Sloan. *Women, Marriage, and Motherhood.* London: Cassell and Co., 1913.

Chishom, Alec H. *The Story of Elizabeth Gould.* Melbourne: Hawthorn, 1944.

Chrisman, Laura. "Empire, Race, and Feminism at the Fin de Siècle." *Cultural Politics at the Fin de Siècle.* Ed. Sally Ledger and Scott McCracken. Cambridge: Cambridge UP, 1995. 45–65.

Christie, John, and Sally Shuttleworth, eds. *Nature Transfigured: Science and Literature, 1700–1900.* Manchester: Manchester UP, 1989.

Cobbe, Frances Power. "Criminals, Idiots, Women, and Minors." *Fraser's Magazine* 78 (1868): 777–94.

———. "Dogs Whom I Have Met." *Cornhill Magazine* 26 (1872): 662–78.

———. "The Duties of Women." *Free and Enobled: Source Readings in the Development of Victorian Feminism.* Ed. Carol Bauer and Lawrence Ritt. Oxford: Pergamon, 1979.

———. "The Ethics of Zoophily." *Contemporary Review* 68 (1895): 497–508.

———. *Life of Frances Power Cobbe by Herself.* Boston: Houghton Mifflin, 1894.

———. "The Little Health of Ladies." *Contemporary Review* 31 (1878): 276–96.

———. *The Modern Rack: Papers on Vivisection.* London: Swan Sonnenschein and Co., 1889.

———. "*Schadenfreude.*" *Contemporary Review* 81 (1902): 655–66.

Cohen, Roy, ed. *Studies in Historical Change.* Charlottesville: UP of Virginia, 1992.

Coles, Gladys Mary. *The Flower of Light: A Biography of Mary Webb.* London: Duckworth, 1978.

Cooter, Roger and Stephen Pumfrey. "Separate Spheres and Public Places: Reflections of the History of Science Popularization and Science in Popular Culture." *History of Science* 32 (1994): 237–67.

Crane, Walter. *Baby's Own Aesop.* London: G. Routledge and Sons, 1887.

Crary, Jonathan. *Techniques of the Observer: On Vision and Modernity in the Nineteenth Century.* Cambridge: MIT P, 1990.

Creese, Mary R. S. "British Women of the Nineteenth and Early Twentieth Centuries Who Contributed to Research in the Chemical Sciences." *British Journal for the History of Science* 24 (1991): 275–305.

Cronin, Helena. *The Ant and the Peacock: Altruism and Sexual Selection from Darwin to Today.* Cambridge: Cambridge UP, 1991.

Dance, Peter. *The Art of Natural History: Animal Illustrators and Their Work.* Woodstock, NY: Overlook Press, 1978.

Darwin, Charles. *The Origin of Species* [selections]. 1859. *Darwin: A Norton Critical Edition.* Ed. Philip Appleman. 2nd ed. New York: W. W. Norton, 1979. 35–131.

——. *The Descent of Man and Selection in Relation to Sex.* 2 vols. London: John Murray, 1871.

Darwin, Erasmus. *Plan for the Conduct of Female Education in Boarding Schools.* 1797. New York: S. R. Publishers, Ltd., 1968.

Daston, Lorraine, and Peter Galison. "The Image of Objectivity." *Representations* 40 (1992): 81–128.

Desmond, Ray. *Dictionary of British and Irish Botanists and Horticulturalists, Including Plant Collectors and Botanical Artists.* London: Taylor and Francis, 1977.

Dew-Smith, Alice. *Confidences of an Amateur Gardener.* London: Seely and Co., 1897.

——. *Tom Tug and Others: Sketches in a Domestic Menagerie.* London: Seely and Co., 1898.

Dickens, Charles. *Our Mutual Friend.* London: Chapman & Hall, 1865. Vol. 10 of *The New Oxford Illustrated Dickens.* 21 vols. Oxford: Clarendon, 1951–62.

Dictionary of National Biography. London: Oxford, 1921–22.

Dijkstra, Bram. *Idols of Perversity: Fantasies of Feminine Evil in Fin-de-siècle Culture.* Oxford: Oxford UP, 1986.

Dillard, Annie. *Pilgrim at Tinker Creek.* New York: Harper's, 1974.

Dixie, Florence. *Gloriana; or, The Revolution of 1900.* London: Henry and Co., 1890.

——. "The Horrors of Sport." *Westminster Review* 137 (1892): 49–52.

——. *Isola; or, The Disinherited, a Revolt for Woman and All the Disinherited.* London: Leadenhall Press, 1903.

——. *Songs of a Child.* London: Leadenhall Press, 1902.

"The Dog." In "Lives That Bless." *Shafts.* 3 Dec. 1892: 67.

Doughty, Robin W. *Feather Fashions and Bird Preservation: A Study in Nature Protection.* Berkeley: U of California P, 1975.

Dowling, Linda. *Hellenism and Homosexuality in Victorian Oxford.* Ithaca: Cornell UP, 1994.

Duffin, Lorna. "Prisoners of Progress: Women and Evolution." *The Nineteenth-Century Woman: Her Cultural and Physical World.* Ed. Sara Delamont and Lorna Duffin. London: Croom Helm, 1978. 57–91.

Dyhouse, Carol. *No Distinction of Sex? Women in British Universities, 1870–1939.* London: UCL Press, 1995.

Early, Julie English. "The Science of Work, Life, and Text: Margaret Fountaine's Captures / Capturing Margaret Fountaine." *Women's Writing: The Elizabethan to Victorian Period* 2.2 (1995): 183–97.

——. "The Spectacle of Science and Self: Mary Kingsley." *Natural Eloquence: Women Reinscribe Science.* Ed. Barbara T. Gates and Ann B. Shteir. Madison: U of Wisconsin Press, 1997. 215–36.

Eastlea, Brian. *Science and Sexual Oppression: Patriarchy's Confrontation with Women and Nature.* London: Weidenfeld and Nicolson, 1981.

Eden, K. F. *Juliana Horatia Ewing and Her Books.* Detroit: Gale Research Co., 1969.

Edgeworth, Maria. *Letters for Literary Ladies.* London: J. Johnson, 1795.

Egerton, George [Mary Chavelita Dunne]. "A Cross Line." *Keynotes.* 1893. London: Elkin Matthews, 1894.

Eliot, George [Mary Ann Evans Cross]. *Middlemarch.* Ed. David Carroll. Oxford: Clarendon Press, 1986.

———. *The George Eliot Letters, Volume 1 (1836–1851).* Ed. Gordon S. Haight. New Haven: Yale UP, 1954.

Ellis, Havelock. *Man and Woman: A Study of Secondary Sexual Characters.* London: Walter Scott, 1894.

Ellis, Vivienne Rae. *Louisa Anne Meredith: A Tigress in Exile.* Sandy Bay, Tasmania: Blubber Head Press, 1979.

Elmy, Elizabeth Wolstenholme [Ellis Ethelmer, pseud.]. *Baby Buds.* London: Buxton House, 1895.

———. *The Human Flower: A Simple Statement of the Physiology of Birth and the Relations of the Sexes.* London: Buxton House, 1895.

———. *Phases of Love.* London: Buxton House, 1897.

———. *Woman Free.* Congleton: Women's Emancipation Press, 1893.

Erlich, Gretel. *The Solace of Open Spaces.* New York: Viking Penguin, 1985.

Ewing, Juliana Horatia. *"A Great Emergency" and Other Tales.* London: Bell and Son, 1911.

———. *"Mary's Meadow" and "Letters from a Little Garden."* London: Society for Promoting Christian Knowledge, 1886.

Fairly, Robert. *Jemima: The Paintings and Memoirs of a Victorian Lady.* Edinburgh: Cannongate, 1988.

Fausto-Sterling, Anne. *Myths of Gender: Biological Theories about Women and Men.* New York: Basic Books, 1985.

Fee, Elizabeth. "The Sexual Politics of Victorian Anthropology." *Clio's Consciousness Raised: New Perspectives on the History of Women.* Ed. Mary S. Hartman and Lois Banner. New York: Harper and Row, 1974. 86–102.

Fenn, Elleanor Frere. *The Rational Dame; or, Hints towards Supplying Prattle for Children.* London: John Marshall, c.1800.

Ferguson, Moira. *Animal Advocacy and Englishwomen, 1780–1900: Patriots, Nation, and Empire.* Ann Arbor: U of Michigan P, 1998.

Fitch, Walter. "Botanical Drawing." *Gardeners' Chronicle.* 1869. *The Art of Botanical Illustration.* Ed. Wilfrid Blunt. London: Collins, 1950.

Foster, Muriel. *Muriel Foster's Fishing Diary.* New York: Viking, 1980.

Fountaine, Margaret. *Love among the Butterflies: The Travels and Adventures of a Victorian Lady.* Ed. W. F. Cater. Boston: Little Brown, 1980.

Frank, Katherine. *A Voyager Out: The Life of Mary Kingsley.* Boston: Houghton Mifflin, 1986.

Frawley, Maria. *A Wider Range: Travel Writing by Women in Victorian England.* Rutherford, NJ: Fairleigh Dickinson UP, 1991.

Frazer, James. *The Golden Bough: A Study in Comparative Religion.* London: Macmillan, 1890.

Freeman, Barbara Claire. *The Feminine Sublime: Gender and Excess in Women's Fiction.* Berkeley: U of California P, 1995.

Frye, Northrop. *A Study of English Romanticism.* New York: Random House, 1968.

Gaard, Greta, ed. *Ecofeminism: Women, Animals, Nature.* Philadelphia: Temple UP, 1993.

Gage, Andrew Thomas, and William Thomas Stearn. *A Bicentenary History of the Linnean Society of London.* London: Academic Press, 1988.

Galton, Francis. *Essays in Eugenics.* London: Eugenic Education Society, 1909.

———. *Hereditary Genius: An Inquiry into Its Laws and Consequences.* London: Macmillan, 1869.

Gates, Barbara T. *Victorian Suicide: Mad Crimes and Sad Histories.* Princeton: Princeton UP, 1988.

Gates, Barbara T., and Ann B. Shteir, eds. *Natural Eloquence: Women Reinscribe Science.* Madison: U of Wisconsin P, 1997.

Gatty, Margaret. *Parables from Nature.* London: George Bell, 1880. New York: Garland Pub. Co., 1976.

Geddes, Patrick, and J. Arthur Thompson. *The Evolution of Sex.* London: Walter Scott, 1889.

Gilbert, Elliot. "The Female King: Tennyson's Arthurian Apocalypse." *PMLA* 98 (1983): 863–78.

Ginzberg, Ruth. "Uncovering Gynocentric Science." *Feminism and Science.* Ed. Nancy Tuana. Bloomington: Indiana UP, 1989. 69–84.

Gosse, Philip Henry. *The Aquarium: An Unveiling of the Wonders of the Deep Sea.* London: J. Van Voorst, 1854.

Gould, John. *The Birds of Great Britain.* 5 vols. London: John Gould, at Taylor & Francis, 1862–73.

Gould, Peter C. *Early Green Politics: Back to Nature, Back to the Land, and Socialism in Britain, 1880–1900.* New York: St. Martin's, 1988.

Gould, Stephen Jay. "The Invisible Woman." *Natural Eloquence: Women Reinscribe Science.* Ed. Barbara T. Gates and Ann B. Shteir. Madison: U of Wisconsin P, 1997. 27–39.

Graham, Frank, Jr. *Since Silent Spring.* Boston: Houghton Mifflin, 1970.

Grand, Sarah [Frances McFall]. *The Beth Book.* 1897. London: Virago, 1980.

Green, Martin. *Dreams of Adventure, Deeds of Empire.* New York: Basic Books, 1979.

Greene, Rev. H. *As in a Mirror.* Leaflet no. 2. London: Society for the Protection of Birds, 1898.

Greville, Robert Kaye. *Algae Britannicae.* Edinburgh: MacLachlan & Stewart, 1830.

Grey, Maria, and Emily Shirreff. *Thoughts on Self-Culture, Addressed to Women.* Boston: Crosby and Nichols, 1851.

Griffin, Susan. *Woman and Nature: The Roaring inside Her.* New York: Harper and Row, 1978.

Günther, Albert. *Introduction to the Study of Fishes.* Edinburgh: Adams and Charles Black, 1880.

Gwynn, Stephen. *The Life of Mary Kingsley.* London: Macmillan, 1932.

Hack, Maria. *Harry Beaufoy; or, The Pupil of Nature.* 1821. London: Darton and Harvey, 1845.

Haggard, Rider. *She.* 1887. New York: Dover, 1951.

Hall, Ruth. *Passionate Crusader: The Life of Marie Stopes.* London: Harcourt, Brace, Jovanovich, 1977.

Haraway, Donna J. "A Game of Cat's Cradle: Science Studies, Feminist Theory, Cultural Studies." *Configurations* 1 (1994): 59–71.

———. *Primate Visions: Gender, Race, and Nature in the World of Modern Science.* New York: Routledge, 1989.

Harding, Sandra. *The Science Question in Feminism*. Ithaca: Cornell UP, 1986.

————. "Women's Standpoints on Nature: What Makes Them Possible?" *Women, Gender, and Science: New Directions*. Ed. Sally Gregory Kohlstedt and Helen E. Longino. Spec. issue of *Osiris* 12 (1997): 186–200.

Harvey, William H. *A Manual of British Algae: Containing Generic and Specific Descriptions of All the Known British Species of Sea-Weeds*. London: J. Van Voorst, 1841.

Havely, Cicely Palser. *This Grand Beyond: The Travels of Isabella Bird Bishop*. London: Century, 1984.

Haweis, Mary. *Words to Women: Addresses and Essays*. Ed. Reverend H. R. Haweis. London: Burnet and Isbister, 1900.

Hay-Cooper, L. *Josephine Butler and Her Work for Social Purity*. London: Society for Promoting Christian Knowledge, 1922.

Heyck, Thomas William. *The Transformation of Intellectual Life in Victorian England*. London: Croom Helm, 1982.

Hill, Octavia. "Colour, Space, and Music for the People." *Nineteenth Century* 15 (1884): 741–52.

————. *The Life of Octavia Hill as Told in Her Letters*. Ed. C. Edmund Maurice. London: Macmillan, 1913.

————. "Natural Beauty as a National Asset." *Nineteenth Century and After* 58 (1905): 935–41.

————. *"Our Common Land" and Other Short Essays*. London: Macmillan, 1877.

Hirsch, Pam. "Barbara Leigh Smith Bodichon: Artist and Activist." *Women in the Victorian Art World*. Ed. Clarissa Campbell Orr. Manchester: Manchester UP, 1995. 167–86.

Hobusch, Erich. *Fair Game: A History of Hunting, Shooting, and Animal Conservation*. New York: Arco Publishing Co., 1980.

Holden, Edith. *Country Diary of an Edwardian Lady*. New York: Holt, Rinehart and Winston, 1977.

Holton, Sandra Stanley. "Free Love and Victorian Feminism: The Divers Matrimonials of Elizabeth Wolstenholme and Ben Elmy." *Victorian Studies* 37.2 (1994): 199–222.

Hope, Frances. *Notes and Thoughts on Gardens and Woodlands*. Ed. Anne J. Hope Johnstone. London: Macmillan and Co., 1881.

Hopkins, Gerard Manley. *The Journals and Papers of Gerard Manley Hopkins*. Ed. Humphry House. London: Oxford UP, 1959.

Horn, Pamela. *Victorian Countrywomen*. Oxford: Basil Blackwell, 1991.

Horton, Susan. "Were They Having Fun Yet? Victorian Optical Gadgetry, Modernist Selves." *Victorian Literature and the Victorian Visual Imagination*. Ed. Carol T. Christ and John O. Jordan. Berkeley: U of California P, 1995. 1–26.

Hudson, W. H. *Feathered Women*. Leaflet no. 10. London: Society for the Protection of Birds, 1902.

————. *Green Mansions: A Romance of the Tropical Forest*. London: Duckworth, 1904.

————. *Green Mansions*. Ed. John Galsworthy. New York: Knopf, 1916.

————. Letter to the editor. *Times* [London] 17 Oct. 1893.

Huxley, Thomas Henry. *Evolution and Ethics*. New York: D. Appleton, 1894.

————. *"Man's Place in Nature" and Other Anthropological Essays*. 1863. New York: Appleton, 1902.

————. "On the Physical Basis of Life." *Lay Sermons*. London: Macmillan, 1871. 120–46.

Jameson, Anna. *Sisters of Charity and the Communion of Labour: Two Lectures on the Social Employment of Women.* London: Longman, Brown, Green, Longmans, and Roberts, 1859.

Jann, Rosemary. "Darwin and the Anthropologists: Sexual Selection and Its Discontents." *Victorian Studies* 37.2 (1994): 287–306.

———. "Revising the Descent of Woman: Eliza Burt Gamble." *Natural Eloquence: Women Reinscribe Science.* Ed. Barbara T. Gates and Ann B. Shteir. Madison: U of Wisconsin P, 1997. 147–63.

Jay, Eileen, Mary Noble, and Anne Stevenson Hobbs, eds. *A Victorian Naturalist: Beatrix Potter's Drawings from the Armitt Collection.* London: Frederick Warne, 1992.

Jeffreys, Sheila. *The Spinster and Her Enemies: Feminism and Sexuality, 1880–1930.* London: Pandora, 1985.

Jekyll, Gertrude. *Children and Gardens.* London: Country Life, 1908.

———. *Colour Schemes for the Flower Garden.* 1908. Salem, NH: Ayer Company, 1983.

———. *Wall and Water Gardens.* 1901. Salem, NH: Ayer Company, 1983.

———. *Wood and Garden.* 1899. Salem, NH: Ayer Company, 1983.

Jersey, M. E. (Lady Jersey). "Ourselves and Our Foremothers." *Nineteenth Century* 27 (1890): 56–64.

Jex-Blake, Sophia. *Medical Women: A Thesis and a History.* Edinburgh: Oliphant, Anderson and Ferrier, 1886.

Johnston, Judith. "The 'Very Poetry of Frogs': Louisa Anne Meredith." *Natural Eloquence: Women Reinscribe Science.* Ed. Barbara T. Gates and Ann B. Shteir. Madison: U of Wisconsin P, 1997. 98–115.

Jordanova, Ludmilla J. "Gender and the Historiography of Science." *British Journal for the History of Science* 26 (1993): 469–83.

———. "Natural Facts: A Historical Perspective on Science and Sexuality." *Nature, Culture, and Gender.* Ed. Carol MacCormick and Marilyn Strathern. Cambridge: Cambridge UP, 1980. 42–69.

———. *Sexual Visions: Images of Gender in Science and Medicine.* Madison: U of Wisconsin P, 1989.

Journal of Psychological Medicine and Mental Pathology 4 (1851): 8–50.

Kaplan, Carla. "Reading Feminist Readings: Recuperative Reading and the Silent Heroine of Feminist Criticism." *Listening to Silences: New Essays in Feminist Criticism.* Ed. Elaine Hedges and Shelley Fisher Fishkin. Oxford: Oxford UP, 1994. 168–94.

Keith, Thomas. *Man and the Natural World: Changing Attitudes in England, 1500–1800.* London: Allen Lane, 1983.

Keller, Evelyn Fox. *Reflections on Gender and Science.* New Haven: Yale UP, 1985.

Kenealy, Arabella. "Woman as Athlete." *Nineteenth Century* 45 (1899): 636–54.

Kestner, Joseph. *Mythology and Misogyny.* Madison: U of Wisconsin P, 1989.

Kidwell, Peggy Aldrich. "Women Astronomers in Britain, 1780–1930." *Isis* (1984): 534–46.

Kingsford, Anna. "Unscientific Science: Moral Aspects of Vivisection." *Spiritual Therapeutics.* Ed. William Colville, Jr. 1883. Chicago: Educator Pub. Co., 1890. 290–308.

Kingsford, Anna, and Edward Maitland. *The Perfect Way; or, The Finding of Christ.* 1881. 2nd ed. London: John M. Watkins, 1923.

Kingsley, Charles. *Glaucus; or, The Wonders of the Shore.* Cambridge: Macmillan, 1855.

———. *Madame How and Lady Why; or, First Lessons in Earth Lore for Children.* London: Macmillan & Co., 1869.

Kingsley, Mary H. *Travels in West Africa.* 1897. Boston: Beacon, 1982.

———. *West African Studies.* New York: Barnes and Noble, 1964.

———. Letter to Mrs. Farquharson. 26 November 1895. Kingsley Papers. Royal Geographic Society, London.

———. Letter to George Macmillan. 18 December 1894. Macmillan Papers. Correspondence. Manuscript Collection. British Library.

Knoepflmacher, U. C., and G. B. Tennyson, eds. *Nature and the Victorian Imagination.* Berkeley: U of California P, 1977.

Kohlstedt, Sally Gregory, and Helen E. Longino, eds. *Women, Gender, and Science: New Directions.* Spec. issue of *Osiris* 12 (1997).

Krasner, James. *The Entangled Eye: Visual Perception and the Representation of Nature in Post-Darwinian Narrative.* New York: Oxford UP, 1992.

Kroeber, Karl. *Ecological Literary Criticism: Romantic Imagining and the Biology of Mind.* New York: Columbia UP, 1994.

Kropotkin, Petr. *Mutual Aid: A Factor in Evolution.* London: William Heinemann, 1902.

Krueger, Christine L. *The Reader's Repentance: Women Preachers, Women Writers, and Nineteenth-Century Social Discourse.* Chicago: U of Chicago P, 1992.

Kuklick, Henrika, and Robert E. Kohler, eds. *Science in the Field.* Spec. issue of *Osiris* 11 (1996).

Lang, W. D. "Mary Anning and the Pioneer Geologists of Lyme." *Presidential Address to the London Geological Society* (21 Feb. 1939): 142–64.

Lansbury, Coral. *The Old Brown Dog: Women, Workers, and Vivisection in Edwardian England.* Madison: U of Wisconsin P, 1985.

Laslett, Barbara, Sally Gregory Kohlstedt, Helen Longino, and Evelynn Hammonds, eds. *Gender and Scientific Authority.* Chicago: U of Chicago P, 1996.

Ledger, Sally, and Scott McCracken, eds. *Cultural Politics at the Fin de Siècle.* Cambridge: Cambridge UP, 1995.

Lee, Sarah Bowdich. *Excursions in Madeira and Porto Santo.* London: George B. Whittaker, 1825.

———. *Fresh-Water Fishes of Great Britain, Drawn and Described by Mrs. T. Edward Bowdich.* London: Printed for the Authoress, 1828.

———. *Taxidermy; or, The Art of Collecting, Preparing, and Mounting Objects of Natural History for the Use of Museums and Travellers.* London: Longman, Brown, Green, and Longmans, 1843.

Lee, Vernon [Violet Paget]. *Genius Loci.* London: Grant Richards, 1899.

———. *The Handling of Words and Other Studies in Literary Psychology.* London: Bodley Head, 1923.

———. *Laurus Nobilis: Chapters on Art and Life.* London: John Lane, 1909.

———. "Lizard in the Abbey Church." *"The Tower of Mirrors" and Other Essays on the Spirit of Place.* London: John Lane, 1914.

———. *Renaissance Fancies and Studies, Being a Sequel to Euphorion.* London: Smith, Elder and Co., 1896.

———. *The Sentimental Traveller: Notes on Places.* London: John Lane, 1908.

———. *The Spirit of Rome: Leaves from a Diary.* London: John Lane, 1906.

———. *"The Tower of Mirrors" and Other Essays on the Spirit of Place.* London: John Lane, 1914.

———. "Vivisection: An Evolutionist to Evolutionists." *Contemporary Review* 41 (1882): 788–811.

Lee, Vernon [Violet Paget], and Clementina Anstruther-Thomson. *"Beauty and Ugliness" and Other Studies in Psychological Aesthetics.* London: John Lane, 1912.

Lees, Edwin. "Observations on the Popularity of Natural History." *Naturalist* 3 (1838): 291–301.

Lemon, Mrs. Frank E. [Margaretta Louisa Smith Lemon]. *The Bird of Paradise.* Leaflet no. 20. London: Society for the Protection of Birds, 1895. Rev. ed. 1899.

———. *Dress in Relation to Animal Life.* Leaflet no. 33. London: Society for the Protection of Birds, 1899.

———. "The Story of the R.S.P.B. [Royal Society for the Protection of Birds]." *Bird Notes and News* 20.5–8 (1943): 67+.

Levine, George. *Darwin and the Novelists: Patterns of Science in Victorian Fiction.* Cambridge: Harvard UP, 1988.

———. "Objectivity and Death: Victorian Scientific Autobiography." *Victorian Literature and Culture* 20 (1992): 273–91.

———. *One Culture: Essays in Science and Literature.* Madison: U of Wisconsin P, 1987.

———, ed. *Realism and Representation: Essays on the Problem of Realism in Relation to Science, Literature, and Culture.* Madison: U of Wisconsin P, 1993.

Levine, Phillipa. *Feminist Lives in Victorian England: Private Roles and Public Commitment.* Oxford: Basil Blackwell, 1990.

Lewes, George Henry. *Sea-Side Studies at Ilfracombe, Tenby, the Scilly, and Jersey.* 1858. 2nd ed. Edinburgh: Blackwood, 1860.

Lightman, Bernard. "Constructing Victorian Heavens: Agnes Clerke and the 'New Astronomy.'" *Natural Eloquence: Women Reinscribe Science.* Ed. Barbara T. Gates and Ann B. Shteir. Madison: U of Wisconsin P, 1997. 61–75.

———. "The Gendered Nature of Victorian Science: Recent Works." *Victorian Studies Association Newsletter* 48 (1991): 15–21.

———, ed. *Victorian Science in Context.* Chicago: U of Chicago P, 1997.

Lines, William J. *An All-Consuming Passion: Origins, Modernity, and the Australian Life of Georgiana Molloy.* Berkeley: U of California P, 1994.

Linton, Elizabeth Lynn. "Wild Women as Politicians." *Nineteenth Century* 30 (1891): 79–88.

———. "Wild Women as Social Insurgents." *Nineteenth Century* 30 (1891): 596–605.

Lipshitz, Susan. *Tearing the Veil: Essays on Femininity.* London: Routledge and Kegan Paul, 1978.

Lock, Margaret. "Decentering the Natural Body: Making Difference Matter." *Configurations* 5.2 (1997): 267–92.

Lombroso, Cesare. *Female Offender.* New York: Appleton, 1895.

Longshore-Potts, Mrs. A. M. *Discourses to Women on Medical Subjects.* London: Published by the Author, 1887.

Lorimer, Douglas. *Colour, Class, and the Victorians: English Attitudes to the Negro in the Mid-Nineteenth Century.* Leicester: Leicester UP, 1978.

Loudon, Jane. *British Wild Flowers.* London: William S. Orr & Co., 1846.

———. *The Ladies' Flower-Garden of Ornamental Annuals.* 1840. London: W. S. Orr, 1849.

———. *The Lady's Country Companion.* London: Longman, Brown, Green and Longmans, 1845.

———. *The Young Naturalist; or, The Travels of Agnes Merton and Her Mama.* London: Routledge, Warne, and Routledge, 1863.

————. *The Young Naturalist's Journey.* London: William Smith, 1840.

Lowerson, John. *Sport and the English Middle Classes, 1870–1914.* Manchester: Manchester UP, 1993.

Lowry, Delvalle. *Conversations in Mineralogy.* London: Longman, Hurst, Rees, Orme and Brown, 1822.

Lyell, Charles. *Elements of Geology.* London: J. Murray, 1838.

————. *Principles of Geology.* 11th ed. 3 vols. New York: Appleton, 1890.

MacKenzie, John M. *The Empire of Nature: Hunting, Conservation, and British Imperialism.* Manchester: Manchester UP, 1988.

Maitland, Edward. *Anna Kingsford: Her Life, Letters, Diary, and Work.* Vol 1. London: George Redway, 1896.

Malchow, H. L. "Public Gardens and Social Action in Late Victorian London." *Victorian Studies* 29 (1985): 97–124.

Manos, Nikki Lee, and Meri-Jane Rochelson, eds. *Transforming Genres: New Approaches to British Fiction of the 1890s.* New York: St. Martins's, 1994.

Manton, Jo. *Elizabeth Garrett Anderson.* London: Methuen, 1965.

Marcet, Jane. *Conversations on Chemistry, Intended More Especially for the Female Sex.* London: Longman, Hurst, Rees and Orme, 1805.

————. *Conversations on Natural Philosophy.* London: Hurst, Rees, Orme and Brown, 1819.

Martin, Annie. *Home Life on an Ostrich Farm.* London: George Philip and Son, 1890.

Martineau, Harriet. *Our Farm of Two Acres.* London: Cottage Farm Series, 1865.

"Mary Anning, the Fossil Finder." *All the Year Round* 13 (1865): 60–63.

Matthews, L. H. "The Zoo: One Hundred Fifty Years of Research." *Zoos and Animal Rights: The Ethics of Keeping Animals.* Ed. Stephen St. C. Bostock. London: Routledge, 1993.

Maudsley, Henry. "Sex in Mind and Education." *Fortnightly Review* 15 (1874): 466–83.

Mazuchelli, Nina. *The Indian Alps and How We Crossed Them, by a Lady Pioneer, Illustrated by Herself.* New York: Dodd, Mead, and Company, 1876.

Meeker, Joseph W. *The Comedy of Survival: Studies in Literary Ecology.* New York: Charles Scribner's Sons, 1974.

Mellor, Anne. *Romanticism and Gender.* New York: Routledge, 1993.

Merchant, Carolyn. *The Death of Nature: Women, Ecology, and the Scientific Revolution.* San Francisco: Harper and Row, 1980.

————. *Earthcare: Women and the Environment.* New York: Routledge, 1996.

Meredith, Louisa Twamley. *My Home in Tasmania during a Residence of Nine Years.* London: John Murray, 1852.

————. *Notes and Sketches of New South Wales during a Residence in that Colony from 1839–1844.* London: John Murray, 1844.

————. *Our Island Home.* London: Marcus Wood, 1879.

————. *Our Wildflowers Familiarly Described and Illustrated.* 1839. London: John Murray, 1844.

————. *The Romance of Nature; or, The Flower Seasons Illustrated.* London: Tilt, 1836.

————. *Tasmanian Friends and Foes: Feathered, Furred, and Finned.* London: Marcus Ward, 1880.

Merrill, Lynn L. *The Romance of Victorian Natural History.* Oxford: Oxford UP, 1989.

Mills, Sara. *Discourses of Difference: An Analysis of Women's Travel Writing and Colonialism.* New York: Routledge, 1991.

———. "Knowledge, Gender, and Empire." *Writing Women and Space: Colonial and Postcolonial Geographies.* Ed. Alison Blunt and Gillian Rose. London: Guilford, 1994. 29–50.

"Miss North's Paintings of Plants." *Times* [London] 8 June 1882: 4.

Moore, Marianne. "Poetry" (longer version). *The Complete Poems of Marianne Moore.* New York: Viking, 1967. 266–67.

Morgan, Susan. *Place Matters: Gendered Geography in Victorian Women's Travel Books about Southeast Asia.* New Brunswick: Rutgers UP, 1996.

Morton, Peter. *The Vital Science: Biology and the Literary Imagination, 1860–1900.* London: George Allen and Unwin, 1984.

Moscucci, Ornella. *The Science of Woman.* Cambridge: Cambridge UP, 1990.

Mosedale, Susan Sleeth. "Science Corrupted: Victorian Biologists Consider 'the Woman Question.'" *Journal of the History of Biology* 2 (1978): 1–55.

Murray, Heather. "Frances Hodgson Burnett's *The Secret Garden:* The Organ(ic)ized World." *Touchstones: Reflections on the Best in Children's Literature.* Ed. Perry Nodleman. Vol. 1. West Lafayette, IN: Children's Literature Association, 1985. 30–43.

Myers, Greg. "Fictions and Facts: The Form and Authority of the Scientific Dialogue." *History of Science* 30 (1992): 221–47.

———. "Fictionality, Demonstration, and a Forum for Popular Science: Jane Marcet's *Conversations on Chemistry.*" *Natural Eloquence: Women Reinscribe Science.* Ed. Barbara T. Gates and Ann B. Shteir. Madison: U of Wisconsin P, 1997. 43–60.

———. "Science for Women and Children: The Dialogue of Popular Science in the Nineteenth Century." *Nature Transfigured: Science and Literature, 1700–1900.* Ed. John Christie and Sally Shuttleworth. Manchester: Manchester UP, 1989. 172–200.

———. *Writing Biology: Texts in the Social Construction of Scientific Knowledge.* Madison: U of Wisconsin P, 1990.

National Trust. *Report* 30 (April 1895).

Nightingale, Florence. *"Cassandra" and Other Selections from Suggestions for Thought.* Ed. Mary Poovey. New York: New York UP, 1992.

Noble, Mary. "Beatrix Potter and Charles McIntosh, Naturalists." *A Victorian Naturalist: Beatrix Potter's Drawings from the Armitt Collection.* Ed. Eileen Jay, Mary Noble, and Anne Stevenson Hobbs. London: Frederick Warne, 1992.

North, Marianne. *Recollections of a Happy Life.* Ed. Mrs. John Addington Symonds. 3 vols. London: Macmillan and Co., 1892–94.

———. Letter to Dr. Allman. 4 November 1883. Marianne North Collection. Kew Library, London.

"The North Gallery at Kew." In "London's Hidden Treasures." *Morning Post* [London] 25 Dec. 1905.

Ormerod, Eleanor. *Eleanor Ormerod, LL.D., Economic Entomologist: Autobiography and Correspondence.* Ed. Robert Wallace. New York: E. P. Dutton, 1904.

Ortner, Sherry B. "Is Female to Male as Nature Is to Culture?" *Woman and Values: Readings in Recent Feminist Philosophy.* Ed. Marilyn Pearsall. Belmont, CA: Wadsworth, 1985. 62–75.

Outram, Dorinda. "New Spaces in Natural History." *Cultures of Natural History.* Ed. N. Jardine, J. A. Secord, and E. C. Spary. Cambridge: Cambridge UP, 1996. 249–65.

Paley, William. *Natural Theology; or, Evidences of the Existence and Attributes of the Deity, Collected from the Appearances of Nature.* London: R. Faulder, 1802.

Parks, Fanny. *Wanderings of a Pilgrim in Search of the Picturesque.* 2 vols. London: Pelham Richardson, 1850. Rpt. London: Oxford UP, 1975.

Phillips, Mrs. E. *Destruction of Ornamental-Plumaged Birds.* Leaflet no. 1. London: Society for the Protection of Birds, 1897.

———. *Mixed Plumes.* Leaflet no. 22. London: Society for the Protection of Birds, 1895.

Phillips, Patricia. *The Scientific Lady: A Social History of Woman's Scientific Interests, 1520–1918.* London: Weidenfeld and Nicholson, 1990.

Philpot, Mrs. J. H. *The Sacred Tree.* London: Macmillan, 1897.

Pierson, Stanley. *British Socialism: The Journey from Fantasy to Politics.* Cambridge: Harvard UP, 1979.

Plues, Margaret. *Rambles in Search of Ferns.* London: Houlston and Wright, 1861.

Poovey, Mary. *Uneven Developments: The Ideological Work of Gender in Mid-Victorian England.* Chicago: U of Chicago P, 1988.

Porter, Roy, and Leslie Hall. *The Facts of Life: The Creation of Sexual Knowledge in Britain, 1650–1950.* New Haven: Yale UP, 1995.

Potter, Beatrix. *Complete Tales of Beatrix Potter.* London: F. Warne and Co., 1989.

———. "Hedgehogs." Ms. BP 1306. Victoria and Albert Museum Library, London.

———. *The Journal of Beatrix Potter from 1881 to 1897.* Transcribed, from her code writings, by Leslie Linder. London: Frederick Warne, 1966.

———. *Beatrix Potter's Letters.* Ed. Judy Taylor. London: Frederick Warne, 1989.

Pratt, Anne. *Chapters on the Common Things of the Sea-Side.* London: Society for Promoting Christian Knowledge, 1850.

Pratt, Annis. *Archetypal Patterns in Women's Fiction.* Bloomington: Indiana UP, 1981.

Pratt, Mary Louise. *Imperial Eyes: Travel Writing and Transculturation.* New York: Routledge, 1992.

Probyn, Elspeth. *Sexing the Self: Gendered Positions in Cultural Studies.* London: Routledge, 1993.

Pykett, Lyn. *The "Improper" Feminine: The Women's Sensation Novel and the New Woman Writing.* New York: Routledge, 1992.

Rachels, James. *Created from Animals: The Moral Implications of Darwinism.* Oxford: Oxford UP, 1990.

Reade, Charles. *A Woman Hater.* 1877. New York: Harper and Brothers, 1898.

Rev. of *Recollections of a Happy Life,* by Marianne North. *Athenaeum* 27 Feb. 1892: 270.

Richards, Evelleen. "Darwin and the Descent of Woman." *The Wider Domain of Evolutionary Thought.* Ed. David Oldroyd and Ian Langham. London: D. Reidel, 1983. 57–111.

———. "Huxley and Woman's Place in Science: The 'Woman Question' and the Control of Victorian Anthropology." *History, Humanity, and Evolution: Essays for John C. Greene.* Ed. James R. Moore. Cambridge: Cambridge UP, 1989. 253–84.

———. "Redrawing the Boundaries: Darwinian Science and Victorian Women Intellectuals." *Victorian Science in Context.* Ed. Bernard Lightman. Chicago: U of Chicago P, 1997. 119–42.

Richmond, Marsha L. "'A Lab of One's Own': The Balfour Biological Laboratory for Women at Cambridge University, 1884–1914." *Isis* 88 (1997): 422–55.

Rigby, Elizabeth (Lady Eastlake). "Lady Travelers." *Quarterly Review* 76 (1845): 98–137.

Riley, Norman. "Margaret Fountaine, 1862–1940." Unpublished Memoir. Fountaine Papers. Castle Museum, Norwich.

Ritchie, David. *Darwinism and Politics*. 1890. New York: Charles Scribner's Sons, 1909.

Ritvo, Harriet. *The Animal Estate: The English and Other Creatures in the Victorian Age*. Cambridge: Harvard UP, 1987.

Roberts, Mary. *Voices from the Woodlands, Descriptive of Forest Trees, Ferns, Mosses, and Lichens*. London: Reeve and Bentham, 1850.

Romanes, George. *Animal Intelligence*. New York: D. Appleton, 1884.

———. "Mental Differences between Men and Women." *Nineteenth Century* 21 (1887): 654–72.

Rowold, Katharina. *Gender and Science: Late-Nineteenth-Century Debates on the Female Mind and Body*. Bristol: Thoemmes Press, 1996.

Rudwick, Martin. "Minerals, Strata, and Fossils." *Cultures of Natural History*. Ed. N. Jardinecult, J. A. Secord, and E. C. Spary. Cambridge: Cambridge UP, 1996. 266–86.

Ruether, Rosemary Radford. *Gaia and God: An Ecofeminist Theology of Earth Healing*. San Francisco: Harper San Francisco, 1992.

Ruskin, John. *Proserpina: Studies of Wayside Flowers*. 2 vols. Sunnyside, Orpington, Kent: George Allen, 1879.

Russett, Cynthia Eagle. *Sexual Science: The Victorian Construction of Womanhood*. Cambridge: Harvard UP, 1989.

Sackville-West, Vita. *Some Flowers*. 1937. New York: Harry N. Abrams, 1993.

Saleeby, C. W. *Woman and Womanhood*. London: William Heinemann, 1912.

Sand, George. "To Gustave Flaubert." 8 July 1874. *Flaubert-Sand: The Correspondence*. Trans. Francis Steegmuller and Barbara Bray. New York: Knopf, 1993. 351.

Savory, Isabel. *A Sportswoman in India: Personal Adventures and Experiences of Travel in Known and Unknown India*. London: Hutchinson, 1900.

Sayce, A. H. *The Principles of Comparative Philology*. 2nd ed. London: Trubner, 1875.

Scarry, Elaine, ed. *Fins de Siècle: English Poetry in 1590, 1690, 1790, 1890, 1990*. Baltimore: Johns Hopkins UP, 1995.

Schaaf, Larry. *Sun Gardens: Victorian Photograms*. New York: Hans Kraus, 1985.

Schiebinger, Londa. *Nature's Body: Gender in the Making of Modern Science*. Boston: Beacon Press, 1993.

Schreiner, Olive [Ralph Iron, pseud.]. *The Story of an African Farm*. 2nd ed. Boston: Roberts Brothers, 1889.

Scott, Carole. "Clothed in Nature or Nature Clothed: Dress as Metaphor in the Illustrations of Beatrix Potter and C. M. Barker." *Children's Literature* 22 (1994): 70–89.

Seaton, Beverly. *The Language of Flowers: A History*. Charlottesville: UP of Virginia, 1995.

Selous, Frederick Courteney. *Travel and Adventure in South-East Africa*. 1893. London: Century Publishing, 1984.

Shapin, Steven. *A Social History of Truth: Civility and Science in Seventeenth-Century England*. Chicago: U of Chicago P, 1994.

Sharp, William. *"The Gold Key" and "The Green Life."* Ed. Elizabeth Sutherland. London: St. Edmundsbury Press, 1986.

Sheets-Pyenson, Susan. "Popular Science Periodicals in Paris and London: The Emergence of a Low Scientific Culture, 1820–1875." *Annals of Science* 42 (1985): 549–72.

Shinn, Terry, and R. Whitley. *Expository Science: Forms and Functions of Popularisation.* Dordrecht: D. Reidel, 1985.

The Shooting Party. Dir. Alan Bridges. Castle Hill, 1984. 96 min.

Shore, Emily. *Journal of Emily Shore.* Ed. Barbara Timm Gates. Charlottesville: UP of Virginia, 1991.

Showalter, Elaine. "Feminist Criticism in the Wilderness." *The New Feminist Criticism: Essays on Women, Literature, and Theory.* New York: Pantheon, 1986. 243–70.

———. *Sexual Anarchy: Gender and Culture at the Fin de Siècle.* New York: Viking, 1990.

Shteir, Ann B. *Cultivating Women, Cultivating Science: Flora's Daughters and Botany in England, 1760–1860.* Baltimore: Johns Hopkins UP, 1996.

Smith, Charlotte. *Rural Walks in Dialogues Intended for the Use of Young Persons.* London: T. Cadell and W. Davies, 1795.

Soloway, Richard Allen. "Feminism, Fertility, and Eugenics in Victorian and Edwardian England." *Political Symbolism in Modern Europe: Essays in Honor of George L. Mosse.* Ed. Seymour Drescher, David Sabean, and Allan Sharlin. London: Transaction Books, 1982. 121–45.

Somerville, Mary. *On the Connexion of the Physical Sciences.* 3rd ed. London: J. Murray, 1836.

———. *Personal Recollections, from Early Life to Old Age, of Mary Somerville.* Boston: Roberts Brothers, 1874.

Spencer, Herbert. *Education: Intellectual, Moral, and Physical.* London: Williams and Norgate, 1861.

———. *The Principles of Ethics.* 2 vols. London: Williams and Norgate, 1892–93.

———. *Study of Sociology.* New York: Appleton, 1873.

Stafford, Barbara. "Voyeur or Observer? Enlightenment Thoughts on the Dilemma of Display." *Configurations* 1.1 (1993): 95–128.

Stetz, Margaret D., and Mark Samuel Lasner. *England in the 1880s: Old Guard and Avant-Garde.* Charlottesville: UP of Virginia, 1989.

———. *England in the 1890s: Literary Publishing at the Bodley Head.* Washington, D.C.: Georgetown UP, 1990.

Stevenson, Catherine Barnes. *Victorian Women Travel Writers in Africa.* Boston: Twayne, 1982.

Stopes, Marie Carmichael. *A Journal from Japan: A Daily Record of Life as Seen by a Scientist.* London: Blackie and Son, 1910.

———. *Married Love: A New Contribution to the Solution of Sex Difficulties.* New York: Eugenics Publishing Company, 1931.

Suleri, Sara. *The Rhetoric of English India.* Chicago: U of Chicago P, 1992.

Swiney, Rosa Frances. *The Ancient Road; or, The Development of the Soul.* London: G. Bell and Sons, 1918.

———. *The Bar of Isis; or, The Law of the Mother.* London: C. W. Daniel, Ltd., 1912.

———. *The Cosmic Procession; or, The Feminine Principle in Evolution.* London: Ernest Bell, 1906.

———. *The League of Isis. Rules (of Observance).* London: National Union of Women's Suffrage Societies, n.d.

———. *Science and Women: The Missing Factor.* London: National Union of Women's Suffrage Societies, n.d.

———. "The Tender Mercies of the Vicious." *Awakener* 26 July 1913: 5, 8.

————. *Woman and Natural Law.* London: C. W. Daniel, 1912.

Taylor, Barbara. "Religious Heresy and Feminism in Early English Socialism." *Tearing the Veil: Essays on Femininity.* Ed. Susan Lipshitz. London: Routledge and Kegan Paul, 1978. 119–44.

Taylor, J. E. *The Sagacity and Morality of Plants.* London: Chatto and Windus, 1891.

Taylor, Judy, Joyce Irene Whalley, Anne Stevenson Hobbs, and Elizabeth M. Battrick, eds. *Beatrix Potter, 1866–1943: The Artist and Her World.* London: Frederick Warne, 1987.

Tennyson, Alfred. *The Poems of Tennyson.* Ed. Christopher Ricks. London: Longmans, Green and Co., 1969.

Thomas, Hilary M. *Grandmother Extraordinary: Mary De la Beche Nicholl, 1839–1922.* Barry: Steward Williams, 1979.

Thornburn, John. *Female Education from a Physiological Point of View.* Manchester: J. E. Cornish, 1884.

Tonge, Mrs. O. F. *Sketchbooks of Mrs. O. F. Tonge.* Circa 1908–13. Ms. presented to the Library of the British Museum of Natural History by Lt. Col. H. F. Hobbs.

Torrens, Hugh. "Mary Anning (1799–1847) of Lyme: 'The Greatest Fossilist the World Ever Knew.'" *British Journal for the History of Science* 28 (1995): 257–84.

Trimmer, Sarah. *An Easy Introduction to the Knowledge of Nature, and Reading the Holy Scriptures, Adapted to the Capacities of Children.* London: Longman, Robinson and Johnson, 1780.

————. *Fabulous Histories, Designed for the Instruction of Children, Respecting Their Treatment of Animals.* London: Longman, Robinson and Johnson, 1796.

Tuana, Nancy. *Feminism and Science.* Bloomington: Indiana UP, 1989.

————. *The Less Noble Sex: Scientific, Religious, and Philosophical Conceptions of Woman's Nature.* Bloomington: Indiana UP, 1993.

Tuchman, Gaye. *Edging Women Out: Victorian Novelists, Publishers, and Social Change.* New Haven: Yale UP, 1989.

Turner, James. *Reckoning with the Beast: Animals, Pain, and Humanity in the Victorian Mind.* Baltimore: Johns Hopkins UP, 1980.

Twining, Elizabeth. *Illustrations of the Natural Orders of Plants with Groups and Descriptions.* 1849–55. London: Sampson Low, Son, and Marston, 1868.

Tyacke, Mrs. R. H. *How I Shot My Bears; or, Two Years' Tent Life in Kullu and Lahoul.* London: Sampson, Low, Marston, 1893.

Tylor, E. B. *Primitive Culture.* 2nd ed. 1873. New York: Holt, 1889.

Tyndall, John. *Fragments of Science: Being a Series of Detached Essays, Addresses, and Reviews.* 1879. 6th ed. New York: A. L. Burt, 1925.

Valenze, Deborah M. *Prophetic Sons and Daughters: Female Preaching and Popular Religion in Industrial England.* Princeton: Princeton UP, 1985.

Vickery, Alice Drysdale. "Discussion on Restrictions in Marriage and on Studies in National Eugenics," *Sociological Papers* 2 (1906): 21–22.

Wakefield, Priscilla. *Domestic Recreation; or, Dialogues Illustrative of Natural and Scientific Subjects.* Philadelphia: Robert Carr, 1805.

Wallace, Alfred Russel. "Human Selection." *Fortnightly Review* 54 (1890): 325–37.

————. *Alfred Russel Wallace: Letters and Reminiscences.* Ed. James Marchant. New York: Harper and Brothers, 1916.

Wallington, Emma. "The Physical and Intellectual Capacities of Woman Equal to Those of Man." *Anthropologia* 1 (1874): 552–65.

Ward, Hon. Mrs. *The Microscope*. London: Groombridge and Sons, 1870.

Ware, Vron. *Beyond the Pale: White Women, Racism, and History*. London: Verso, 1992.

Webb, Mary. *Gone to Earth*. New York: Dutton, 1917.

———. *Mary Webb: The Spring of Joy*. Intro. Walter De La Mare and Martin Armstrong. New York: Dutton, 1937.

Weeks, Jeffrey. *Sex, Politics and Society: The Regulation of Sexuality since 1800*. London: Longman, 1981.

Weiskel, Thomas. *The Romantic Sublime: Studies in the Structure and Psychology of Transcendence*. Baltimore: Johns Hopkins UP, 1976.

Westermarck, Edvard. *History of Human Marriage*. London: Macmillan, 1891.

Whewell, William. Rev. of *On the Connexion of the Physical Sciences*, by Mary Somerville. *Quarterly Review* 51 (1834): 54–68.

———. "On Leonardo da Vinci and Correggio." *Blackwood's Magazine* 48 (1840): 270–80.

Whitley, Richard. "Knowledge Producers and Knowledge Acquirers: Popularisation as a Relation between Scientific Fields and Their Publics." *Expository Science: Forms and Functions of Popularisation*. Ed. Terry Shinn and Richard Whitley. Dordrecht: D. Reidel, 1885. 3–28.

Wilde, Oscar. *The First Collected Edition of the Works of Oscar Wilde*. Ed. Robert Ross. 15 vols. 1908–22. London: Routledge, 1993.

Wollstonecraft, Mary. *Original Stories from Real Life; with Conversations Calculated to Regulate the Affections and Form the Mind to Truth and Goodness*. London: J. Johnson, 1783.

———. *Vindication of the Rights of Woman*. 1792. Ed. Carl H. Poston. New York: W. W. Norton, 1975.

"Woman in her Psychological Relations." *Journal of Psychological Medicine and Mental Pathology* 4 (1851): 8–50.

Women in Professions, Being the Professional Section of the International Congress of Women. London: T. Fisher Unwin, 1900.

"Women's Manifesto." *Daily News* [London] 31 December 1869.

Wood, J. G. *The Boy's Own Book of Natural History*. London: George Routledge and Sons, 1883.

Wood, Neville, ed. *The Naturalist*. Vol. 3. London: Whittaker and Co., 1838.

Woolf, Virginia. *The Mark on the Wall*. Richmond, Surrey: Hogarth Press, 1919.

Woolford, John. "Elizabeth Barrett and the Wordsworthian Sublime." *Essays in Criticism* 45 (1995): 36–56.

Wordsworth, William. *The Poetical Works of William Wordsworth*. Ed. E. De Selincourt and Helen Darbishire. 2nd ed. 5 vols. Oxford: Clarendon Press, 1952–59.

Yaeger, Patricia. "Toward a Female Sublime." *Gender and Theory: Dialogues on Feminist Criticism*. Ed. Linda Kauffman. Oxford: Basil Blackwell, 1989. 191–212.

Zornlin, Rosina M. *Outlines of Geology for Families and Schools*. London: John W. Parker and Son, 1852.

———. *Recreations in Geology*. 1839. 3rd ed. London: John W. Parker and Son, 1852.

———. *Recreations in Physical Geography; or, The Earth as It Is*. 1840. 5th ed. London: John W. Parker and Son, 1855.

———. *The World of Waters; or, Recreations in Hydrology*. 1843. 3rd ed. rev. London: John W. Parker and Son, 1855.

INDEX